MENDED SPEECH

P. Joseph Cahill

MENDED SPEECH

THE CRISIS OF RELIGIOUS STUDIES AND THEOLOGY

CROSSROAD · NEW YORK

The author expresses his thanks to Canada Council
for a leave and a research grant
which made work on this book possible.

1982

The Crossroad Publishing Company
575 Lexington Avenue, New York, NY 10022

Printed in the United States of America

Library of Congress Cataloging in Publication Data

Cahill, P. Joseph, 1923–
    Mended speech.

    Includes bibliographical references.
    1. Religion—Study and teaching. 2. Theology—Study
and teaching. I. Title.
BL41.C33   200'.7   81-19582
ISBN 0-8245-0421-6   AACR2

CONTENTS

INTRODUCTION

Writers who discuss the history of religions and theology agree generally that there is a field of study called religious studies, that the history of religions is the principal and constitutive discipline within this field, and that theology should have some sort of separate existence consonant with its confessional presuppositions, origin, and environment. There is likewise a general and largely precritical consensus that some sort of historical and comparative approach constitutes the history of religions and therefore defines the field of religious studies. The presupposition of faith generally present in the practice of theology is felt to be inconsistent with the historical and comparative approach of the history of religions. The history of religions is assumed to be pluralistic in object, whereas theology is considered as unitary. These suppositions are ornamented by the old distinction that says that the history of religions is nonnormative while theology is normative.

Biblical studies, or indeed literary and historical studies of any religiously authoritative text or tradition, when undertaken by a person with confessional affiliation or background, are held to be participations in the theological or even the ecclesiastical enterprises. But infection by association is not thoroughly convincing. First, the historical-critical method, now indigeneous to the history of religions, was introduced, practiced, and highly developed by biblical exegetes whose methods were palpable enough to constitute a history of religions school. The method is now the common, if at times uncomfortable possession of all reputable biblical scholars. Second, Western intellectual history from the latter part of the nineteenth century to the present testifies to the

discomfort felt by many theologians, believers, and ecclesiastical authorities when biblical scholars resolutely practiced the canons of the historical-critical method. Readers need not be reminded of the history of religions school of the late nineteenth and early twentieth century and
the tremors its practitioners caused in theological and ecclesiastical circles. The field of biblical studies, therefore, seems to fall somewhere in
the no-man's-land between the history of religions and theology. Its
method is indistinguishable from that employed by any historian of religion. But its context and supposed presuppositions taint whatever academic deference its method may warrant. At the same time, its method
appears to systematic theologians and troubled churches at most a
deadly foe, and at least a very uncomfortable nuisance.

Such volatile moods suggest a conceptual obscurity that can be neither denied nor evaded. Boundary lines and border zones appear arbitrary or capricious. Concerned parties react differently. The university
accepts a practical solution: it approves accepted usage, lives with an
uneasy peace, and consigns any further discussion to appropriate com-
mittees, which then mirror contemporary chiaroscuro and ultimately,
with a sigh of relief, consign the theoretical and methodological problems to their departments or faculties of religious studies. Ecclesiastical
authority has no direct sanction over the secular university and tends to
limit its interventions to what its particular religious tradition generally
regards as blatant excess. Rarely now does any ecclesiastical power concern itself with the world of theory and the new horizons opened by the
historical-critical method, except where this world and horizon have immediate and palpable effects on either authority or the life of the faithful. The results are occasional skirmishes but no prolonged battles, for
the historical-critical method appears to be an idea whose time has
come.

Historians of religion can remove themselves from the conflict in almost direct proportion to the esoteric nature of the religions they study
or to the temporal distance they create between the object of their study
and current religious belief. No one seriously objects when the scholar
applies the historical-critical method to the religions of the Akkadians,
Sumerians, or Laplanders. Exegetes and literary interpreters can allow
the demands and discipline of their work to absorb their total interest
and confine whatever adjustments their method suggests to the private
theater of personal theological synthesis. Theologians, on the other
hand, if they are to be more than biased or vulgar apologists, cannot

long avoid feeling much like an inhabitant of the inner city who watches the movement of neighbors to the suburbs. Despite articulate protestation, his familiar world has been despoiled, almost under cover of night.

Moreover, it is evident that the field of religious studies (and the same may be said of the history of religions insofar as it identifies itself as religious studies) prospers from a relatively recently won academic respectability and from the more convincing approbation of increasing student enrollments. In most North American universities religious studies enjoys as well the administrative approbation and equipment that accompanies departmental status in a fiscally sound secular university. This rather consequential respectability has so permeated the larger educational and cultural atmosphere that, to take but one small example, certain provinces in Canada have introduced rather sophisticated courses in religious studies on the high school level. So assured was the success of the program from the very nature of the topics that at least one province tacitly assumed the interest in religious studies to be similar to natural resources that should instantly be developed for the benefit of both party and people. While the intrusion of religious studies into the high school curriculum in this particular fashion is a very mixed blessing indeed, it is nonetheless one more sign of assumed prosperity.

Theology, on the other hand, seems to have endured a withering sort of sirocco, in which the desert emerges and those huddled around a small oasis see the shadowy and disappearing figures of departed theological giants. Nor is there a heartening hint of outside approbation suggesting the introduction of theology into either universities or high schools. Occasionally one invokes the sanguine hope of a remnant reminiscent of the Old Testament. Where theology has the compliant approbation of tradition, as in the German universities, or the support of the civilly established religion, as in Britain, it is widely accepted as a strictly confessional discipline but one strengthened by culturally established presuppositions and canons.

Some originally confessional universities in North America, either reading the signs of the times or seeking to avoid either direct obloquy or the more demeaning state of simply being ignored, have changed departments of theology to departments of religion or of religious studies. Some theological societies have ongoing seminars and task forces dedicated to the study of deceased but still important figures of what is assumed to be a better day. One senses a certain wistful hope in massive studies of Barth, Brunner, Tillich, Bultmann, or of older living theologians such as Lonergan and Rahner, of theologians of hope, or of process theologians of varying confessions and hues. It is almost like a hope of regaining lost ground or halting a tide that rolled in quietly while no one was watching. Theologies of revolution and liberation and hearty efforts in theological methodology are as much attempts to fill a void as they are rallying points. It is not quite an exaggeration to say that even where the necessity of theology is tacitly affirmed the discipline suffers a form of dignified destitution—like the British castles recalling a heroic and rich past but now supported and kept alive by tourist fees. It is, of course, true that affection and a rich intellectual tradition, particularly in Britain, and a sophisticated and effective educational system combined with the need for pastors in countries such as Switzerland and Germany, can currently support theological study. One notes too in Europe a perceptible decline in enrollments in the history of religions and in the religious ethics courses which were so popular a decade ago. Some see a corresponding increase in the study of serious theological disciplines as suggestive of a mild renaissance.

Those who would defend the vitality of theology and who find the above description unnecessarily gloomy have not really noticed the gradual loss of their goods, a loss that antedates the emergence of religious studies and which may even have provided some occasion for the success of religious studies. Becker's words of 1932 are perhaps as accurate today as they were then. "Theology, or something that goes under the name, is still kept alive by the faithful, but only by artificial respiration. Its functions, the services it rendered in the time of St. Thomas, have been taken over, not as is often supposed by philosophy, but by history—the study of man and his world in the time sequence."[1] The emergence of historical consciousness has been an intellectual current favorable to a religious studies that characterizes itself by a historical and comparative approach. On the other hand, historical consciousness, as we shall later see in more detail, has been inimical to a theology which was formed, developed, and grew within a classical and normative culture and has thus far not been able to rearrange itself to meet the demands of the historical-critical method and literary strategies. Nor are certain theological fashions or recourse to studies in methodology any substitute for the serious theological revisions demanded by the emergence of historical consciousness and its paratactic concomitants, particularly literary and artistic interpretive procedure.

The intensity of the theological crisis varies with the location of the student's vested interest. One might take comfort in the fact that the long scroll of history gives indications of theology's survival capacity. But survival is not prosperity. On the other hand, religious studies cannot conceal a certain evident patchwork in its hardly timeless architecture. Its accidental success, which almost amounts to being in the right place at the right time, now demands justification by reflective self-definition and clarification of its constitutive components.

The primary concern of this book is to clarify the relation between the history of religion and theology and to place these two disciplines in a coherent and intelligible field of religious studies. The stimulus for such an attempt has a long history. Persistent theoretical concerns were reshaped by participation in articulating graduate theological programs, by coordinating attempts to establish theological centers, and finally by the exacting task of constituting a particular department of religious studies and justifying its conceptual structure not only to faculties of arts and sciences but also before the court of public religious and secular concern. Like so many seemingly discrete practical affairs, the background shadow became the substance: the theoretical attempt to state some manifest foundations for the disciplines that came together under the rubric of religious studies. We began with the broad question, What exactly are religious studies? Many participants in the long dialogue felt that they knew what the history and comparison of religions was. But are these activities constitutive of religious studies? Are there methods by which one can distinguish this field from, for example, sociology, anthropology, philosophy, or psychology? Is the subject matter of religious studies sufficiently distinct to establish a field, to confer a specific identity on a particular perspective? As discussions proceeded, there was a long, faltering agreement that theology was clearly to be excluded from religious studies. And yet one had to ask if theology or any study determined or influenced by a theological perspective or interest of commitment was automatically to be excluded. If so, why?

An example is illuminative. Book reviews by historians of religion frequently note that articles or books by anthropologists or sociologists and sometimes by theologians, commendable as they are, lack the perspective of the historian of religions. But what exactly is meant by this frequent observation? Is the sacred as sacred or the holy as holy inaccessible to the anthropologist or the sociologist? Does belief in a particular manifestation of the holy exclude the theologian from the field of religious studies? Does this implication suggest that independence from religious belief and from the subject matter of religion is an indispensable requirement for the interpreter? It would seem that the only possible basis for distinguishing perspectives with which the interpreter approaches religious reality would be in some relation that the interpreter has to the subject matter and to the forms in which the subject matter is mediated. But what is such a relationship? What is meant by subject matter? And how does one define the forms by which subject matter is mediated?

Such evident questions indicate that if one is to study the relationship between theology and the history of religions and the relation of each to religious studies, one is soon drawn into a larger arena. The reader, I hope, will notice that my primary intention is to specify the relationship between theology and the history of religions, and the relationship of these two disciplines to the field commonly called religious studies. Answers to all the questions above are presented in the light of the principal intention. The first four chapters (part 1) develop a context. With this context as background, I proceed to brief presentations of the history of religion, theology, and an operation of mind called theological. The first four chapters are the scenario in which the last three chapters (part 2) become intelligible.

The point toward which this essay moves is the conclusion that there are four specific mental operations which constitute the field of religious studies: the literary, the historical, the comparative, and the theological. These operations are mediated by a prior relationship of the interpreter to the subject matter of religion. By existential self-analysis, the interpreters must articulate their relationship to the subject matter. And the subject matter of religious studies is intentionality and ultimate meaning directed to final transcendence. By proposing four operations as constitutive of religious studies, it must be noted that there are other operations consecutive to, consequent on, and auxiliary to the constitutive operations. Among the latter are the sociological, anthropological, psychological, and philosophical operations, which do not demand a prior relationship of the interpreter to the subject matter of religion.

The above recapitulation was not the beginning point of the study but rather the term of a process that began with very pedestrian demands: the need to make some sense out of the introduction of religious studies in a large university where most members of the academic community involved in the appropriate committee work were sympathetic, thought the idea was good, but were not quite sure why. The process involved the more complex issues of the impact of circumstances on both the definitions of the history of religions and on theology, and consequently the effect of environment on those who approach religious studies as a university discipline. Hence it is that I begin with a chapter on historicity, which is part of a matrix that nurtures intellectual innovations in the field of religious studies and, at the same time, kills the progeny and inheritance of an earlier era. I do not intend by the stress on Heidegger to imply or suggest that my conclusions depend on a particular form of existentialist philosophy. They do not. But Heidegger does offer a realistic, coherent, and comprehensible analysis of the ordinary experience of historicity. He has explored, elaborated, and refined a structure proportionate to historical consciousness.

Historicity leads directly to its affiliate, cognitional theory. So we move first to the cognitional theory underlying the period before the emergence of historical consciousness. This nonhistorical cognitional model, initiated in the West by Aristotle, received compelling endorsement through Descartes and then through the thought of Kant. This inherited cognitional paradigm was an instrument of precision and symmetry and owes its permeation of the Western world not so much to theory as to the uncompromising clarity and success it bestowed on the empirical sciences and their ever accelerating derived technologies. The exploration of this cognitional paradigm in chapter 2 suggests its inadequacy and the modifications needed to develop a cognitional paradigm suited to the anthropological sciences. How one conceives knowing is very influential—indeed almost decisive—in the formation of concepts about the history of religions, theology, and the relationships of the two to the larger field of religious studies.

But if one takes historical consciousness and its cantilevered cognitional paradigm seriously, then it almost inevitably follows that each tradition and culture seems to have equal historical status and validity. And one might push the conclusion a bit further by noting that apparently only a person raised within a particular tradition has the capacity to understand that tradition. So religious traditions seem to be isolated objective phenomena with little or no basic underlying symmetry. With a certain relentless logic, historical consciousness moves into the interpreting subject and suggests that only a convinced member of a religious tradition is capable of understanding that tradition. These are cryptic but real objections. So chapter 3 moves on to the internalized world of the interpreting subject, where the unity of the disciplines in the field of religious studies is ultimately to be found. Understanding is, first of all, a hermeneutic activity. Explicit reflection on this theme not only incorporates historical consciousness and its accompanying theory of cognition, but also leads directly to the self-interpretation required on the part of the interpreter. This self-interpretation will disclose a relationship of the interpreter to the subject matter of religion. It is this relationship to the subject matter of religion that ultimately differentiates the disciplines generally assumed to have a relationship to religious studies. It is this relationship to the subject matter that enables one to distinguish operations of the interpreter, varied approaches to one and the same subject. Only by careful attention to the interiorized state of consciousness can one clearly distinguish perspectives. Thus chapter 3 is a direct turning to the interpreter.

Chapter 4 then turns to the problem opened up by historical consciousness: the seeming relativity of all traditions and the implication that traditions are not mutually intelligible. In this chapter, I note that there is a common structure to all tradition and a common structure to the consciousness that both creates and later studies religious tradition. This suggests a symmetry without proposing that religious traditions are all in fact the same and are only distinguished by accidental variations. Symmetry does not preclude essential differences.

Today one cannot discuss tradition, particularly religious tradition, without considering the almost amorphous nature of many religious traditions today. This is a problem of dissonance. Such dissonance in individual traditions proceeds not only from the conflict between innovation and continuity within religious traditions, but also from the perceived multiplicity of religious and nonreligious traditions, no one of which is considered to have a monopoly on truth. These historical and psychological factors influence the certainty and assurance with which one confesses or asserts his own tradition. Perceived dissonance is but a concrete form of the problem of historicity. Nor can one speak of perceived dissonance without some comment on the restructuring of consciousness that has taken place under the influence of the communications media as they have moved through their oral, scriptorial, print, and electronic phases. The schematic presentation and consideration of tradition concludes the background of this essay and prepares for the direct consideration of the history of religion in chapter 5.

The history of comparative religion indicates the growing assumption that theology is virtually unrelated to the history of religions and frequently opposed to the way in which the historian of religion should work. This anachronistic assumption is strengthened by the so-called normative approach of theology as well as by the confessional presuppositions of the theologian. Each presupposition has left a scar and a lingering suspicion of the theological enterprise. While the history of religions has profited from the climate of historical consciousness, this benign atmosphere has intensified the problem of the unity and diversity of religions and has thus left the history of religions presiding over an empire of almost disparate entities. The symmetry of tradition (chapter 4) can only be upheld by a further dialectic that maintains both the unity and the diversity of religions. The unity appears in the intentionality and ultimate meaning directed to final transcendence; the diversity, in the mediation of this meaning by diverse cultural symbolic systems. Here Schuon's theory is a helpful beginning in finding an alternative to either pure relativism or an oversimplifying univocity.

A brief history of theology in chapter 6 attempts to locate the cause of theology's disaffiliation from the history of religions in certain practices and theories of theology that gave some ground for regarding it with suspicion. Still, even this history indicates that a proper theology lives best in conjunction with rather than in hostility to the history of religions. This is a virtually self-evident proposition. First, a sound theology—and particularly theology properly related to the historical-critical method—necessarily operates in a historical, literary, and comparative context, that is, the context of religious studies in general and the history of religions in particular. Second, the historian of religion studies not history in general but a religious history; and this history is mediated by theological belief systems which seek to elaborate particular faith postures. Thus, if the field of religious studies is to be truly exhaustive, it must include more activities than the simple study of history or the supposedly simple act of comparison. Any suggestion that the historical operation combined with a supposedly simple comparative operation is adequate for the study of religions is meretricious. Any affirmation that the theological operation can be pursued independently of historical, literary, and comparative procedures takes theology completely out of the present world.

Analysis of what should take place in the field of religious studies suggests a fourfold constitutive operation: literary, historical, comparative, and theological. Each is specified by a dimension or aspect of the subject matter. Other mental operations are consequent on the first four, that is, they follow either in time or by definition the constitutive operations. The consequent and auxiliary operations are the anthropological, the sociological, the philosophical, the psychological, and any others that do not demand on the part of the interpreter a fully articulated prior relationship to the subject matter of religion. The distinction of operations within the field of religious studies is grounded in the epigenetically differentiated consciousness of the interpreting subject. This epigenetically differentiated consciousness is itself based on the intentionalities and meanings that people have historically given to ultimate transcendence. These themes are discussed in the two final chapters, which proceed from theology and the other operations of religious studies to the location of the operations in the larger hermeneutic field made up of elements (the interpreter, the religious community, the world), subject matter (the search for ultimate meaning), and operations proportionate to the field and heuristic to the elements and subject matter (literary, historical, comparative, theological). More time is dedicated to the theological operation both in relation to the other operations and in relation to the hermeneutic field because it is the theological dimension that has been most obscured and problematic in discussions of religious studies.

If this book terminates in the internal world of consciousness and supposes some attention on the part of the reader to this interiorized world, it may be worthwhile to add some concluding remarks about determinations of consciousness and indeed include the general state that we characterize as historical consciousness. The conjunction of these highly elusive terms necessitates some introductory observations.

It was the Enlightenment and the understanding of humanity that it generated that marked, as Troeltsch pointed out,[2] the beginning of the modern period characterized by an evolved consciousness of historicity, hermeneutic, understanding, and their inter-connections.[3] One might write separate treatises on any one of these topics, but that is not my intent here.[4] My aim is simply to develop as economically as possible the themes that form the context of religious studies and thus to establish some conceptual framework, to outline some heuristic structure that may define or open and enlarge the horizon within which discussions about the history of religions, of theology, and of religious studies generally may be conducted more profitably and more clearly.[5] Even this modest effort, however, demands the discussion of consciousness.

We not only locate the unity of religious studies in the epigenetically differentiated consciousness of the individual interpreter but likewise in the communal consciousness of the interpreting community. As religious activity concomitantly modifies consciousness, so too does the attempt to understand this religious consciousness shape the interpreter's and the community's consciousness. In the higher achievements of the human race, in those moments that encapsulate our noblest aspirations, it is generally the case that the interpreter must rise to the level of the mediated subject matter. This demands transformations of consciousness.

We know, of course, that consciousness in the technical sense, "does not occur unconditionally and as a matter of course."[6] Consciousness in the medical sense is a minimal state and is the opposite of unconsciousness; it is valued precisely because it is a sign of life and the required beginning point for consciousness in the more technical sense. The awareness accompanying every act of knowing, believing, thinking, conceiving, judging, and imagining is largely implicit. When the awareness becomes explicit, the person is properly a subject.

In addition to explicit perception of consciousness there is the awareness that consciousness goes through stages; it develops, it differentiates degrees of personal growth and development and simultaneously provides various ways of conceiving and understanding reality. This procedure is most clear in the growth of the infant, who rapidly proceeds from a relatively undifferentiated consciousness to the differentiations required for intersubjective understanding, locomotion, and language apprehension. The latter learning process indicates new structures of consciousness, new ways of conceiving of reality, particularly as the child proceeds from the oral world to the alphabet and chirography. Such new structures develop gradually and are not easily accessible to introspection. Writers speak of the heightening of consciousness, of the transit from the unconscious to the conscious, of the change from the naive to the reflective, of the development from the precritical to the critical. Authors as diverse as Heidegger, Lonergan, and Ricoeur agree that it is the increasingly differentiated consciousness that produces the truly human subject. Such observations, however brief and fleeting, on consciousness are the prelude to finding the principle of unity common to the history of religions, theology, and religious studies in the differentiated consciousness of the interpreter[7] and of the interpreting community. Fortunately, Josiah Royce, a neglected thinker indeed, has developed excellent notions of interpretation and interpreting communities. Explicit elaboration of a community of interpretation and of the communal consciousness following communal interpretation are unnecessary because Royce has done this work.

Our observations on consciousness should not be construed by the reader as a type of fetching philosophical or psychological speculation of no real practical use or concern. The psychoanalytic literature on moral growth and on the learning procedure as such illustrates the concrete and practical dimensions of such seemingly abstract considerations. "As we know from the study of psychology, the earlier stages are not replaced, but developed according to an epigenetic principle—that is, they are absorbed into a hierarchic system of increasing differentiation. As the individual proceeds developmentally from the moralism of childhood through the ideology of adolescence to some adult ethics, the characteristic gains and conflicts of the early stages are not abandoned but, in the best of circumstances, renewed and reintegrated."[8] The coherence of epigenetic development can, in general, be measured in terms of the hierarchic differentiations of consciousness that one would expect at certain levels. The differentiations of consciousness both accompany and are determined by the forward motion, so to speak, of the individual as he moves from inactivity to activity. So the child goes from relative quiet to motions of the individual members of the body, to crawling, walking, talking, and so on. In the adult, the development of the subject proceeds (or does not) by what Kierkegaard described as ventures—ventures in which possibility becomes actuality.

It is important to comprehend not simply the meaning of differentiation of consciousness but the fact that differentiations are measured against the practical norm and model of a "subject," that is, one who performs activities expected of him as a subject. Adequate development and integration is termed healthy; its opposite, characterized by a failure of growth and a deficiency of integration, is called arrested development, an unhealthy state, a condition inappropriate to the standard or criterion of expectation suitable to a specified stage in the growth of the human person. It is, I think, safe today to say that the becoming of the human person is equivalent to freedom so that healthy personality development is motion toward freedom. "The distinctive characteristic of the human being in contrast to the merely vegetative or the merely animal, lies in the range of human possibility and in our capacity for self-awareness as possibility."[9] Whatever the varieties of explanation about either what a subject is or how consciousness is constituted, and whatever the disagreements about standards of discrimination, there is substantial agreement that persons are constituted by the possibilities that they actualize in their own existence; one's being is becoming; one can be. But differentiations in consciousness accompany, manifest, and constitute becoming. While the integrity of religious studies is grounded in a certain seemingly objective unity found within religions, the final unity of religious studies ultimately resides in the epigenetically differentiated consciousness of the interpreter who performs a series of operations appropriate to the understanding of a religion. As there are differentiations within individual consciousness, so too may it be affirmed that there are differentiations in the communal consciousness, a consciousness that is different and distinct from the consciousness of the individual, a point to which I return in the chapter on tradition. So Müller's affirmation that myth is a disease of language is today commonly rejected, and it is clearly affirmed that myth is a necessary and valid carrier of human meaning.

If the above observations are primarily psychological, Lonergan uses a more metaphysical and traditional type of distinction. Here the human being is distinguished as substance and as subject. The substance, the person when asleep, is potentially a subject whose being is characterized by becoming.[10] The subject is the one who moves from dependence to autonomy and ever higher degrees of differentiation in consciousness. Thus a subject is one who achieves authenticity, becomes what one potentially is, actualizes possibilities of existence, and therefore expands one's world and one's horizon. It is the apprehension of the differentiations in consciousness that constitutes the unified subject. So the appropriation of the differentiations of consciousness required for the field of religious studies is the ultimate source of unity in religious studies and the basis for distinctions in the operations of the human subject.

Erikson stresses the psychological growth of the subject from basic trust or mistrust to the eighth stage of integrity where all the prior stages are incorporated and sublimated. Polanyi expands the personal, historical, and emotional dimensions to include even the empirical sciences and particularly the intimate involvement of the subject in the object studied.[11] The subject becomes a subject insofar as there is an awareness of and an appropriation of this self-involvement. Polanyi suggests that the unity of even the empirical sciences is to be found more within the subject than in any objective criteria external to the interpreter. Ong, following McLuhan and others, indicates that the development of the communications media leads to a restructuring of the psyche or the sensorium. The movement from an aural-oral culture through the alphabet, printing, and the electronic means of communication can tend to an increasingly differentiated subject. This subject can become more truly human, more a subject in direct proportion to the intensity of the world of interiority he or she is now capable of experiencing.[12] It is therefore not out of place today to think that it is in the world of interiority that the disciplines of religious studies will find both their unity and principles of distinction and discrimination.

The citation of authors of quite different background, interest, and training is quite deliberate. The reader need not adhere to the confines of one particular philosophical tradition to assent to what emerges from a convergence of agreement. It would be beyond the scope of this book to point out this convergence as a possible basis for agreement with certain tendencies in Eastern religious thought. The Western consensus, if this is not too broad, affirms that the human subject is constituted by the autonomous appropriation of a suitably differentiated consciousness. The distinctions within and the appropriation of the differentiated consciousness transpires in the world of interiority. Transition to the world of interiority is a large factor in the constitution of historical consciousness. Historical consciousness, an irreversible state, must operate in any attempt to distinguish or relate the work of the historian of religion, the theologian, and the student of religious studies.

Bianchi[13] is one of the very few historians of religions to affirm first that there exists a cultural and religious differentiation of consciousness, and second, that later stages of consciousness are advances on earlier stages. His first reference is to the ethnologists of the historical-cultural school who would see the essence of religion in the primitives without written records, indeed an early stage in human consciousness. "It is as if the achievements of Christian history, or of religious India, or of Greek religious thought were less meaningful, from this point of view, than the 'stammerings' of a savage, and not something new and infinitely greater than these."[14] He then points out that the history and comparison of religions should specify "the original, unique and progressive creation of human and cultural values which, if on the one hand potentially implicit in common human nature, are on the other hand historically localized and real in a history which leaps, or at least marches, forward at its own pace."[15] But to point out "the original, unique and progressive creation of human and cultural values" involves not only a forward motion within the "creation of human and cultural values" but also a sufficiently sophisticated development within the consciousness of the interpreter, differentiated enough at least to affirm from his own experience epigenetically differentiated consciousness as this appears in history.

Whether from the philosophical, the psychoanalytic, the psychological, or the historical viewpoints, there is a rather striking unity in the general affirmations that the person becomes a human subject by the development and appropriation of epigenetically differentiated consciousness. It is not unnatural, therefore, that understandings of the history of religions, theology, and religious studies should proceed in accord with the relatively modern thematic shifts to the subject and to the world of interiority that have accompanied the emergence of historical consciousness. Historical consciousness is perhaps best defined by turning directly to historicity, which not only colors all modern intellectual life but also provides the environment in which the history of religions and theology presently have their existence.

PART ONE

·1·

HISTORICITY

Historicity, according to Heidegger, is an attribute of *Dasein* that follows what he calls the *existenzialia,* the characteristics of specifically human existence.[1] "Being in," "being alongside the world," is the primary *existenzial,* or characteristic of human existence. All other possibilities of human existence are possible because the person is in a world. "Taking up relationships with the world is possible only *because Dasein,* as Being-in-the-world, is as it is."[2] This is later described by Heidegger as the "world-hood" of *Dasein.*[3]

This is obviously a different approach to the study of human existence from that which seeks to distinguish human beings from the animal world in terms of genus and species and thus yields a definition such as "rational animal" or a paraphrase of Boethius's *"substantia individualis naturae rationalis."*[4] The person thus defined is one entity in a hierarchic chain of being, differentiated from below by rationality and from above by the capacity for substantial change. Reflections on what a person later does, as, for example, the study of religion or theology or, indeed, any other significant activity, will vary in accord with the presuppositions one has about what people are, how they are related to the universe, and of what they are therefore capable. Heidegger's *Dasein* is quite different from the inherited Greek anthropology.

Heidegger presents other structures of *Dasein* which are equally "equiprimordial with Being-in-the-world: *Being-with* and *Dasein with* (*Mitsein und Mitdasein*)."[5] This being-in-the-world, being-with, and being-there imply instantly, of course, a "they" which is also an *existenzial.*[6] Being-there and with a "they" involves a state of mind, which

state of mind[7] is further described as fear[8] and, more importantly for
our purposes, is defined as "understanding."[9] Understanding, which is
identified with *Dasein,* is already interpretation.[10] This, of course, means
that assertion, or what in another understanding of reality is called
"predication," is really a derivative mode of interpretation[11] (most later
hermeneutical discussions center on this point). It is "Being-there" that
is already understanding and interpretation and that subsequently generates discourse and language.[12]

For our purposes, then, Heidegger is saying that historicity, hermeneutic, and understanding are fundamental *existenzialia,* that is, what
would be called in another mode of discourse attributes of human existence, intrinsic characteristics of human existence, essentials of *Dasein.*
Each of these terms, unfortunately, is inaccurate in its connotation. Any
form of attribution involves the priority of that to which some quality
or capacity is attributed, e.g., substance to which certain accidents are
attributed. This priority, and subsequently, importance, appears from
the terms themselves: substance, accidents. In this scheme, time and
place are accidents. And one must go through an unusual amount of
juggling to preserve the accidents as somehow necessary to the substance or nature.

In contrast, Heidegger affirms that *existenzialia* are modes of *Dasein's*
Being.[13] Thus the whole tenor of Heidegger's existential analysis is to
analyze being, "whose essence it is to be historical."[14] What were earlier
conceived as accidents are now constitutive. Historicity enters the
human constitution. It is not simply accidental to this man that as this
man he is black and lives in a particular time and place, any more than
the concrete person is an instance of universal person. Heidegger sees
the individual as such to be historical in makeup and essence. This is
what was meant in the discussions in the late 1920s and early thirties in
Germany when the writers again and again stated that they were beginning with existence. Only, however, with the emergence of historical
consciousness on the broader scale could persons perceive in an explicit
fashion their historicity in a radical fashion. Some writers would see historicity "as man's realization that individually he is responsible for the
life he leads and collectively he is responsible for the world in which he
leads it."[15] While consequentially true, the statement is an oversimplification. Heidegger is speaking of historicity on a much more radical
level: a person's being is *Sein-können.* Authentic being is or is not
achieved through decision made in concrete historical situations, which

themselves allow a certain defined field for effective historical choice. Thus the power to be (*Sein-können*) is restricted not only by the historicity of the individual as individual, but also by the historicity of the temporal and societal structure in which the individual lives: one could not have been, for example, an astronaut in the fifteenth century.

Authentic existence is that in which one realizes the historical possibilities of existence by decision. One achieves authentic existence, becomes concretely what one is, only insofar as one "grasps the meaning and directs the destiny of its (*Dasein's*) true temporality. Unauthentic existence hides the real meaning of time as the expression of Being. From the interplay of the two is born the continuing drama of history...."[16] Thus, the impetus of Heidegger's thought is that if one misunderstands what *Dasein* really is—historical in the radical sense—then *Dasein* cannot achieve authenticity because *Dasein* will understand and therefore be something other than it is. The dimension of thinking that Heidegger here exercises is what Langan called a personal type of philosophizing.[17] The approach is developed out of an analysis of everyday existence, the concrete, ontic level at which one actually lives. It is then formulated on the existential and ontological level.

One need not totally appropriate the recondite terminology of Heidegger nor attempt to follow his later oversimplifications in his subsequent poetic phase. But one must take seriously the fact that Heidegger represents a current of thought (largely emanating from the Renaissance's development of historiography and the Enlightenment's emphasis on human autonomy) and a manner of analysis that not only corresponds to experience but also provides the conceptual equipment or a heuristic structure capable of dealing with that experience. Heidegger's analysis of human existence, his return to being, has had on our age an impact equal to that of Hegel on his own era. The impact is not limited to the details of the system or bound to passing incidentals. Heidegger provides the conceptual framework and a new urgency for ideas that were in the air long before his time. These ideas, which predate the Enlightenment period, ultimately had their roots in the Greek idealistic image of the person, which saw the human essence as mind, and in the Christian vision of the person as will. The decisive element of will was added by Christianity. In this sense Heidegger is developing and purifying a tradition. With the emphasis on will "the historicity of man begins to be recognized, although it is not yet clearly perceived."[18]

Later, Romanticism, with its stress on elements peculiar to the individual, who is seen as unfolding in a mysterious but unique fashion, becomes another step towards understanding the historicity of the person.[19] The realistic view of humanity enters the horizon of the West via the Bible and provides at least a background for the very movement that has recently caused so much perturbation in Western religions, particularly Christianity. Bultmann is quite correct in citing Auerbach's *Mimesis*,[20] which holds that it was by "the Christian understanding of man that the realistic view of life enters into high literature. Now for the first time the everyday life of man is seen as the field of serious problematic and tragic happenings."[21] The understanding of historicity evolves slowly and perceptibly within a tradition.

Historical consciousness emerges with historical experience. So, for example, Heidegger's description of historicity is primarily addressed to the possibilities of individual choice and decision in a temporally determined existence. The focus is primarily on the individual, who accepts responsibility for individuality in a relatively monochromatic society. Since his writing, historical consciousness has broadened its horizon to include the historicity of particular societies in which the individual's capacity for historical existence—one's field of effective choice—can be greater or less, according to the type of institutionalized society in which one lives. Repressive societies restrict the possibilities for effective personal choice. Historical consciousness therefore is a mental differentiation that evolves and admits variations in intensity or degree.

Bultmann notes that *"Historical narrative* proper arises when a people experiences the historical processes by which it is shaped into a nation or state."[22] Historical consciousness, in contrast to mythical consciousness, depends on a phonetic alphabet, chirography, a moveable printing-press process, and, later on, the electronic media of communication. These vehicles progressively extend human memory far beyond the range of the story, the legend, the saga, the myth. Accompanying each stage is a corresponding reorganization of the sensorium, which is a concrete dimension of human historicity. Attending the development of the means of communication are larger historical movements that are frequently characterized as revolutions, such as the agricultural, industrial, scientific and the communications revolutions. Finally, the result of the confluence of these movements is the revolution of expectations.[23] As experienced by nations, these are all historical processes that demand and generate new conceptual structures in dialectical operation with the ongoing reorganization of human consciousness.

Heidegger represents a thematization of human existence as historical. This explicit elaboration is a basic insight and a differentiation of consciousness of major proportions.[24] In the light of this differentiation, one may note some who early prepared the ground: for example, Vico (*Nuova Scienza,* 1725, 1730[2], 1744[3]); Lowth (*De sacra Poesi Hebraeorum praelectiones,* 1753); Michaelis, who annotated the first German edition of Lowth in 1758, as well as Heyne, Eichhorn, and Gabler. Herder is important not merely for his direct contribution to hermeneutics and his influence on Goethe, but also for his advanced observations on the historicity of language (*Origin of Language,* 1772).

Heidegger operated within this tradition. He began lecturing in 1915 in Freiburg on the pre-Socratics, Kant, and, in 1916, on Aristotle. He published *Sein und Zeit* in 1927. His competencies were within the ancient classical tradition. And about the time that Heidegger was beginning his lecturing career, Freud, likewise trained in the classical tradition, was slowly discovering that individuals were far less rational and more historical than hitherto supposed.[25]

The Enlightenment's emphasis on the human autonomy met perhaps its strongest enemy in the hold that historical determinants exercised in the history of the individual. The history embodied in the person's attitudes and psychological patterns was every bit as relentless as the more generalized historicity of culture. Freud's patients behaved in rigid, stereotyped, and predictable fashion, as if driven by some inexorable stimulus-response pattern. Otherwise seemingly intelligent and capable people were held in dreary captivity to the influence of forgotten historical events, either real or imaginary. And their rationalized defense systems, perfected by long practice, made the original historical events even less accessible to any type of scrutiny. An event of very early life could provide its own historicity, hermeneutic, and understanding not only in the unconscious realm but in the conscious sphere of pseudo-justification. Freud's work is significant not only for his topographical analysis of the conscious and, in relation to the conscious, the divisions of the unconscious and preconscious, but perhaps more so for its dramatic illustration of the influence, pertinacity, and pervasiveness of historicity. Freud's significance can be best understood as working against the "compartmentalization of personality in the nineteenth century."[26] The attempt to compartmentalize was an effort to escape historicity and the conceptual difficulties that historical consciousness was to introduce into virtually every area of human living and human thought.

But so powerful was historicity in the life of Freud's patients that each of his attempts to establish a scientific methodology made only small inroads on the hermeneutic and understanding so elaborately and pertinaciously bolstered by what we now know to be defense mechanisms. In clinical practice Freud discovered on the ontic level what Heidegger was to orchestrate and spell out on the ontological level. In light of the insights of Freud and Heidegger, the words of Gadamer, uttered at a much later date, sound less the property of a theoretician of hermeneutics. "Actually, history does not belong to us, rather we belong to it. Long before we understand ourselves in retrospect we understand ourselves as a matter of course in the family, society and state in which we live. . . ."[27] Interpretation and whatever measure of freedom is available to us depend on coping with historicity.

The implications of Freud's discovery are not confined to the treatment of emotionally troubled persons or to the lives of individuals clearly classifiable as neurotic or psychotic. Rather, historicity as a constitutive element in human existence is of most significance in what Heidegger calls the "everydayness" of human existence. Historicity in the neurotic is but a dramatic instance of all historicity. If we admit this, then we will not assume that reflective consciousness is the automatic accompaniment of every human being's existence; it is not simply identified with being awake. We are therefore in a position to distinguish between substance, so to speak, and subject.

A further implication of Freud's work is the awareness that both the individual and the community require a certain delicate emotional balance before rationality is free to operate, a fact that requires no more concrete verification than attention to our own internal states. Jung, for instance, notes that, "Rational argument can be conducted with some prospect of success only so long as the emotionality of a given situation does not exceed a critical degree."[28] Discussion of emotionality and its potential influence is illustrative not only because of the transparent and instantaneous historicity, hermeneutic and understanding that the emotions imperiously dictate, but also because the emotions themselves normally have a definite and historical cause, either genetic or environmental. The influence of prior history on the emotions is as historical as the current activity of any emotion.

Because this is so, most people are convinced of Jung's comment that the individual or group can be "ruled by effective judgments and wish fantasies,"[29] though rare are the people who are reflectively conscious of this in their own particular case or who are even willing to admit its possibility in a concrete personal instance. Hence a group can be in a state of "collective possession," so much so that its members may feel that they are perfectly adapted "and consequently feel quite at home in this historical state of possession."[30] The serious problem here is that when we are subject to what Jung calls a "historical state of possession," we both perceive and justify the state by appeals to the dictates of reason, a process comparable to the defense mechanisms of the neurotic. Though the term possession does not here involve any antiquated religious views, one can readily see why Jung chooses the term, in contrast to the more neutral statement of the philosopher who would say rather that possession is simply the occupation of a hermeneutical field by certain definite presuppositions, attitudes and ideas and the subsequent justification of this occupation. The all pervasive nature of the state, and the firmness with which it is maintained and justified, is clear when writers suggest that only a process as equally intense and radical—conversion—stands any chance of altering the state of possession.

It should not be supposed here that I have any particular states of possession in mind, much less among scholars given to the practice of religious studies or theology. What I am affirming, however, is that what human beings create, as for example, the history of religions, theology and the field of religious studies, is subject to the historicity of the creators and therefore can only be understood in this context. Such states, however mild they may be, are possibilities of human existence. To ignore the possibilities, either in the individual or the community, would be to ignore historicity. This is all the more pertinent in both the actual practice of religion and its study. Here the vested interests of individuals and societies tend to be high, the risk of illusion always threatens, the potential reorganization or denial of a belief system is always frightening, and the introduction of any relativity tends to undermine not only certainty, but also hopes and aspirations. More importantly, any states of disequilibrium in the study of a religion may obscure or deface the understanding of the persistent quest for transcendent meaning.

Because all religions attempt to mediate ultimate meaning, both those who accept the meaning and those who resolutely oppose it, tend to have rather strong views on the nature of religion and on the form and shape of studies of religion: hence the point of discussing emotions and their historicity. Strong emotions were at work at the beginnings of the history of religion and likewise among ecclesiastics and theologians, as we shall later see. To ignore possible emotional coloring is to bypass the pages of history, or, at the very least, to be unrealistic about the place of reason. In matters of religion and its study, civil conversation is the only vehicle for long range hope. And civil conversation has certain prerequisites.[31]

The argument above may seem rather quaint, abstract, and unduly impertinent until one turns to the suggestion that distinctions between theology and religious studies were once made to satisfy the intellectual and/or the religious community, and that once having been made, this is the end of the matter—now the two disciplines should converge.[32] Not only does this suggestion ignore the ramifications of historicity already mentioned, but it tends to treat both religious studies and theology as mere social conventions, or as subjects so remote from vested interest that purely rational criteria become instantly operative. On the contrary, the disciplines of religious studies and the suppositions operative in the establishment and exercise of the disciplines have been as emotionally charged as any political or military conflict. Convergence may work temporarily as an administrative procedure but offers little promise of long-term clarification of the relationships among religious studies, the history of religion, and theology.

Nor can one go on to imply, as is done in justification of the suggestion above, that one is clearly aware that there are presuppositions in every interpretation, that every study has its historicity and that therefore there are presuppositions and historicity in religious studies and theology—as if one simply glanced at one's presuppositions, turned to one's historicity, and all became self-evident. This approach ignores historicity as constitutive of human existence and as the very possibility by which human existence is understood. The subtle shift in perspective characteristic of historical consciousness is that we cannot understand anything outside of its historical setting and that we are part of the historicity we seek to understand. The historical setting does not disclose itself easily to understanding, particularly if one equates understanding with the act of seeing, or interpretation with seeing what is given in a text. "What is peculiar to the modern mind is the disposition and the determination to regard ideas and concepts, the truth of things as well as the things themselves, as changing entities, the character and significance of which at any given time can be fully grasped only by regarding them as points in an endless process of differentiation, of unfolding, of waste and repair."[33] Suggestions of convergence ignore the complexity of historical understanding.

To appreciate the relation of the individual to historicity, we may proceed negatively. Historicity is what would be forgotten in a case of total amnesia, and what would be eliminated if individuating characteristics of the genes were removed. (Both Becker and Lonergan use the example but confine it rather to partial amnesia.) Historicity here is identified with the existence of the human being, with that which makes one capable of carrying on life even at the most elementary level. It is temporality and possibilities within existence that make each person a historical being. And this historical life necessitates the foundation and perpetuation of a tradition. If history is indeed but an extension of the memory,[34] then, potentially at least, those communities where memory is longest are theoretically the most historical (I refer here to communities that have gone through what Ong calls the aural-oral period, the phonetic alphabet, the chirographic culture, the moveable printing-press culture and the electronic period of preserving and recollecting history). Maybe it is no accident that a very high degree of concern for individuals as such appears concomitantly with the growth of the communications media, which detribalize human beings. And these media are either nonexistent or rigidly controlled where ideologies give primacy to the masses over the individual. Even in these cases, however, there are indications of movement toward the same type of orientation in space and time that one finds in most of Western society. This point, at least, was made by C. P. Snow as far back as 1959.[35]

One would naturally expect to find in studies about religion, given the variation of cultures, a relatively high degree of historicity understood as relativity of perspective. With the growth of historical consciousness, both the practice and study of religion are conceived in more relative terms. This may cause a problem for the practice of religion and likewise for the theoretical justification of particular forms of religion, a point to which I will return. In this climate traditional modes of conceiving theology become increasingly irrelevant, while the academic study of religion temporarily benefits from the climate of relativity and the demand that every human construct be studied historically. The multiple problem created by historicity has only been postponed by housing religious studies within the university because it is nonnormative, and theology within the church because it seems to be normative. Such categories are descriptive and typical of a past age.

They describe the ways in which the two disciplines were once practiced. This general obscurity is obvious in the instance of religious studies from the diversity of names given to the discipline—comparative religion, history of religions, phenomenology of religions, etc.—as if nomenclature conferred clarity and identity on the subject matter and its methodology. Meanwhile, theology has been left to itself to make do with the term normative study and its pejorative implications. The fact that even theology now studies religion in a climate formed by historical consciousness receives infrequent attention. Historicity suggests that theology be practiced in a way suited to the developed state of consciousness manifested by historical consciousness. As yet there is no fully developed outline of what a new type of theology should look like. Possibly the best presentation of theological methodology in a context of historicity has been proposed by Gordon D. Kaufman.[36] He notes: "Since the radically constructive character of the theological task has not been clearly recognized in the past, there is little in the tradition to give us guidance on how to proceed methodologically."[37] There is a growing conviction, more operative as background than as principle, that whatever methodology is or will be used should bring theology and the history of religions closer together. To specify theoretically how this conjunction should occur is the large theme of this book.

To summarize: Historical consciousness becomes aware of the historicity of human existence and human creations. Historicity suggests a certain relativity. Diverse meanings may be attributed to human existence and human creations. Seemingly contradictory authorities may be cited. Nonetheless there is an agreement that one's being as such is a continual becoming within the scope of self and one's culture's possibilities. For religious studies, the history of religions, and theology the concrete implications of historicity seem to insinuate at the very least a reconsideration of the field and its disciplines in the light of historical consciousness. This is by no means a simple task since historical consciousness is both developing and operating. In its first stages, historical consciousness disclosed what influenced me as opposed to the Hindu, the Easterner, the one from a developing nation, the underprivileged. A new factor, which can be only briefly mentioned here, has recently been felt. This is the fact that, to a certain extent, identical historical forces are influencing and forming everyone and all cultures. Some of these forces are scientific activity; sophisticated technology; rapid long-distance transportation; economic interdependence; electronic communications; the accepted classification of areas of the world as underdeveloped, developing, and developed; the urgent need to reconcile national disputes, and the right of all people to a truly human existence. An early fruit of historical consciousness is its capacity not only to recognize the influence of individuating factors on individuals but also its capacity to grasp the influence of identical historical factors upon virtually all individuals and nations. This latter point suggests the interesting possibility that whereas historical consciousness at first highlighted differences it is now grasping similarities and indeed agreements about the authority of historical forces working universally.

While historicity may insinuate a certain relativity of perspective with regard to both the present differences among societies and the discordances between the present and the past, the historical individual and the historically determined societies are not at all totally discrepant entities or isolated units (a point to which I will return). For there exists in every individual the adaptation to the world he or she inhabits, a world sustained by the various forms of propaganda and mythology destined to maintain the status quo, to make the business of everyday living proceed at least with minimal satisfaction. But there is likewise resident within all individuals a view of the world that they would like to have and inherit. It is this world of desire that leads to forms of civilization, which Northrop Frye describes as the human form given to nature.[38] The shape of the society one would like to live in is, of course, projected by the imagination and usually emerges in the art forms. The limits of achievement are set by definite historical and personal forces. While the historical determinants may vary from age to age, the constant is human desire and human imagination. These invariables anchor what may at first glance seem to be purely arbitrary and haphazard historical influences, without at the same time suggesting the fallacy that there is a sort of constant and eternally invariable human nature, everywhere and at all times the same. There is rather a dialectic between human desire, its expression through imaginative projection, and the concrete historical and temporal structure in which desire and imagination operate. Residual and identifiable constancy is dialectically present amid an almost infinite temporal evolution typified by the shifts of caprice and accident. Meaning, therefore, is a process "requiring continual revision."[39] This conclusion itself continues to be refined by historical consciousness.

But our task at this early point it not to develop this philosophical, historical, and literary concept but rather to locate religious studies, the history of religions, and theology in the ecological system of historical consciousness. I will discuss in chapter 6 the world created by desire and the artistic worlds created by imagination, particularly the world of literature.

However, since the history of religions, theology, and the field of religious studies involve the process of knowing or understanding, which, while being a dimension of historical consciousness, is nonetheless a procedure with its own suppositions and history, it is useful now to turn to the dominant cognitional paradigm inherited by Western culture, the model influential in determining what is meant by knowing and understanding in general, and therefore a structure that has exercised considerable influence in determining the accepted categories of knowing and understanding in the field of religious studies. It will then appear, I think, that the inherited paradigm is in considerable conflict with the data provided by historical consciousness.

·2·

A COGNITIONAL PARADIGM

W hen we speak of historicity and of its accompanying hermeneutic, that is, the way in which historicity operates as understanding, we are instantly involved in the larger realm of cognitional and epistemic theory. One cannot speak of historicity without explicit attention to the major cognitional paradigm that has been influenced, modified, developed, or sometimes contradicted by historical consciousness. Descartes proposed the paradigm that was in keeping with the intellectual inheritance of Aristotle and scholastic intellectualism. The subject permits only the briefest development here.

Thinkers such as Heidegger do not simply differ in degree with the tenets of classical intellectualism developed by Descartes, but rather almost in kind.[1] Historicity played no role whatsoever in the transcendental ego or the *res extensae* established as epistemic principles of clear and distinct ideas. Descartes, of course, could not totally ignore historicity, at least in the format of his discourse, which was an address to a particular reader. Yet the transcendental ego was isolated from its historical determinants and thus overcame not only relativity but uncertainty. Such isolation fostered not only the clarity and distinctness of ideas but also eliminated the contingent, the accidental, and so led to absolutely certain judgments. The gains for the empirical sciences were incalculable. But isolated, autonomous reason has turned out to be largely a fiction when applied to the study of man or when used as the exclusive cognitional paradigm.

Thought, in this model, in some sense preceded existence and was in some respect foundational. Descartes then had to be occupied with a bridge from the knowing subject to the existent object. Rational thought, as the criterion of human existence, deliberately excluded the social and historical determinants of human existence. This Cartesian model has been determinative in Western civilization—either in itself or with Kantian and neo-Kantian modifications. Strangely enough, Descartes, rather than contradicting the classical epistemic intellectualism that finds its roots in Aristotle, actually reinforced and developed this tradition. Thus, to take an instance, Christian apologists in the sixteenth and seventeenth centuries could build their systems on Cartesian presuppositions without feeling they were in any way out of step with the Aristotelian and scholastic traditions. Aubert, for instance, provides a splended example of how Cartesian intellectualism could be applied to the foundations of Christian faith and to the act of faith itself.[2] Thus Cartesianism created a religious apologetic that made religious assent the terminal point of intellectual understanding among people "of good will"; the only factor to explain why seemingly intelligent people did not make the religious assent, particularly in certain forms of Christianity, was bad will. This apologetic procedure was highly indebted to classical intellectualism.

Put quite simply, "classical intellectualism explains human knowledge as proceeding out of a matrix of senses through conceptualization to judgement to communication."[3] The intellect understands data that are presumably identified with the reality in question and makes judgments about this data. It is in the judgment that truth resides. Later writers standing in this tradition added the dimension of decision to the level of judgment. This emphasis, of course, led one at least to the threshold of historicity since decisions are usually pertinent to choices between historical contingencies. But since decisions fall immediately and directly into the realm of personal history, one can easily understand how the notion of decision was not included in the classical synthesis.

The truth attained in the judgment is described as some type of parity of intellect and object (*adaequatio intellectus et rei*), whether the truth be formal, ontological, moral, or logical. The emphasis here is on the intellect and a potentially intelligible world. Science was then conceived of in a univocal sense as knowledge of necessary, immutable, eternal truths—truths unaffected by the capricious currents of history. The knowledge is certain because attained by an understanding of the causes; universal because causal historical determinants are eliminated;

timeless because of precision from any individuating characteristics. The later Kantian and neo-Kantian positions, even with their a priori categories do not vary that much from the classical model. Truth in the classical synthesis is not adequately developed to include historicity, the social character of knowledge, or the social construction of reality, much less the linguistic mediation of reality.

In fact, the classical synthesis, which began to break up in the early sixteenth century with the work of Copernicus, was related to a cosmology that tells us as much about cognitional process as did the Cartesian explanations. The seven celestial spheres—Moon, Mercury, Venus, Sun, Mars, Jupiter, and Saturn—revolved around the earth and provided a palpable cosmological symmetry. The soul ascended through the spheres and was purified of its dross elements. The seven days of the week were named after the spheres. The diatonic scale developed from the spheres and their harmony. The seven branches of learning in the Middle Ages were associated with the spheres: the trivium (grammar, dialectic and rhetoric) dealt with the words, the vocables (*voces*); the quadrivium (arithmetic, music, geometry and astronomy) worked on the form and nature of things. While the trivium prepared one to understand the meaning of the words, the quadrivium was dedicated to the understanding of things. Knowledge distinguished a perceptible form (*forma visibilis*) from a hidden essence (*natura invisibilis*), and all earthly knowledge was derived from and ordered to the divine wisdom: *"Omnes itaque artes subserviunt divinae sapientiae et inferior scientia recte ordinata ad superiorem conducit."*[4] Symmetry and hierarchic differentiation characterized the ontology and the epistemology.

The classical synthesis did not disintegrate immediately but rather yielded slowly and over a long period of time to different epistemic principles. That the harmony of the classical synthesis has been displaced rather than replaced needs no further development here. But whatever the challenge to the cosmology and its accompanying epistemology, one does not successfully eliminate all effects of the synthesis either abruptly or permanently. Here it is sufficient to note the classical structure, its undeniable coherence and charm, and its evident incompatibility with any cognitional structure that takes historicity seriously.

One sign of the endurance of the classical synthesis is present in the work of Kant. I refer here to his tacit equation of knowing with the visual paradigm of seeing. This equation was begun by Plato, reinforced by the scholastic emphasis on the beatific vision (*visio Dei*) as the ultimate end of humanity and climaxed by its rigorous application in the philosophy of John Locke. There is some linguistic evidence at least that Kant took one of the senses and made it paradigmatic for all knowledge. How much this emphasis was due to the Greek and Hellenistic tradition of true knowledge proceeding from the distance of perception (*theoreo*) could only be determined by detailed historical study. In any case, the identification of knowing as such with vision or any type of visual model does tend to deny the social and historical character of knowledge as well as the interiority of knowledge. For knowledge transcends all merely visual models and owes its certainty to basic and internal historical orientations in human living that are prior to the act of seeing, radically different from seeing, and that transcend the capacity of sight. Yet once one thinks in terms of *phenomena* then almost necessarily the distinction and contrast to *noumena* suggests itself. Here language proposes not only the problem but also the solution. By definition, sight must confine itself to the outward, to the external, to the surface, to the appearance, to the *phenomena*.[5] One may, of course, take issue with this explanation and its basis within Kantian epistemology. But it seems relatively clear that the popular and residual effect of Kant would be such as I have described it. While development of these points would go beyond the scope of this book, one can hardly ignore the influence of the visual model in generating a literal mindedness which "gives the priority entirely to seeing."[6] Historical consciousness, almost by the very obscurity of its wording, does, linguistically at least, take models of knowing out of the realm of vision and into the world of internal consciousness, the world of interiority, the internal world in which the process of religious apprehension ultimately resides.

Associated with the stress on real knowledge as seeing is the supposition that systematic and theoretical thought that can be seen, intellectually or visually, is an advance on the oral or literary presentations of religious thought. It is as if Sophocles or the Yahwist or Shakespeare were imperfect stages along a road tending to a more typically human form of thought identified as the systematic presentation of religious thought. It is this system that is commonly transmitted to students, usually in a seminary, who wish to learn theology. The process of apprehension is assimilated to the procedures of ocular vision. Such a pedagogic assumption makes for tidiness of understanding but vitiates the religious text as a form of direct address. For instance, it is highly questionable whether the so-called systematic and theoretical language of Nicaea, Ephesus, and Chalcedon and their subsequent tertiary symbolic articulations are an advance on the vertical and horizontal Christology of the Fourth Gospel.[7] Better to regard the conciliar elaborations in their historicity as attempts to clarify meaning for a particular period. This would construe the biblical literature as a genre that is not transcended or superseded by any other thought modality. Moreover, if conciliar elaborations may be interpreted primarly according to modes of ocular vision, this is an indication that Christianity has never quite resolved its Greek and Hellenistic inheritance, based on the apprehension of truth by seeing, and its Judaic and New Testament emphasis on the apprehension of truth primarily by hearing and all that this latter term connotes. One thing that is quite clear is that the diversity of emphasis constitutes two quite different types of religion.[8] Whether many theological systems are really more akin to Gnosticism, Hellenism, Stoicism, or Aristotelianism than to New Testament thought is an intriguing question: there is a growing body of biblical studies that makes one wonder who baptized whom.

Before moving on, it might be well to catalog a series of differences evident in contrasting the aural with the visual model of cognition. Hearing suggests an internal orientation while seeing suggests the confrontation of exteriors. In hearing, the subject apprehends the subject, while in seeing the subject apprehends an object. Therefore hearing suggests proximity and seeing distance. Hearing locates the principal meaning in what the subject invests in the object—the subject's reaction—whereas seeing implies that the major meaning is in the perceived object. The act of hearing generates and creates the language through which the world is meaningfully organized and hence stresses the volitional aspect. The act of seeing organizes the world in hierarchies and hence stresses the intellectual aspect. Hence, seeing ultimately tends to place language in space whereas the principal medium in hearing is time. Hearing is preceded by believing, hoping, loving, mutuality, and the need for help. It is therefore productive of genuine community. Seeing is preceded by simple existence of the subject and the object and is productive primarily of individuality and isolation. Both models, of course, are necessary in human living and are complementary. The issue here is simply that the stress on one or the other develops quite different intellectual systems. And the inheritance in the West has largely stressed the visual image.

Visual models of cognition are pertinent to any intellectual procedure whereby the person seeks to objectify to understand. But such models are not paradigmatic for cognitional procedure as such.

Even a superficial consideration of the actual genesis of knowlege in the human being makes it rather clear that the active process of knowing "moves between two (or more) minds rather than simply between mind and thing or world."[9] I would qualify the statement to read "persons" instead of mind. While the university professor, the philosopher, and empirical scientist may feel comfortable with the Cartesian model, children would not recognize the Cartesian description as the way in which they learn. For learning, and the knowledge acquired through the learning process, occurs among individuals who are historically conditioned and determined, individuals formed by a tradition and attempting to pass on the tradition with mostly minor deviations. Learning begins in the infant with the predispositions of belief, hope, and love. Unless, of course, these predispositions are reciprocated there is a corruption of the learning process and a distortion of the learner. Knowledge is an activity and term of some form of dialogue within a community and within a tradition. Only very specialized forms of knowledge approach the Cartesian model. Thus, in contradistinction to classical Western intellectualism in its main thrust, knowledge "is triadic in its structure rather than dyadic."[10] Acknowledgment of the triadic constitution of knowledge must inevitably lead to a recognition of the role of historicity in the knowing process as well as to a consideration of the social aspects of the knowing process and the dispositions requisite to the procedure taking place in an appropriate fashion. Such observations lead immediately to worlds of intentionalities and worlds of meanings. But one cannot always deal adequately with meanings and intentionalities by recourse to a visual model of knowing.

If one examines further the social context of knowledge, particularly at its beginnings in the infant, it is clear that there is a dynamism at work, a dynamism not simply "to know," but rather to know that someone is there to help. No observant parent can miss this orientation. Thus the individual is directed to community, to "an other." A part of that help, of course, is in facilitating knowledge. But the need for help on a larger scale, a help to survive and develop, is more basic and comprehensive than the desire to know. The desire to know is first the desire to know someone, someone who is reliable, someone who is the object of hope. The need for help, so evident in the human organism, is accompanied by and generates a hope—hope that help is forthcoming. As this expectation continues to be realized, there follows a trust, a belief.

Correspondingly, in the mother or the one who helps there is likewise an orientation of hope and trust accompanied by love. Thus there is a complementary series of acts and orientations which precede and determine knowing and likewise determine the characteristics of knowledge and the knowing process as such.

In this instance of the child who is at the beginning of his being, which is becoming, what seems to be evident is a wishing, a hoping for help that is desire, an expectation that is absolutely necessary for human development. It is this wishing and hoping, this human desire that creates and enlarges reality. This hope, which seems at first present in a sort of compulsive and instinctual fashion, actually seems to be creative, generating a type of evidence. If the hope is not realized then one is frustrated to the core of one's being, so much so that one experiences a futility, a despair, and ultimately a type of death. This basic human orientation becomes extremely important in religious thought, where we shall see that it is the hope and trust of the believer that confers meaning on the religious symbolism. No doubt these ideas are well enough known not to need further elaboration except to observe that such realities are slighted in the strictly visual paradigm of knowledge.

There is still another way of approaching the triadic nature of knowledge, an approach that does not stress the community of knowers, as does Royce, nor the orientation of the knower to hope, but rather the mediating powers of language. Thus the knowing subject apprehends the object or the world of reality by the mediating powers of language, of symbol. This position is summarized by Wheelwright:

> There has been an increasing disposition in the twentieth century to bring the problem of language into the very center of philosophical studies. That is to say, language has come more and more to be regarded not only as a necessary means by which philosophical thought may be developed and communicated, but also as a basic ingredient of such thought. Consequently the traditional Cartesian dualism of mind vs. matter . . . has begun to yield in many quarters to a threefold thought-structure, in which subject, object, and linguistic medium play irreducible and inter-causative roles in the formation of what, for want of a better name, we may call reality.[11]

This approach too not only affirms the triadic structure of knowledge but also the historicity of the language, symbols, and speakers.

The triadic and social structure of the knowing process is clear where one seeks definitions of religious studies. One looks for or encounters what a particular writer says or what a tradition affirms.[12] Yet any description or definition we uncover by research, understand by interpretation, and judge by historical investigation is historically conditioned—not only by the one who propounds the definition but also in the language he uses. The tradition in which the definition is uttered is, of course, likewise historically conditioned. All past definitions are adequate for the present only insofar as they correspond to the historicity of the present, are suited to the differentiations of consciousness of the present. Thus, on principle, there is no one past definition of the disciplines of religious studies that will remain static for a very long period of time. If, for instance, historical consciousness becomes an effective differentiation of consciousness in the modern world, then the disciplines of the history of religion and theology, and the field of religious studies will be conceived in a new context. If historical consciousness suggests modifications and revisions of the Cartesian cognitional paradigm, then quite clearly religious studies cannot be defined exclusively in Cartesian terms or with Cartesian presuppositions. And if the modern understanding of tradition—a subject to which I will turn in the next chapter—is more evolved than it was, say, in the time of Max Müller or Schleiermacher, then modern definitions of religious studies and its constitutive disciplines cannot be based upon definitions or methodologies appropriate to the nineteenth century. (I am deliberately bypassing discussion of the development of new methodologies that accompanies the new context, for these methodologies are concrete effects of taking historicity seriously. As the context of religious studies changes, so too will the methodologies and the presuppositions. That I am speaking here of what was once called substantial change or a total alteration from one form to another will become clear as we go on.)

It is evident in a context of historical consciousness, of pluralism in content and methodology, that the student is beset by the uncertainty accompanying the relativity of traditions, by the variety of approaches to one and the same subject matter, and by the inevitable fact that no one world view has a monopoly on truth. The university and the printed word it generates provide a diversity of opinions, hypotheses, and judgments on a variety of subjects. At first, the history of religions benefits from the context of relativity in which one abstains from any type of value judgment or evaluative hermeneutic. In fact, many historians of religions have found the character of the history of religions to reside in the fact that it pursues the discipline "scientifically"—which

means, among other things, that it abstains from an evaluative hermeneutic or a classification of religions into higher and lower. "What it
(the history of religions) does not propose to do, is to rank them (the
religions) as higher and lower—which cannot be done in terms of scientific reasoning."[13] However clear this statement, it is apparent that its
accuracy depends on a particular interpretation of what is meant by scientific reasoning. Although one may attempt to secure the scientific
character of the history of religions in the employment of a method
common to all historical disciplines, this would be to assume tacitly
that a religion is quite the same as what could be called a past secular
occurrence. If indeed a religion has the aspect of personal address—and
more so than most historical occurrences—then it is not so evident that
the study of religions is exactly the same as the history of more secular
events. My point here is not to suggest a resolution, but rather to indicate that the history of religions has enjoyed a certain prosperity that it
owes to the primacy of historical method in the study of humanity and
human creations. But the primacy of historical method, particularly in
its beginnings, was established by its close connection with the Cartesian paradigm of cognitional process. The later growth of historical
consciousness has at the very least suggested that there is an intimate
involvement of the knowing subject in what it knows and that without
this involvement knowledge in certain areas is impossible.

The theologians have also been judged by the Cartesian canons. Even
though they utilize a historical and comparative methodology, their
normative presuppositions seem to exclude them from the real world,
where each historical and religious tradition is assumed to have validity.
It is almost as if a cultural caprice, either of birth or choice, has conferred on one tradition an absolute validity that is outside the pale of
scientific consideration. On grounds of presupposition theology has
generally been excluded as an academic discipline within the university—particularly in North America. Whether this exclusion is now
theoretically sound is questionable. In fact, it is possible that the theologians' presuppositions and commitment to the subject matter of their
tradition may be a requisite for the understanding of religious subject
matter in general. One can here readily distinguish the subject matter of
a religious tradition from the form in which this subject matter is mediated. It would be an error to identify the subject matter with the particular cultural form in which this subject matter is mediated, a point
to which I will return.

To clarify the matter one may distinguish *Sachexegese* (exegesis of the subject matter) and *Sachkritik* (criticism of the subject matter), a distinction introduced more than fifty years ago. Exegesis of the subject matter is largely identified with a traditional historical exegesis: the identification and understanding of what was said, what was done, what happened, and who the agents were. This type of interpretation, which is identified with Leopold von Ranke, attempts to parallel the objectivity obtained in the empirical sciences. To this method the anthropological sciences owe much of their current reputability. Instances of this type of interpretation abound in introductory textbooks in the history of religions.[14] Quite naturally this austere presentation of the so-called facts has eliminated much of the controversy attending earlier discussion of religions that were largely apologetic. So too has exegesis of the subject matter purified individual belief systems of accretions and misunderstandings that have accumulated through an arbitrary interpretation of religious texts and traditions.

On the other hand, the growth of historical consciousness has suggested the necessary involvement of the interpreter in the act of interpretation. One does not free oneself from either presuppositions or other forms of involvement with the texts. Rather, historical consciousness proposes that one become aware of these influences on interpretation. As the interpreter approaches a religious tradition with a series of prior involvements in the subject matter, so too the founders of a tradition had their own presuppositions that must be taken into consideration. Words and actions likewise have effects that go beyond the intentions of the subjects. Thus, in addition to exegesis of the subject matter, there is a type of historical interpretation that one may call criticism of the subject matter. This type of interpretation "comes to what is meant by what is said, and yet measures what is said by what is meant."[15] Frequently, particularly in simple matters of fact, the two modes of interpretation may coincide. But criticism of the subject matter and its possibilities reside ultimately in the interpreter's relation to the subject matter, for example, Bach's to music or Einstein's to mathematics.

Without a genuine relation to the subject matter one can nonetheless arrive at what was said, what was done, who the agents were, when and where the events took place: hence the great number of articles and books on the same subject; hence the small number of books that become classics. One does not necessarily arrive at the world of meaning, even though one may have full control of the data required for understanding the meaning. Exegesis of the subject matter is required for criticism of the subject matter, but the two are quite distinct in most cases. "What is available to the interpreter depends on how responsive he is to the range of human possibility," on "what sort of interpretation . . . the exegete has of himself as a man."[16] Buddhism, for example, will find very little resonance in an interpreter who has not experienced life as suffering and human desires as the primary cause of this suffering. Yet the exegete of the subject matter is quite capable of preparing a lecture or paper on the subject of suffering and desires. Ultimately all historical and textual

> interpretation is determined by self-interpretation. The romanticist interprets texts aesthetically, since he understands man's essence to be form. The idealist sees the texts as a gradual unfolding of spirit because he already interprets the essence of man as reason and the intellectual evolution of ideas. The psychologist apprehends texts in terms of "psychic conditions, moods, and experiences," for he defines man in psychological categories. All these projected self-interpretations view man in general terms, as a particular instance of a universal law, as a member of a species! . . . Without conscious intent the interpreter shapes the texts to his design.[17]

A glaring instance of this, of course, is the interpretation of religious realities and religious terminology by logical positivism and empiricism. Because of a prior self-interpretation that demands that all terms be univocal and empirically verifiable in the world, the language of religious reality, as well as the world of myth and poetry, becomes meaningless.

As a principle of interpretation, criticism of the subject matter demands a relation of the interpreter to the subject matter, **a relation** that is suitable to the manner in which religious texts or religious history present the subject matter. So the interpreters must first grasp their own existence as historical in the sense that their existence is possibility, their being is becoming. Particular religious traditions (and today some political systems) are potential possibilities for existence understood as historical. In a generic and abstract sense these are the boundaries of religious subject matter. If the interpreter has no relationship to the various possibilities for making human existence accessible to human beings, then it would seem that he or she is incapable of exercising a criticism of the subject matter, regardless of proficiency in the exegesis of the subject matter. In this instance much of the work will turn out to be what one interpreter has called "busy work";[18] the blind man speaks of color.

In a sense, therefore, one of the presuppositions of the theologians is their prior relationship to the subject matter of religion. They are, at least in theory, prepared to understand religion, as opposed to this particular form of religion. Given the prior relationship to the subject matter of religion, criticism of the subject matter must inevitably lead to the problems constituted by a plurality of religious traditions and by any claim to universal validity made by one's own particular confession. If theology has been banned from the university, at least in North America, the reason has not been the theologian's prior relationship to the subject matter of religion, but rather that theologians in the past have suggested an absolute equation between the historical form of a particular confession and the subject matter of all religion. Likewise, theology has been under suspicion in academic circles because it has at times employed the homiletic use of theology—quite valid within the liturgical, creedal, and apologetic confines of a particular confession—in the academic context, where such a use of theology is inappropriate. Such use would be both an intellectual and a diplomatic error. Lapses of judgment and incidental failures to comprehend theology in the totality of its functions do not erase the fact that theology is a perfectly reputable intellectual discipline. Nor can the theologian's relation to the subject matter of religion or commitment to a particular historical embodiment of that subject matter be sufficient ground for excluding theology from the university any more than would be the relationship of the musician to music or the historian to history.

If religion is indeed a possibility within human existence, then the theologian's relationship to the subject matter of religion is a required disposition for understanding the subject matter of religion, as the artist's relationship to art is a prerequisite for the understanding of art. Such at least is the suggestion not only of historical consciousness but also of common sense. In a real sense, therefore, the confessional commitment of the theologian is closer to the cognitional paradigm formed by historical consciousness than is the stance of the historian of religion whose posture is based on the Cartesian cognitional paradigm. Of course, theologians may at times have to purify their relationship to the subject matter of religion to eliminate its dross elements.

If one distinguishes between the exegesis of the subject matter and the criticism of the subject matter, one asserts that it is ultimately a disposition of the interpreter that enables an interpreter to move from exegesis of the subject matter to criticism of the subject matter. What is the nature of this disposition? If criticism of the subject matter seeks the meaning of what is said or done, what is the hermeneutic presupposition to criticism of the subject matter? Or, what is meant by suggesting that the outcome of interpretation, particularly in the instance of religious traditions, depends on the kind of interpretation the interpreter has of himself or herself as a person?[19] Or, the next topic, what is the relationship of hermeneutics and understanding?

·3·

HERMENEUTICS
AND UNDERSTANDING

Primarily through the work of Schleiermacher, Dilthey, Husserl, Heidegger, Bultmann, Gadamer, and Ricoeur have we come to acknowledge the hermeneutic structure common to all human consciousness: hermeneutics and understanding are coextensive.[1] The act of interpretation includes in itself a prior disposition that is also a particular and historical type of understanding. One comes to the subject matter of one's investigation with a preexisting orientation. This orientation will in large measure determine the outcome of study. The modern shift is away from a paradigm that equates knowing with seeing, away from knowledge as a process that begins with the presentation of an object to a subject, away from what is called the alienation of objectivity and the distance therein implied. If the interpreters approach the subject matter of interpretation with a preunderstanding that is an integral part of their own self-understanding, so too can the subject matter, mediated in either written or oral discourse, alter the interpreter's self-understanding. In this context, meaning exists primarily in an internal world, the world of interiority, the world of intentionality. Meaning is what the subject intends and the subject matter mediates. Thus is the subject involved in the subject matter of the quest.

An illustration of this involvement is offered by the study of the preliterate religions: for example, the study of the Amerindian traditions. The predispositions that the historian of religion brings to this investigation are typical of a civilization that has gone through the oral-aural stage to the more sophisticated stages of communication. The interpreter is better equipped to understand traditions in which oral discourse has been confined to the written word, where the medium of the word is space—words on a printed page—rather than time. Even where it is suggested that story is a category more appropriate to understanding authoritative religious texts, as, for example, in the biblical tradition,[2] the story is usually encountered as written, not orally narrated.

However, the interpretation of preliterate cultures demands that the interpreters encounter not only the oral form but that somehow their symbolic consciousness be so altered that they are able to revert to an ontogenetic state in which the primary medium of the word is time rather than space. All modern Western education is intended to replace or elevate this earlier stage of development, both in the human race and in the individual, with a literacy characterized by the appropriation of the alphabet as written and printed. Western society invests an enormous psychological capital in this endeavor.

When literate interpreters approach an Amerindian tradition, they do so with a psychological structure primarily developed within the literate tradition. Success or failure in understanding the native traditions does not depend on a methodology easily accessible to all Western interpreters but rather on the interpreters' capacity to alter their preunderstanding and prior relationship to the subject matter of religious studies. This change of symbolic consciousness will begin with the experience of the culture in question; in the case of preliterate traditions that still exist, the experience will be characterized by extensive listening until such time as the interpreter is capable of reverting to the characteristics of the aural-oral period of human development. The point here is that the alterations of the interpreter's prior consciousness only become possible in the context of intersubjectivity. The interpreters cannot exclusively read their way into the understanding of native traditions. Nor can they assume the distance involved in the Cartesian cognitional paradigm. Natives immediately sense both approaches even though they might not be able to say precisely why an interpreter fails to grasp their tradition.[3]

At this point one encounters what seems to be a fundamental difference between the empirical sciences, which tend to operate from an objective distance, and the more anthropological disciplines. This was the problem that Dilthey sought to solve. Dilthey, utilizing Droysen's terms, attempted to distinguish between disciplines which study *Natur,* the world of objects, and those which study *Geist,* the world of human subjects. He sensed that there was a mode of understanding appropriate to the *Naturwissenschaften* and another suitable to the *Geisteswissenschaften.* Husserl developed the differentiation in the intentionality[4] of the knowing process and its consequent psychological dimensions.[5] Though this transition did not found or establish a principle of distinction, it did move knowledge more to the realm of the internalized experience and consciousness of the knowing subject. This was a step toward overcoming the distance created by any model which described knowing in terms of an object perceived by a subject. Husserl's work further stressed the role of meaning in human existence so that Heidegger could later describe authentic human existence as existence which was basically concerned with "things of an intentional kind."[6] Heidegger could then, after his existential analytic, identify *Verstehen* with *Dasein.*[7] Thus, understanding itself is a sort of preexisting state of a subject and does not begin when the adult subject—generally considered as a tabula rasa—turns to a field of investigation. So *Auslegung,* the activity of interpretation, is a "laying out" or "interpretation of there-being."[8] Hermeneutic is then *"sich aus-bilden,"* a "building out of understanding."[9] One makes explicit and articulate what was already there. "The process of explicating There-being's antecedent comprehension of Total meaningfulness (World) Heidegger calls 'interpretation' (*Auslegung*) which, as we have seen, he in turn designates as 'hermeneutic.'"[10] In Heidegger's own words, interpretation is "the working-out and appropriation of an understanding."[11] The appropriation of an understanding is the subject's conscious awareness of the predispositions he or she brings to the subject matter and the concomitant working out of these predispositions. In the case of literate interpreters faced with the work of understanding Amerindian or other native traditions, the interpreters not only work out or develop the predispositions characteristic of the highly literate state but also must gradually work their way out of the negative implications that such a literate state suggests about an aural-oral culture. The process is complex precisely because the requisites for literacy have formed the psychological structure of the interpreter over a long period and because these prerequisites have achieved considerable success in the understanding of literate traditions. But even to the task of understanding literate traditions, the interpreter brings prior dispositions.

"Every interpretation has its fore-having, its fore-sight, and its fore-conception,"[12] which must be *worked out* and all of which are them-selves understandings. One notes here a type of language characteristic of the therapeutic situation, which has recognized that the fore-having, the fore-sight, and the fore-conception play determinative, if unconscious or preconscious, roles in understanding. It is the task of a hermeneu-tic—exercised in any discipline that is involved in interpretation—to make explicit and conscious the interpretation and understanding that has taken place long before the interpreters are aware of it and long be-fore interpreters turn to what they commonly call their work.

Bultmann turned the theoretical Heideggerian existential analytic to the more concrete activity of New Testament interpretation. Indeed, he turned the existential analytic into a vehicle that should be applied to any type of textual interpretation.[13] Gadamer moved further in the ar-ticulation of the universality of hermeneutics. Hermeneutics seeks to dissipate the alienation of objectivity. This alienation has hitherto been found in the realms of aesthetics and of the philosophy of history, and in the understanding of language." The claim to universality is sup-ported by the *language-dimension* of all experience, for language is the universal *medium* which expresses and articulates the fundamental expe-rience of dependence-on and belonging-to. . . . Hermeneutics, then, is the discourse which tells how *belonging-to* language provides the univer-sal medium of *belonging-to* being."[14]

Wheelwright studies the aspects of "What Is," and its relation to a responsive mind through the vehicle of language. His distinction be-tween a steno-symbol and a tensive symbol has become part of modern interpretation. In addition to his suggestive linguistic considerations, he reflects on "the characteristics of reality insofar as it is an object of tensive language and of the responsive wonder that expresses itself through such language. From this standpoint the principal characteris-tics of living reality appear to be three: it is presential and tensive; it is coalescent and interpenetrative; and it is perspectival and hence latent, revealing itself only partially, ambiguously, and through symbolic in-direction."[15]

For Ricoeur, hermeneutics is the activity characteristic of "an inquiry about the art of understanding involved in the interpretation of texts. . . . My task will not be to give a hermeneutics *of* the text, but a hermeneutics *based on* the problematics of the text. This problematic will be organized around four poles: the text as a relation between writ-ing and speaking; the text as a structured work; the text as the *projection* of a world; and the text as the mediation of self-understanding."[16] Each of Ricoeur's four points suggests detailed development. The thread of continuity from Bultmann to Ricoeur, for our purpose at least, is the agreement that it is insufficient to view texts with the same type of objectivity that one employs in astronomy. Ricoeur is repeating what Bultmann said some fifty years ago when he noted that "the text remains a discourse said *by* someone and addressed *to* someone. In this sense reading is a kind of *response* to what the text says. In modern language it is an appropriation, a term which underscores the movement from the alien to the proper."[17] It is obvious that the language of religious literature admits of multiple approaches. But if one is to arrive at the religious dimension of the literature, that is, the aspect of transcendent meaning accessible to human living, the text must be considered as a mode of personal address. Reading or study, to be accurate, must be "a kind of *response* to what the text says." But if the reading or study is to be a response, the interpreter must have a relationship to the subject matter mediated under the form of direct address.

There is no such thing as a religion or a religious tradition that presents itself primarily as a subject for curiosity or for study from a safe distance. Nor are there instances of founders of classic religions whose primary intention was to establish an aesthetic system. Even Chinese philosophers, such as Confucius and Lao-tzu, whose teachings are perhaps capable of the most systematic and harmoniously symmetric presentation intend that the students respond to the teaching as address. Even the doctrine of *paticcasamuppada* ("dependent origination") of the Theravada school, while addressed first to the intellect for understanding, directs itself to the experience of the reader for personal verification. It is, I think, safe to say that all religious traditions have a prophetic and apocalyptic dimension. Either the founder or his followers feel that the prophet has been sent to execute a commission, to give humanity a new understanding of itself, a transcendent meaning. Judaism, Christianity, and Islam refer to the authority of a God who addresses humanity and validates the message by His authority. Confucianism, Buddhism, and Hinduism, to take a few more examples, are based on an intrinsic authority—the authority of the person's life or message, or the authority of the tradition itself—that demands a personal response. Religious traditions ask each person, "How is your life to be understood?"

If the possibility of understanding religious texts lies in the relationship of the interpreter to the subject matter of the texts—part of which will include approaching the texts as forms of direct address—then some sort of existential self-analysis is clearly required of the interpreter. Hence the importance of Heidegger is not that he is the founder of a particular philosophical school—which may or may not be the case—but rather that he has developed an existential analysis suitable to interpretation.

Concretely, Heidegger's phenomenological analysis of *Dasein* is the process "through which the authentic meaning of Being, and also those basic structures of Being which *Dasein* itself possesses, are *made known* to *Dasein's* own understanding of Being."[18] This is the hermeneutic which is an interpretation of self and at the same time an interpretation of the subject matter mediated through texts in most cases. Heidegger specifies three tasks here. First the specifically hermeneutical task; second, the working out of "the conditions on which the possibility of any ontological investigation depends,"[19] and third, an analytic of the "existentiality of existence."[20] The third task may be considered, says Heidegger, as the primary philosophical effort. Even though Heidegger specifies the third task as philosophical, it is clear that all interpreters of religious texts must be engaged in the three acts. The second and third tasks demand a particular conceptual structure. And whether an interpreter adverts consciously to the second and third act, some conceptual structure will inevitably be employed. What is necessary here is that the interpreter become conscious of that structure.

A graphic instance is found in the correspondence between Barth and Bultmann. Of Barth's *Dogmatik*, Bultmann says: "It renounces either a tacit or thorough confrontation with modern philosophy and naively assumes that old metaphysics from patristic and scholastic theology."[21] In theory, Barth seems to have conceded that an existential analysis and a consciously adopted philosophical structure were necessary. But for his own reasons Barth chooses to pursue another path.[22] That the Bultmannian approach has won the day is clear not just from the fact that Barth's theory of interpretation has found virtually no following in theories about hermeneutics but also from the fact that many modern interpreters are repeating what Bultmann said as early as 1925 and developed in a series of later essays.[23] Thus, reference to Bultmann is not made in the context of a particular New Testament exegete working within the German Evangelical tradition, but rather in the larger dimensions of hermeneutics in which Bultmannian thought continues to be a force even where not acknowledged as such.

Development of hermeneutics in recent times has been determined through the works of Gadamer and Ricoeur. It is, I think, to Gadamer that we owe the direct switch to language as the mode of understanding typical of humanity and to the stress on language as the vehicle through which conception and understanding are possible. Language is the fundamental mode of access to reality, the foundation of semantic action.[24] (This train of thought is not the exclusive possession of recent philosophical thought. Oscar Wilde had proposed similar ideas, stressing not only the permanency of language but its powers to serve as a surrogate for past events: "yet, every day the swanlike daughter of Leda comes out of the battlements and looks down at the tide of war."[25])

Gadamer asks, *"Wie ist Verstehen moglich?"*[26] ("How is understanding possible?")—a question that presumes the Heideggerian contribution. Gadamer's own answer, that *"Sein, das verstanden werden kann, ist Sprache"*[27] ("Being that can become understood is language"), acknowledges the validity of the Heideggerian temporal analytic of human *Dasein,* in which Heidegger has effectively indicated that understanding is not just one activity or attitude of the human subject but is rather the very *Sein* of *Dasein.*[28] Thus, what we have described as historicity enters the constitution of understanding and hermeneutics that makes historical understanding possible. In the present context it is not necessary to outline the contributions of Ricoeur's splendid analyses of the act of understanding as this act takes place with written texts, except to recall that his efforts are the most developed contributions to the actual act of interpretation and its concomitant hermeneutic and understanding.[29]

While the term hermeneutic or hermeneutics is susceptible of various definitions, it is helpful to recall that the history of the term is best depicted adjectivally, in the sense of "hermeneutical reflection," a description that stresses the "function accomplished in all bringing of something to a conscious awareness."[30] A reflection that one describes as hermeneutical recalls the origin of the term hermeneutics. And at its origin, hermeneutics always signified, in a spatial metaphor, the process of bringing something distant a bit closer, of overcoming the strangeness of what is distant, of building a bridge "between the once and the now."[31] (It was a later development that suggested that dispositions of the interpreter—certainly in a topographical sense, near or identified with the interpreter—could also be psychologically distant and therefore the legitimate and necessary subject of hermeneutical reflection.)

That hermeneutical reflection is necessary in understanding is particularly significant for the field of religious studies, where distances of both types are evidenced. In fact, one might distinguish at least three types of distance with an accompanying state of psychological tension. There is first of all one's distance as the interpreter from oneself, the distance from a full and conscious appropriation of self. Second, there is the distance of the interpreter from other religious traditions. And this distance is twofold: a distance in time and a cultural distance. Third, there is a distance of the tensive symbol from what it intends to define, describe, indicate, or suggest. While distances in the first two instances must be narrowed for successful interpretation, distance in the third case must remain. For in the third species, distance is constituted by the subject matter of religions—ultimate and transcendent meaning—as well as by the transcendent within the human being. This transcendence may be simply defined as the individual's capacity of "raising further question."[32]

In a certain sense, the unknown—whether it be of temporally or culturally remote religions—can become known, given the proper hermeneutical reflection. But our orientation to transcendence, toward going beyond the present state of knowledge, presents the yet unknown as mysterious. Much of what today is considered to be mysterious will be known at some future date. But "the field of mystery" can be narrowed with the advance of knowledge without at the same time eliminating mystery from human living.[33] Therefore, beyond the present horizon or on the periphery of the horizon remains what is yet to be known. This is the generic realm of transcendence and mystery. What distinguishes religion from other human activities is that religions and their symbols point beyond every present or communal horizon to the realm of the permanently mysterious, which will not be contracted by further advances in knowledge. Yet the religious symbol must contain some meaning within a present horizon. This paradoxical symbolic state creates greater tension within the study of religion than within the practice of religion, where symbols obtain their efficacy and validity from an intersubjective relationship to the transcendent toward which the symbols point. Here the religious experience is its own confirmation, as is clear from either personal experience or from a careful study of mystical writings in all traditions.[34] The person described as religious is one who does not need a confirmatory reasoning process.

But people who study religions have a more difficult task, for they are engaged in an effort to domesticate an intractible transcendence. Or, if you will, they seek to close distances between symbols and the reality to which they point without at the same time reducing the tensive symbol to the steno-symbol. If the student of religion reduces religious symbols to the status of steno-symbols—the realm of absolute univocity and therefore of absolute clarity—then religion becomes detached from ultimate and transcendent meaning, the meaning that is on the edge of every individual and communal horizon. Such reduction of the tensive symbol to a closed language has been described by one interpreter:

> Briefly there are two ways in which steno-language or closed language, language consisting of static terms, may arise: by habit and by prescription. Language becomes closed and static by habit when the imagination fails, so that the same words are repeated without examination or critical integrity. Such language has lost its vitality, as when a person talks too much about God or love or duty, or any other great theme. Language that is closed in this manner, by default, may be indefinitely susceptible of ambiguities. . . . When language is closed by stipulation, on the other hand, as is done in scientific and logical usage, the aim is to get rid of ambiguity as far as possible and to establish semantic precision combined with sharability. . . .[35]

Hermeneutical reflection, therefore, is the process whereby the interpreter brings to conscious awareness the tripartite distance. This state of conscious awareness then suggests and proposes the appropriate means to narrow or preserve the distance as measured by the interpreter's relation to the subject matter of religion.

The beginning point of hermeneutical reflection is in the interpreter's reflection on his or her own tradition. This is a transit from the naive to the critical, from the implicit to the explicit, from the unthematized to the thematized. In this process interpreters will soon discover that the tradition that formed them and which they unconsciously assumed for purposes of identity is not completely identified with the tradition they uncover by their scientific study. What slowly emerges is a gap between an assumed tradition and an authentic tradition, coming from the conflict between authentic and inauthentic appropriation. Whether the process of critically appropriating and judging one's own tradition authentically is first called hermeneutic and subsequently understanding is of little importance. What is important is the fact that hermeneutical reflection uncovers complexity in a realm that has been for a long time considered to be simple, namely, the explicit appropriation of one's own tradition. The prior disposition, which assumed that one's own tradition was a body of knowledge easily understandable, is contested by a hermeneutic that very soon discloses the problem of distinguishing between the authentic and the inauthentic, between what was hitherto assumed and what in fact has been actually operative. (Further description is beyond the scope of this book, but there is a parallel in the critical appropriation of one's own tradition. The ordering principle is the old Aristotelian concept of wisdom, or the prior disposition, that regulated and controlled the acquisition of all later knowledge. Erikson, for example, describes an understanding that is beyond knowledge.[36] The action is a hermeneutical transposition of consciousness, which is necessary if one is to proceed to the study of religious traditions and cultures different from one's own.)

Hermeneutics first demands self-interpretation. This is the attempt by discrete acts of consciousness to discover how one has become what one is. Self-interpretation suggests the conscious appropriation (whether by form of acceptance or rejection or substantial modification makes little difference) of one's own tradition(s)—for tradition confers identity. Appropriation of one's own tradition grounds the possibility of understanding other traditions. Thus we are not forced into Dilthey's suggestion that we abolish the obstacle of historicity. The critical appropriation of historicity through hermeneutical reflection in one instance becomes the basis for understanding historicity in other instances. This is close to Gadamer's proposal summarized in the phrase *"wirkungsgeschichtliche Bewusstsein"* ("efficacious historical consciousness"). It differs from Gadamer in implying that the basis for understanding diverse traditions derives from a perceived identity of cognitional structure, a perceived symmetry in the structures of traditions, and, in the case of religious traditions, an identity of relationships to the subject matter of religion. Diversity, as will become clear in the following chapter, exists in the contents of cognition, of tradition and, in many instances, in the symbolic articulation of the contents.

But even the symbolic articulations of religious subject matter are strikingly similar when one proceeds to a careful hermeneutical reflection on one's own tradition. For all religious traditions begin with an experience that is articulated in myth: thus could Malinowski call myth the language of religion par excellence. Because of the universality of myth as religious language, Vico and Herder both held that myth springs from the depths of human nature, and is a valid, necessary, and universal carrier of meaning.[37] They both perceived the necessity for conscious self-transformation if an interpreter in an age of scientific and discursive consciousness is to understand myth. A later generation took the step that Vico and Herder did not take—the acknowledgment that mythical consciousness actively permeated both the Judaic and Christian traditions.[38] This conjunction of religious traditions can only appear when the Western interpreter is dedicated to serious and prolonged interpretation of the inherited religious tradition and of the Judeo-Christian tradition, which has so strongly influenced Western civilization.

The validity of myth as a carrier of human meaning was confirmed by the comparative study of religion, a point to which I will turn shortly. This acceptance of myth as a necessary carrier of meaning led initially to the early success of the history of religions but had the opposite effect on Christian theology, which continued to identify myth as falsehood. Nor has Christian theology yet totally freed itself from the consequences of this identification. For confirmation of this statement one need only read Gunkel's classic commentary on Genesis and compare his conclusions, if they may be so called, with the generally accepted dogmatic tenets of most speculative Christian theology.[39] We see in Gunkel's work an example of the historical-critical method at its best. The results of this historical-critical method have yet to be incorporated into systematic and speculative theologies, though a beginning may be found in the work of Schillebeeckx. This problem within the discipline of theology accounts for many of the difficulties in the relations between theology and the history of religions.

Hermeneutical reflection not only directs itself to conscious self-appropriation, to explicit criticism of one's own tradition(s), but also to the discovery of myth as a universal and necessary carrier of meaning. In the more objective world of the religious symbol, such reflection discovers the double intentionality of the symbol. This double intentionality of the symbol, a theme suggested by Bultmann in 1925 and only recently entertained in the arena of critical study,[40] confirms the need for the serious and continued use of the historical-critical method and yet stresses a subjective dimension within all interpretation. Thus the interpreter could employ the scientific methods worked out in the historical-critical study of literary documents and at the same time avoid the pitfalls of eisegesis that accompany an uncontrolled subjectivity. Resident in the very nature of the religious symbol is a second intentionality that evokes a response from the interpreter: and it is then the interpreter whose role it is to confer meaning on the symbol. But any response to a religious symbol assumes a critical self-appropriation on the part of the interpreter. And the critical self-appropriation of the interpreter will center mainly on the relationship of the interpreter to the subject matter with which the symbol deals. Obviously, an interpreter who has no relationship whatsoever with the subject matter the symbol intends to mediate will be incapable of understanding the symbol.

The act of interpretation or the hermeneutic of interpretation is broader now than it was in the past. So theologians who remain untouched by direct Heideggerian influence and who specialize in fields other than biblical studies can describe the act of interpretation as a functional specialty in their own proposed theological methodologies. And more importantly, they can describe interpretation as a function that understands the object (*die Sache*, "the subject matter"), the words, the author, and the self who is doing the interpreting.[41] This act of interpretation I have called hermeneutical reflection to remind the reader of the breadth of the activity. In any case, hermeneutical reflection is a circular activity in which self-appropriation begins to be achieved through critical apprehension of one's own tradition(s), through critical understanding of the religious symbol, particularly in its second intentionality. It should again be noted that the believer invests the second intentionality with meaning. This investiture is based on the primordial orientation of the individual to a hope—a hope that there is someone there to help. This is the same hope that is basic to the entire learning process and is so clearly operative in childhood. As an interpreter, one must see how this primordial orientation operated within oneself in the assumption of one's own tradition. The delicate process of analysis is the remote preparation for the understanding of a tradition different from one's own.

If this chapter has been preoccupied with the internal world of the interpreter and the manner in which this internal world must be developed, there remains something to be said about the more externalized world of tradition and the relation of interpreters to traditions other than their own. This is the commonly discussed question of whether an interpreter who is committed to one tradition or educated in a particular religion can truly understand another tradition.

·4·

TRADITION

We have thus far suggested that the interpreters of any religious tradition should have a consciously developed understanding of their own relationship to their particular religious tradition and to the traditions that have decisively shaped the world in which they live. Such an existential analysis will necessarily disclose the relationship of the interpreter to the subject matter of religion. The subject matter of religion is generally mediated through particular historical forms called tradition and is understood by a type of reflection described as hermeneutical. It suffices for now to describe the subject matter of religion as ultimate and transcendent meaning.

The attempts to mediate the subject matter of religion become historical and cultural codes called tradition. So there is a Christian tradition, a Hindu tradition, a Buddhist tradition, even though there may be disagreements about the elements that constitute the traditions. "The fundamental codes of a culture—those governing its language, its schemes of perception, its exchanges, its techniques, its values, the hierarchy of its practices—establish for every man, for the very first, the empirical orders with which he will be dealing and within which he will be at home."[1] Thus a religious tradition, even though it be distant now from the original experience that generated it, is a way of organizing human experience. This systematization is a communal possession. Its continual reaffirmation, particularly in monochromatic cultures and subcultures, provides stability within the society and, for the believer, an effective mode for organizing personal life. Rarely, however, in modern Western society is a tradition found in pure and simple form. Normally a religious tradition contains within itself a superstructure, a structure, and a substructure. To distinguish among these elements is the task of hermeneutical reflection. This is a problem that exists primarily within a tradition. While clarification of one's own relationship to a tradition is sufficiently complex, it is nonetheless specifically distinct from the problem generated by the simple multiplicity of religious traditions.

What immediately confronts the serious interpreter is the striking diversity of religious traditions, the variety of cultural codes—each of which claims a legitimacy and a certain degree of absolutism. Even when accompanied by hermeneutical reflection, historical consciousness seems to canonize pluralism and to insinuate a state of relativity. What is true for the Hindu is not necessarily true for the Muslim. Striking dissimilarities among religions suggest a lack of underlying symmetry. Such dissimilarities have often enough been described as irreconcilable contrasts in symbolic consciousness and mental procedure: so one distinguishes mythical from scientific, prelogical from logical, an intuitive from a discursive mode, and an Eastern from a Western approach. Where differences and distinctions among cultures and religious traditions are so explained and legitimated by historical consciousness, all cultures and traditions are assumed to possess equal status and validity, for there are no scientific categories capable of rating or hermeneutically evaluating cultures or religious traditions.

Such a hermeneutic evaluation, of course, is made even more difficult by the epistemological assumption that students of one tradition simply cannot understand another tradition. Theoretical justification for the assertion comes from accepting historicity as constitutive of human existence. If, as Heidegger maintains, knowing is a mode of being, knowledge varies with the historical mode of existence proper to each individual. That there is a certain degree of truth here is quite clear, if only from the wide variety of protest movements decorating the social scene during the last decade or more: these movements are generally intended to generate an understanding of particular viewpoints and would be pointless if the protestors really felt their own personal experiences had already been comprehended. Whether the ineluctable portion of truth in the statements above arises from historical consciousness as such or from the relatively opaque and mysterious nature of the individual as such,[2] is a question beyond the scope of this book. What we are concerned with is first, whether religious traditions are communicable and intelligible to those outside the tradition, and second, whether particular religious traditions may endow their adherents with certitude sufficient to withstand competitive claims. Both questions suggest a study of tradition. This chapter is concerned with the first question; the second question arises within the larger context of comparative religion, the topic of the next chapter.

If a tradition is to be intelligible to an outsider, there must be something common to the traditions and something common to the act of understanding that appropriates and understands tradition. One can begin by noting that there is a common structure to all tradition and likewise a common structure to the consciousness that creates and attempts to understand tradition. But more evident than these broad similarities is the fact that all traditions play a specific role in the creation of the identity of the individuals within the traditions. There is, therefore, also a communality of function among traditions.

Human persons are not socialized simply by being instructed into a tradition; they are also constituted by the tradition. The temporality and historicity of the individual is specified by the tradition. The individuating tradition and its subtraditions are conveyed by presuppositions, unspoken assumptions, speech, gesture, customs, laws, cultural and religious values, constancy of environment, music, art, and personal relationships, which mediate the tradition under the perceptible aspects of *la langue* and *la parole*. It is the *la langue* aspect of the tradition, the social part of the language, the systematized set of conventions that the individual as such can neither create nor change, that gives an objective temporal stability to the tradition. In the concrete, of course, the tradition is identified with the individuals on whom the tradition originally confers identity. The stability and universality of the mode in which tradition confers identity on the individuals standing within the tradition makes the understanding of traditions possible, for the *la langue* aspect of a tradition is embodied primarily in objectified and permanent symbols. All traditions are stabilized by the conventions and codes that an individual as such can neither create nor alter.

In the active sense tradition gives identity to the individual while at the same time gradually involving one in one's own hermeneutic, one's own choice as to how one will understand oneself within the tradition that initially gave identity. It is the tradition which enables the individual to remember a past and look forward to a future.[3] In both the active and passive senses, there is a noetic structure to tradition. This noetic structure makes the tradition and subsequently, but to a lesser degree, the individual comprehensible. Because of the dynamism of human existence and because of the cultural evolution following this dynamism, tradition is susceptible of change, growth, decline, modification, and sometimes of obscurity or the ambiguous state I will later describe as dissonance. But by definition all mutation is gradual—even in so-called revolutionary societies. There is then a communality in structure and function among all traditions.

Thus individuals are far more comprehensible and intelligible—both to themselves and to outsiders—than is usually thought, precisely because of their own development within a traceable tradition. The tenacity and power of tradition as such is concretely illustrated by the strife in Northern Ireland, the problems in the Middle East, relations between Greeks and Turks, and the dialectic between Hinduism and the attempt to modernize in India. Individuals in these instances are identified by their inherited tradition. How this process occurs is explained by Allport:

> Each person is an idiom unto himself, an apparent violation of the syntax of the species. An idiom develops in its own peculiar context, and this context must be understood in order to comprehend the idiom. Yet at the same time, idioms are not entirely lawless and arbitrary; indeed they can be known for what they are only by comparing them with the syntax of the species.[4]

The tradition therefore can be known precisely because of its own historicity and the historicity of the individuals within the tradition. While the tradition is the syntax of the species, the idiom becomes intelligible by its relation to the syntax and grammar of the tradition. Ultimately this intelligibility derives from the enduring noetic structure of *la langue* primarily, and of *la parole* secondarily. Thus there is a basic symmetry of structure and function among all traditions.

In fact, a genuine tradition in any era and in any culture is the permanent element of the society. It is the backdrop against which human life unfolds. It is tradition that allows one to speak of history. In this sense tradition plays an integrating role by uniting past, present, and future. This unification allows the interpreter to seek an understanding of the society and its members. The monuments required for intelligibility are the symbols used in the language and any other vehicles of meaning employed within the tradition. All societies have symbols and other resources for the transmission of meaning. If the interpreter focuses on the vehicles of meaning and the intentionalities found therein, he will not so easily attempt to explain differences in cultures and traditions by recourse to categorical contrasts in mentalities, such as primitive versus modern, unscientific versus scientific, Eastern versus Western, prelogical versus logical, or holistic versus ratiocinative. Modern research agrees that the human mind, as a property of the human species, is one.[5] The true differences in cultures and traditions are differences in meaning. These differences can be understood because they are differences in meaning. If there is a communality in structure and function among all traditions, so too is the category of meaning common to all traditions. When interpreters of an alien tradition find no meaning, they have not found the tradition.

Meaning in tradition is mediated by symbols appropriate to the tradition. Some symbols are idiosyncratic and difficult to understand, not for intrinsic reasons but rather because of a lack of evidence indicating the force and meaning of the symbols. Here the interpreter will have to proceed cautiously to avoid imposing on an obscure symbol an anachronistic meaning or one suggested by the presuppositions of the interpreter. The explicit appropriation of one's own culture is calculated to make clear how such temptations arise. On the other hand, that there are symbols shared by all cultures is becoming increasingly clear. These are the symbols that Wheelwright has called archetypal and "which carry the same or very similar meanings for a large portion, if not all, of mankind."[6] So, in addition to structural and functional similarities among traditions there is likewise symbolic similarity, a likeness which is basically contentual. The working out of contentual similarities is clearly one of the positive contributions made by the history of religions under its rubric of comparison. A striking instance of this is found in the studies of Mircea Eliade. His works suggest, moreover, not merely the similarities of archetypal symbols shared by diverse cultures but also a similarity among symbols that are culturally differentiated but actually point to the same reality, as will be discussed in the next chapter.

In addition to the permanency and intelligibility of the structure of tradition and its contents considered under the rubric of meaning, and the intelligibility of the proximate formation of tradition by *la langue,* there is a corresponding invariancy within the structure of the consciousness that both creates and understands traditions. By invariant, I mean a structure of cognition and, potentially, of reflective consciousness that is either actually or potentially the same in all people. No one today would seriously assume, for instance, that preliterate persons or so-called primitives had no experiences whatsoever, that they had no understanding of any kind, and that they arrived at no judgments or decisions. Writers such as Lonergan, Polanyi and Popper have developed acceptable theories on the universally shared cognitional structure. This structure is difficult to deny since denial follows the structure it attempts to deny.[7] The particular operations that constitute the process of knowing always occur in historical circumstances, which ground a tradition. The historical situation accounts for diversity of cultures and traditions. The structure of tradition provides the stability and permanency requisite for knowledge. The invariant structure of human consciousness and its ultimate orientation to meaning is the ground for the potential intelligibility of all traditions.

In addition to objective similarities in traditions and in the more subjective dimension of similar cognitional structure and concomitant consciousness, one may postulate a third invariable in the psyche: the realm that has been described topographically by Freud as the unconscious, the preconsious, and the conscious. Not only is the structure common, but the generic type of contents pertinent to the realms is similar as well. Development of this point is particularly relevant in the attempt to understand prophecy, divination, shamanism, miracles, mysticism, magic, epiphanic experience, and cosmic and apocalyptic phenomena.

In proposing a triple invariancy, we are making an attempt to detail what Dilthey described as the shared life-structure, which he maintained makes understanding and interpretation possible. A fundamental and developed analysis of the life-structure enables the interpreter to accomplish more critically what Dilthey has described as "self-transposition," the activity necessary for interpretation. But what he called "self-transformation" I would call self-appropriation and self-transformation, the procedure by which interpreters first consciously appropriate their own tradition, then see in this appropriation the structure and function of all traditions. The full development of this process helps interpreters to grasp the presuppositions with which they approach a tradition different from their own. So I have modified what Dilthey intended by the use of self-transposition, that is, the moving of oneself out of one's own horizon, the escape from one's own horizon. This escape, as we know, is impossible. Therefore the attempt here is to enlarge the horizon of the interpreter to allow the exercise of the self-understanding requisite for the comprehension of other horizons.[8] The foundation for this self-transformation is a strategically developed understanding of historicity, hermeneutics, and tradition.

If one speaks of self-appropriation and self-transformation, one is suggesting a difficult procedure and still one by which the person becomes a subject. For the process to be within reach it must be directed first to a thematic knowledge of one's own tradition, the tradition which gave the interpreter initial identity. Included in this complex existential analysis is the relationship of the interpreter to the subject matter that the tradition intended to mediate. The unthematic and precritical possession of the tradition must be raised to the thematic and critical level. "To be able to understand other religions, I must be able to understand something of my own religion."[9] This is not a superfluous requirement nor a work of supererogation, for any understanding of an alien tradition will always be measured by the interpreter's grasp of the tradition that lies within his or her own experience.

The attempt to appropriate one's own tradition, as well as to distinguish how successfully or unsuccessfully that tradition has mediated the subject matter of religion, will disclose the manner in which traditions are formed, developed and the way in which the tradition confers identity on the individual. Particularly in religious traditions measured by authoritative books, it will become clear that perceptual deficiencies in interpreters have caused misinterpretations of traditions. For instance, an interpreter who has no experience whatsoever of an apocalyptic community or lacks creative imagination will have little success in interpreting books in which apocalypticism is subtle, for example, the Marcan Gospel. Those thoroughly committed to the historical-critical method will encounter problems in understanding the way in which an oral society structures the people within that society. So too will the interpreter who has absorbed a tradition in a noncritical fashion, as indeed must be the case in the beginning, begin to wonder what is constitutive of a tradition and what is merely consequent. This is an issue that goes beyond the ordinary scope of history, which may indeed satisfy itself with reporting what as a matter of fact occurred. Self-appropriation inevitably brings up, if it does not answer, the question of authentic and inauthentic tradition. This question, of course, will obviously have ramifications when the interpreter seeks an understanding of an alien tradition. Whatever the outcome of the process, either in the consideration of one's own tradition or of another tradition, one will have succeeded as an interpreter extending one's own horizon and in revising one's symbolic consciousness. One cannot predict what the term of this revision will be except to say that the procedure is a prerequisite for understanding a tradition different from one's own. This procedure, for both the historian of religion and the theologian, is a much more concrete requisite for the study of religious traditions than the usual exhortations to be sympathetic, to have an open mind, and to be self-critical—suggestions usually found in textbooks for the study of religions. These ordinarily recommended qualities are rather the result of something prior—in this case the transformation of consciousness engendered by a serious attempt to thematize one's own tradition.

It is clear, of course, that the process I have described may well accompany the scholar's study of other religious traditions and may in fact be promoted by such study. It is likewise clear that extraordinarily gifted people may do by instinct or intuition or almost automatically what is here suggested. This merely illustrates the necessity of the procedure as such. That such a practice is required for the historian of religions seems relatively clear from outstanding historians of religions, such as Ichiro Hori.[10]

Direct or indirect self-appropriation is significant for another reason. It is the interpreter's accepted tradition that influences the interpreter in the selection of problems and methodology, and in the reaction to the phenomenon of religion as such.[11] If the study of religious traditions demands transitions from the *vécu* to the *thématique,* the *existentiell* to the *existential,* the *exercite* known to the *signate,* the fragmentarily expressed to the methodically known, the fact to the theoretical explanation, fantasy to rational analysis, the precritical to the postcritical, the nondiscursive symbol to the discursive symbol, the lived relation to the refraction of the relation in representation, the operative to the understood and altered[12]—if all of this is required for the study of religions, then it would seem necessary for the interpreter to have experience of the procedure in the tradition closest to him or her. These internalized differentiations of consciousness are the subject of hermeneutics, which is ultimately historicity taken seriously.[13]

The task of the historian of religion makes it virtually impossible to ignore the polymorphic content of multiple traditions. Such, I would suggest, is likewise the case for theologians who turn seriously to the tradition they have inherited and then must extend their reflection to the realities of pluralism, thus going beyond parochial discussions among sects within the mainstream of their own tradition. Such a proposal does not envisage a multiplication of new disciplines within theology (or of new titles, such as the theology of the unbeliever or the theology of the history of religions). Rather, theology will have to become more sensitive to the exteriorization of knowledge, to the role that such knowledge has on already existing theological systems, to the reconstitution of the psyche in the face of more knowledge about diverse religious traditions, to the reconstruction of the sensorium that has accompanied new modes of storing, structuring, and diffusing knowledge.[14] This is also to say that theology will have to develop new sources, acts, functions, and exigencies of meaning.[15] But new knowledge and different modes of diffusing knowledge not only affect a particular theology in its stance toward other religious traditions, but also modify its introspective posture. Theology will have to develop in the context of historicity and hermeneutics and therefore ask itself what is consititutive in its own tradition and what is consequent.

Both theology and the history of religions have to take seriously the undermining of the Cartesian paradigm of knowledge by historical consciousness. If theology is to extend itself to the broader horizons of world religions and their symbolisms, so too the history of religions must explicitly incorporate the work of the theological community, for a history of religion cannot ignore theological meaning within a religious tradition. (The more precise relationship between the two disciplines is the subject of the last three chapters.)

Therefore one may propose, not the convergence of the two disciplines, but rather that the two disciplines be viewed as integral parts of a community of interpretation. This conjunction is compatible with the newer knowledge paradigms and opposes the Cartesian model of knowing. The complementarity of the two disciplines would render practically ineffectual the Cartesian supposition that the search for truth is primarily "the work and activity of the individual as individual."[16] Such an emphasis would avoid the now obsolete problem of the bridge and the real Cartesian problem of solipsism.[17] The problem today is not the solipsism of the individual knower, but rather the problematic of constructing bridges among traditions and thereby avoiding the greater hazard of cultural solipsism.

If it is true that human knowledge occurs in "the situation of communication between persons, and the self does not know itself nor anything else without 'knowing' other persons in communication,"[18] then it is true, in theory at least, that a parochial theology or a provincial history of religions cannot do justice to the subject matter of the disciplines. In isolation—which I would think is rarely the case today, except in theologies that confine themselves exclusively to the preservation of a faith within one community—neither discipline is capable of understanding religious traditions in a pluralistic environment.[19]

There is an underlying symmetry in tradition and in the structure of the consciousness that attempts first to appropriate a personal tradition and then to understand an alien tradition. There remains likewise the possibility of distinguishing in all tradition a superstructure, a structure, and a substructure. Both theology and the history of religions must take into account this threefold articulation. Beyond this there still remains a peculiarly modern problem, that of dissonance within a religious tradition and among the several religious traditions. This demands some further explanation in the light of what has been said about the symmetry of traditions.

Evolved concepts of historicity, hermeneutic, and understanding, as well as a developed notion of tradition, are currently coming into existence in the developed societies characterized by pervasive and rapid change and distinguished by a conscious awareness of mutations. Tradition, as both term and process, manifests all the ideographs of the larger phenomenon of change. Tradition as open-ended is relatively stable. But the capacity of the substructure and the structure to remain stable allows the secondary features or the superstructure to be variable. The ability of a religious tradition to absorb seemingly alien features is marked in a society where each religious tradition is but one of many traditions by which the society and community live.

Currently, except in cases where isolation from the larger world is fostered and demanded, religious tradition is marked by a certain dissonance and inconcinnity. The dissonance is located in the claim the tradition once made on its followers as contrasted with its current power of persuasion. Dissonance is evident when the terms in which the tradition expresses itself remain clear enough but the force of the terms and its structure is questionable. If one is to appropriate one's own tradition explicitly, it will inevitably be necessary to cope with the problem of dissonance. Dissonance is the chasm between the intelligibility of symbolic structures in the world of theory and their compelling force in the world of practice.

The problem of dissonance is pertinent for both the theologian and the historian of religion. A historian cannot be a historian without understanding the present, as Eichhorn observed.[20] "In general, it can be said that interest in a particular area of history (if the work in it is not purely busy work) rests on a conscious or unconscious choice among the various possibilities of making human existence accessible and that, insofar as this choice results from existential vitality, this vitality will continually be effective in the historical task."[21] That is to say that the common subject matter of both the historian of religion and the theologian is the possible ways of understanding human existence, ways that somehow contribute to humanity's understanding of itself today. Religious traditions are not merely the subject of simple disinterested study. Their meaning is totally found in the meaning and force they have had and may yet have for the present. The so-called disinterested approach may well disclose what was said or what happened but not what was meant. To understand what is meant in a religious tradition requires a preexisting relation to the subject matter of the tradition, as a preexisting relation is required to understand the subject matter of music or art. This concern for the subject matter of the religious tradition is concretely manifested by the interpreter's relationship to his or her own current existential possibilities in relation to the possibilities offered first by the inherited tradition and then by other religious traditions. So the contemporary point of dissonance in religious traditions is relevant to any interpretation of religious traditions that would seek to be more than a presentation of museum pieces.

The relevance of dissonance is seen in the way in which religious traditions confer identity. Religious communities and interpreters exist in time. This implies a past and a future. Recollection of the past involves a certain hermeneutic and understanding. Remembering the past means remembering the tradition. As I have said, it is the tradition that confers on the individual an identity. A religious community, formed by a tradition, is a community of memory and expectation, or hope.[22] Memory and hope are understood by interpretation. The interpretation of a common past and a hoped-for future mediates the tradition and its subject matter. If any of the elements in this process—either memory or hope—is drastically altered, it is possible that the tradition involved will be so fragmented as to be virtually unidentifiable. This is especially true if interpretations within a tradition conflict and therefore lead to uncertainty in the psychological present, or if the current interpretations seem to be at variance with those of the past. If a tradition is not stable enough to be altered in minor ways and yet is persistent enough to exist in questionable form, one experiences dissonance. In such instances, the community lacks a formal identity, though a material identity may still remain.

One lives off the heritage of the past,[23] a situation described so well by Nietzsche. One who is involved in a case of material identity with one's own tradition, a tradition no longer strong enough to claim one's allegiance nor persuasive enough to offer a genuine possibility for understanding and organizing one's own existence, will lack the identity that a strong tradition confers on its adherents. Material identity transmitted by the substructure of a tradition generally indicates that the tradition is residually present but moribund. Where memory may be strong but hope ineffectual, believers become incapable of investing their symbols with appropriate meaning. Thus the tradition and its power to confer identity is thoroughly dissipated.

Material identity, where one is nominally a member of a particular confession, generally occurs where the superstructure of a tradition has been assumed to be the structure of the tradition. As Hori has pointed out of folk religions, "In spite of bewildering changes in the superstructure, the substructure is comparatively stable and follows a course of rather slow changes."[24] But if the superstructure has been identified with the substructure, and if this superstructure is subjected to change, questioning, or even direct assault, the individual believer is left with whatever identity the structure and substructure are able to confer. Whatever identity believers have through their own tradition has been bestowed by the dynamism of the substructure as it makes its influence felt through whatever power it has to permeate some of the superstructure or structure.

The historian of religion may immediately object that such problems of finesse do not pertain to the discipline of history, which merely tabulates the changes of which I am speaking. The objection is sound if one conceives the history of religion exclusively under the rubric of exegesis of the subject matter as opposed to criticism of the subject matter, and if one conceives history in the German sense of *Historie* as opposed to *Geschichte*. But how is one to recognize the power of dissonance in the past if one has not encountered it somehow in the present? And if this dissonance is unrecognized then history must confine itself to the account of what was said, what was done, what happened, and slight the question of what was meant.

For our present purposes, however, it is sufficient to note that when a tradition does not confer a strong sense of identity on the individual, it is because the tradition is in the process of becoming obsolete or because the superstructure of a tradition has long been identified as the structure. When the superstructure is challenged by change, whatever its sources, then the individuals involved in identifying the superstructure with the structure experience the change as dissonance. If the structure of a religious tradition can be meaningfully reinterpreted—as is the case in successful renewals and reformations—then the dissonance gradually disappears and the tradition comes to life again, as was the case in the Protestant Reformation, the effects of which are still being felt. What will happen in the modern cases of dissonance remains to be seen. But clearly the most profound meaning of a religious tradition is present when it is capable of vitally forming and shaping the lives of its adherents.

Neophytes are often introduced to a religious tradition long before they are capable of formally accepting or rejecting the tradition. The learning process takes place usually in the family or small community and is characterized by intersubjectivity and by the dispositions of belief, hope, and love, rather than by any type of Cartesian paradigm. The conviction of the instructors, their reliability and the confirmatory value of the environment bestows power and force on the tradition. Later the adherent may find intrinsic reasons within the tradition to reaffirm its meaning and satisfy the quest for meaning. This dynamic process depends on a whole series of stable and reliable factors.

In the developed societies of the West stability and reliability are not striking characteristics of the traditional religions. The environment in which tradition exists has been altered; there are competitors in the world of meaning. There are disagreements within the traditions themselves as to what is constitutive and what is consequent. The confirmatory force of the environment is diminished or lacking. Transmitters of the tradition are somewhat less than convinced of its efficacy. And there are still cases of the propagation of unhealthy systems that appeal to the unfortunate and sick strata of society. Therefore the vehicles of transmission manifest a certain impotence in normal circumstances.

Two contrasting traditions, Roman Catholic and Amerindian, illustrate this point. In Roman Catholic theology, the former quest for certitude has been supplanted in many instances by what is termed a search for understanding. The professional theologian or student may make the shift with a minimum of discomfort. But for the administrative arm of the church and for the faithful, the change can be shattering. Whatever the psychological reactions, it is clear that the tradition as hitherto conceived is called into question. The long-range benefits of the motion from certitude to understanding cannot forestall the resulting change in perspective. The tradition is perceived as ambivalent, ambiguous, amorphous, or even self-contradictory. Quite simply, former certitude has become incertitude or uncertainty. While one may speak of a shift from the scholastic emphasis on formal objects to an emphasis on a field of study,[25] this shift does not easily or rapidly compensate for that which it seeks to displace. The vast shifts in perspective that are involved in technical theological studies have not been transferred to the general public, except in the sense that the new perspectives have simply worked to invalidate older perspectives. No one can say, not even those who propose new methods of coping with change,[26] what new horizons will be opened by new perspectives. Aspects of this tradition are not merely changing, but may already be in stages ranging from desuetude to extinction.

A similar case is that of Amerindian religion. Recently there has been a movement in Canada to restore the elders to their ancient dignity as teachers and preservers of the "old ways." This effort has been characterized as a return to "the inner dynamics of Indian cultures."[27] The issue, of course, is whether the traditional symbolic forms, particularly the myths, contain enough vitality to support and to re-create Amerindian ways, morals, civilizations, and cultures. Therefore, the situation in Amerindian religion is quite parallel to that of many Christian denominations and, likewise, of other religions in lands affected by technological development or pluralism, as, for example, Hinduism in India and Islam in Iran. The issue today for all the traditions is the viability of particular world views and their concomitant symbolic systems. The outcome is as yet unknown, but it is not out of place to recall Hegel's observation that when reflection occurs it is a sign that some particular historical form of life is at an end.

Ricoeur has stated the problem not so much from the standpoint of the tradition as from the perspective of the thought forms and conceptuality in which the tradition is understood and articulated.

> We must concede that this kind of conceptuality is still lacking, because we have received from the tradition mainly the conceptual expressions of the '*hautes epoques*,' i.e., from the supreme moments when our culture dreamt of its complete integration

and projected these dreams in systems where harmony had over-come war, at least in discourse. Such were the blessed times of the great Neo-Platonic onto-theologies, the Aristotelian-Tho-mistic syntheses, the Leibnizian theodicy, the Hegelian system. In fact, we 'think' with the debris and the offspring resulting from the wreckage of these systems and—perhaps—of the dreams which these systems brought to language.[28]

What was sufficient in a classical culture becomes insufficient in a pe-riod characterized by historical consciousness. The symptom of a transi-tion from one era to the other is dissonance in religious tradition. The dissonance is significant not only in itself but in the way it colors the perspective of both the historian of religion and the theologian.

In other words, the problem facing classical Christianity, Amerindian religion, and religions in the Eastern countries importing Western em-pirical science and technologies, to take some examples, is that of the interrelation of tradition and innovation.[29] A possible interpretation is to see a change in structure rather in content. But a theologian with more historical interests notes that, "Sometime during the period be-tween the Gregorian Reform and the outbreak of the Protestant Refor-mation there began to develop a historical sense which recognized dis-continuity with the past."[30] The discrepancy in the two interpretations resides in the way in which one conceives change. The first opinion seems characterized, despite disclaimers, by the idea of an accidental change according to the Aristotelian inheritance. Institutions, and par-ticularly religious institutions, were thought to have an essence that was stable throughout all accidental change. Such a mental construct sees all change, however radical it may be, as evolutionary: changes in the accidents occur while the substance remains untouched and so con-tinuity within a tradition is preserved. Historical consciousness, how-ever, suggests rather an essence that is really identified with its existence so that the being itself is altered in cases of serious change. The subject of the change may remain identifiable. But at a certain level change does not leave the essence untouched.

If, therefore, the contents or a tradition are altered, so too is the structure altered in the world of real existence. One may speak of a structure or even of a substance that is an idealized concept capable of performing heuristic functions. But it is not this heuristic structure that exists in the real world. One may have the flu, for instance, with-out exhibiting all the usual symptoms of the flu. One may speak of a symmetry of traditions and a symmetry of structure in the conceptual order without suggesting that this symmetry is literally found in the real world of existence. Thus a serious change in traditional contents seems to suggest a corresponding change in structure in the world of everyday reality. It is this type of real change that begets dissonance.

The ultimate cause of dissonance is not simply the transition of the Western world from a classical culture to one characterized by historical consciousness, for this transition has been painlessly accomplished in the empirical sciences and has indeed created a whole series of social sciences with concomitant new human meaning. In the ultimate analysis dissonance in understanding and appropriating religious traditions resides in the unequal acceptance and limited diffusion of the historical-critical method within religious traditions. What thoroughly permeates the technical historical study of all religions has neither been incorporated into systematic theologies nor been integrated into the lives of ecclesial communities. This has led to a demonstrable intellectual schizophrenia, as has happened repeatedly in the past for different reasons.

But dissonance in a tradition is most serious, not simply because one cannot put some intellectual pieces together, but rather because dissonance breaks down hope, trust, and love, which are basic orientations in the human being. It is not surprising that when an unconscious perception of dissonance becomes conscious, expressed, and shared, members of a religious tradition are not only fragmented but intensify the dislocations by accusations, attacks, and vituperation that tend to set believers against each other and against the interpreters and custodians of the tradition. The help that individuals need from the tradition is unavailable and disputes are a manifestation not simply of intellectual dissatisfaction but rather of a kind of despair. Gradually acrimony diminishes and a feeling of futility replaces contentiousness. Then comes a sort of quiet resignation. Without help from the tradition, believers are divested of trust, hope, and love. Without these orientations the common symbols of a religious tradition can no longer be invested with religious meaning. Study of the process of dissonance is therefore enlightening for the interpreter who is interested in the more general phenomenon of the role that religious traditions and their symbolism play in human life.

One of the factors seeming to mitigate the severity of dissonance within religious traditions has been the printed word. Literate students of religion feel that they can always turn to the printed page, to the word as record, to find a genuine tradition. Discrepant positions may be reconciled by intensive study or by the printed contribution of a new Aquinas, Maimonides, Luther, or al-Ghazzali. This is, however, a deceptive fallacy. Assuredly, recovery of a tradition is fully possible if the tradition is, so to speak, recorded in the written or stored word. But a living tradition is present and operative in the minds and hearts of people. If a tradition lies inert on shelves, like the historical facts of which Carl Becker spoke, the tradition may have no real effect whatsoever in the world. Libraries contain the records of past traditions that are completely obsolete. Nonetheless one may maintain that dissonance within a tradition harbors within itself the possibilities of reform and renewal that will diminish or eliminate the dissonance. So one may hope for a new Augustine but one may likewise maintain that the dissonance itself can render the tradition inefficacious and may ultimately lead to disintegration.

One may obviate the problem of dissonance on the theoretical level, particularly in "religions of the book," by discovering that the book, for example, the New Testament, is really a series of diverse reactions to one and the same saving event, that is, that the book is constituted by a series of seemingly discrepant hermeneutical reactions. Pluralism, therefore, is at the heart of the original and definitive interpretations as, for example, is the case in Hinduism. Such a theory was proposed by James M. Robinson some years back and may also be found in the well-known writings of Ernst Käsemann. The position is enticing and indeed in accord with some of the early facts. One of the problems of such an approach is the difficulty the position creates for the historian and the exegete, not to mention the theologian. The interpreter then becomes a recorder of what happened and what was said. This quite easily leads to an omission of the vital questions of what was meant and what was intended—questions suggested under the rubric of criticism of the subject matter. Ultimately there is the danger that the tradition then becomes "whatever happened" and "whatever was said." Although in one sense this is quite correct, it is a beginning point that is meant to lead to the further question of authentic and inauthentic meaning. The difficulty of answering the question should not lead to its elimination as a question.

Once again the printed word manifests the point at issue. The interpreter may hope to retrieve a tradition. And indeed this is perhaps the easiest work, particularly if the tradition is no longer in actual existence. But in the case of existing religions, the task is complex. If the tradition is alive, one need not retrieve it. If the tradition seems to be in a limbo characterized by dissonance, the effort to recover the tradition may be the most significant work that the scholar can perform. But this effort apart from its considerable intellectual impact, usually works indirectly; its contribution to the actual life of a tradition is based on the hope that what is true will ultimately prevail.

However, even where a certain consensus could be achieved as to the exact nature of a particular tradition, the difficulty inherent in the role of the printed word is still operative. For the printed word continues its work of detribalization. It suggests that readers come to their own judgments and decisions once they have done the requisite reading. While isolated readers have the capacity to understand, discriminate, and accept, they likewise have the power to reject, modify, and distort what they have read. Latent in the very nature of the printed word is the power to dissipate the realm of common meaning that grounds a tradition and unites a community. (Few people paid much attention to this problem when the sale of religious books, published in profusion in the 1960s, not only escalated but, in many instances, generated an unconscious hope that religious traditions would suffer less from their earthly forms and bestow rich, new, and unheard of significance on human lives. Disappointment then produced a new series of books lamenting the lost stability and security produced by tradition in earlier days. A graphic illustration of this type of modern lamentation is found in the works of Garry Wills.[31] So too did many Westerners turn to esoteric Eastern religions—thus aiding the growth of religious studies departments—in the wistful hope of finding something they did not experience in Western religious traditions and forms.)

In is therefore not out of place to recall again that many religious traditions today find themselves in the position poignantly illustrated by the Amerindian who is trying to recover and revitalize Amerindian religious tradition through the elders and their contact with the ancient wisdom. Desperation forced the search:[32] the Amerindian quest indicates that a dominantly nonliterate society basically committed to an oral-aural stage of transmission experiences dissonance when confronted by a society that has passed through the oral-aural level, the chirographic stage, the printing phase, and lives with the electronic era of knowledge storage, retrieval, and diffusion. (There are suggestions that the Hindu religious traditions are beset with much the same problem in a slightly different context.[33])

However developed a society may be, oral-aural interaction always remains the earliest and most effective mode of transmitting a tradition and conferring identity on the individual. The exigencies of the learning process from infancy onward necessitate the procedure. Insofar as this process is legitimated and sanctioned by the society at large, the procedure will be effective. For example, it was once the custom in the United States to have every child say the Pledge of Allegiance daily in the presence of the symbol of the nation, the American flag. Children assented to "one nation, under God, indivisible, with liberty and justice for all" long before they could define any of the terms. Students stood for the national anthem, saluted the flag, sang songs such as "God Bless America," and were thereby trained in the American tradition. In later days scholars began to note that this education in a tradition bore the earmarks of civil religion. It might have been far more pertinent to observe that a sufficient number of people felt that the American tradition was important and worthwhile enough to make sure that the tradition was passed on in ways quite similar to transmission of religion.

As long as these oral forms, gestures, symbols, and rituals are the product of prior faith, hope, and love, the tradition will be transmitted. Obviously, the oral tradition and the detailed forms it takes are reinforced by laws and the legal interpretations. But it is highly doubtful whether one could have laws working toward "liberty and justice for all" if there were not a common understanding, acceptance, and assent to the meaning of these terms transmitted by the oral tradition. It is the tradition itself, larger than individuals within the tradition, that is the communal consciousness strong enough to overcome the biases of particularized individual consciousness.

Beyond the influence of the printed word is the dissonance introduced by the very nature of tradition as such, which sooner or later contributes to its being called into question. For tradition of any kind enables the individual to function in a particular sphere: it is the organization of past experience into a particular order and system. Tradition "acquires its status or binding claim only where it appears as the common possession of a nation or of a broad stratum within a nation. . . . But, insofar as it becomes the possession of all, it is in danger of simplifying and generalizing truths which can be generalized only to a certain extent. . . . It is called in question by every contrary experience;

indeed this knowledge can even become one enormous deception to the extent that it tries to shut off the experience of new reality and fights against it where possible."[34]

It is with this fact in mind that extremely conservative and fundamentalist traditions attempt to wall in a religious tradition by excluding, insofar as is possible, contacts with any other tradition, which might legitimate experiences contrary to their own tradition. Alien traditions, therefore, must be in some sense anathematized. Even within a fundamentalist tradition an atmosphere of doubt cannot be countenanced because this would disclose that adherents within the tradition experience the same difficulties and doubts, and thus the tradition would be open to full-scale questioning. In general, therefore, where such questions and contrary experiences are allowed they are classified as difficulties intrinsic to belief. Hence they are to be overcome by a stronger faith, eliminated through prayer, and diminished by orthodox interpretation. Weaknesses intrinsic to tradition as such are diverted from their principal purpose, which is to call the tradition into question and thus perhaps to modify gradually some prior inauthentic interpretations of the tradition.

That we can actually speak of dissonance within a tradition and uncover at least some of its causes is an indication that there is an underlying symmetry in all traditions. If, therefore, one can in principle distinguish in one's own tradition a superstructure, structure, and substructure, then one is presumably more capable of understanding other traditions. This potential intelligibility of tradition, particularly religious tradition, is ultimately resident in the common structure of human consciousness and the common objective structure it creates. Since neither the subjective nor objective structures are detached from temporality, historicity is the constitutive factor in the formation of all traditions. Thus a hermeneutic capable of dealing with historicity is the requisite for understanding an alien tradition.

Whether a religious tradition so influenced by historicity can actually provide believers with certitude sufficient to claim their absolute assent will be discussed in the next chapter in the larger context of the history of religions.

PART TWO

·5·

COMPARATIVE RELIGION
OR THE HISTORY OF RELIGIONS

The preceding chapter was devoted to one aspect of the unity of religious traditions, that is, the capacity of these traditions as intelligible and therefore communicable entities—due consideration being given to dissonance in traditions—to be understood by those outside the tradition. The question still remains as to whether the individually intelligible and communicable religious traditions, even in instances of dissonance, maintain enough power to confer on their adherents sufficient certitude to claim their assent. The question is not simply that of the relevance of a tradition to the religious person as such, but also a question that must receive some kind of answer from professional students of religions, who are required to assimilate consciously, explicitly, and thematically their own religious tradition as a condition of understanding other religious traditions. In general terms, the problem is whether pluralism of religious traditions makes all religions equally uncertain. If so, the matter of choice or continuation of options exercised by one's forebears can indeed be called into question.

Since perceived religious pluralism emerged in the context of the historical study of religions and has become a matter of universal experience it is appropriate first to recall this history, to examine the history of religions as it currently exists, and in this environment to suggest a theory that, at least for the present, will justify the diversity of religions and preserve their individual claims to positive assent while at the same time allowing one to cope with the absolute nature of the religious demand in what seems to be a context of indiscriminate relativism. The enterprise suggests a threefold division: a history of comparative religion, a consideration of some aspects of the history of religions today, and a theory of the unity and diversity of religions.

The History of Comparative Religion

Comparative religion, one of the constitutive disciplines in any definition of religious studies, had its origin as a conscious subject in the late nineteenth century, primarily, though not at all exclusively, in the work of F. Max Müller (1823–1900), who published from 1844 until 1899. His essay "Comparative Mythology," which appeared in 1856, is considered the proximate origin of the history of religions, although all scholars are aware of the debt of religious studies to comparative mythology, not to mention its more remote bond to the extraordinary work of the Jesuits de Nobili and Ricci. Details of these foundational contributions can be found in standard introductory textbooks as well as in the growing literature on mythography.[1]

Dilthey (1833–1911) thematized comparative religion's search for a definition under the broader rubric of the cultural sciences. He sought to develop the lineaments of some intellectual process which would distinguish *Geisteswissenschaften* (the term seems to have been introduced to translate John Stuart Mill's *moral sciences* of 1863) from *Naturwissenschaften*. All of Dilthey's works are concerned with what he called the most difficult problem for the theory of knowledge: the effort to understand something foreign. (His theories of *Nacherleben* and *Nachfühlen fremder Seelenzustände* were less influential in outlining the scientific basis of the history of religion than were the complex and technical procedures used in philology and comparative mythology.)

The effort to name the discipline and to characterize its distinctive methodology played less of a role in the origin of the history of religion than did Darwin's *Origin of Species* of 1859. The climate created by this book, as well as preliminary indications of linguistic growth and development, led to a developmental, if not evolutionary, approach in the emerging field of the history of religions. Thus no matter how much Andrew Lang and Max Müller may have disagreed in their long and literate debate—Müller holding the origin of myths to be in solar, lunar, and astral mythology and that myth itself was really a disease of language, and Lang maintaining that myths derived from an animistic stage of human thinking which personalized the elements[2]—both men accepted an evolutionary or developmental viewpoint of the origin, growth, and advance of religion. By definition, therefore, the history of religions studies a series of nonnormative phenomena. No religion or theology developing out of religion could in fact be normative since it was destined to succession by further development, and this subsequent growth did not necessarily contain the same organic unity evident within one particular living organism. An unexpressed assumption during the early period of the history of religions was that comparisons were to be made either by contrast to a present tradition (Christianity and Judaism were at first exempted from the comparative method) or to what that generation held to be the dictates of reason.

The appearance of comparative mythology, buttressed by a scientific-linguistic apparatus and practiced by men whose talents equalled their industry, led to a secure and widespread feeling of control over the subject matter under investigation and consequently to a conceptual rule that could explain the origin of religion in the use of language, the primitive sense of the numinous, magic, the prelogical mentality, fetishism, totemism, animism, and preanimism. The sense of security and certainty bequeathed by comparative mythology owed as much to its eloquent practitioners as to their methods. The vast influence of Max Müller is illustrative: he came to Oxford in 1849 to translate the sacred books of India and twenty-three years later when he thought of leaving, the thought generated "a special decree at Convocation and a prayerful eulogy from the Dean of Christ Church"[3] that he remain and continue his work within the university. The term *Religionswissenschaft,* introduced in 1867 by Müller, indicated the assumed scientific validity of the discipline.

The traditional dating of the beginning of the history of religions with Max Müller does not quite do justice to two factors that are of some importance in considering the unity of religious studies and theology. First of all, one must remember the Enlightenment's emphasis on a religion of an omnipotent reason, at least as one of the positive postulates of the period. And second, one must attend to the widespread study of *religious* myths. On both counts comparative religion contained a potential antagonism to Christian theology, which had contrasted false religions to true religion in terms of history or gospel versus myth, and which itself was always based on a revelation that in a

certain sense exceeded the powers of natural reason. By the time of
Müller, therefore, the skeptical climate of the Enlightenment, which
had developed with a certain historical relentlessness from Cherbury to
Hume, implicitly, at the very least, opposed religions based on revelation. This opposition was particularly strong in the case of Christianity.
Part of this antagonism came to be reflected in the structure of the theological curriculum, which began with an apologetic affirmation of the
possibility, necessity, and actuality of a divine revelation. A classic example of this approach is found in the writings of Joannes Perrone, specifically his *Praelectiones Theologicae* of 1840. The program was designed
to meet the objections of rationalism. The consideration of myth
within Christianity was proposed by Strauss in 1835 but was disre-
garded until much later. On the other hand, the study of comparative
mythology itself contained what might be considered a deceptive factor,
the assumption that myth was often characteristic of benighted peoples.
As Feldman and Richardson have written, "the firsthand information of
travellers, missionaries and merchants equated 'pagan' religion with
'contemporary savagery.' "[4] They "fed the study of comparative religion
and they weakened, without ever intending to do so, the idea of Revelation."[5]

Before the time of Müller, the British had been avid collectors of
classical artifacts and enthusiasts of travel reports from the East, Near
East, Greece, and Egypt. The "French *Académie des Inscriptions et Belles-
Lettres* was a center for classical and oriental studies; only in 1734 was
the Society of Dilettanti organized in England to support travel, schol-
arly exploration and publication; and the first modern excavations
began at Herculaneum in 1738 and in Pompei in 1748."[6] Because classical philology was hardly established at this time, we may classify this
age as the period of amateur study of religions—a historical circumstance that has had lasting repercussions, as evidenced even among
some members of the university community who feel that common
sense, personal experience, and feelings are sufficient tools for reliable
judgments about religion and its study.

In the late nineteenth century the history of religions was taught at
Leyden, Oxford, Copenhagen, Geneva, and at the Catholic Institute of
Paris. In 1830 the first specialized journal in the history of religions ap-
peared, *Revue de l'histoire des religions.*[7] Bianchi correctly notes the apolo-
getic and anticlerical orientation of the history of religions as taught by
De Broglie and Goblet d'Alviella, and by Labanca in Italy. The history

of religions exhibits a much more tolerant mien today, a tolerance due in some measure to the "discovery of the historicity of man"[8] and to a growing sense of community among those who pursue the academic study of religion.

In addition to the generative period of the nineteenth century, the history of religions is indebted to the studies of ethnologists, classicists, and philologians of an early day. Of particular significance are Fontanelle (1657–1757), Lafitau (1670–1740), Vico (1668–1744), de Brosses (1709–1777), Lowth (1710–1788), Heyne (1729–1812), Herder (1744–1803), Schlegel (1772–1829), and Schelling (1775–1854). The history of religions still bears the marks of these men as well as those of scholars such as Tylor (1832–1917) and Frazer (1854–1941). I have already mentioned some of their contribution to the subjects of historicity, hermeneutic, and understanding, in addition to which one must recall that they attempted a neutrality of approach that assumed as a starting point a certain independence from Christianity and its claims to be the one true religion. By the time of Schleiermacher it was possible to assert the equality of all religions as valid and necessary approaches to the transcendent, a point that was later somewhat ignored by Schleiermacher's extremely conservative interpreters. Intellectual grounds for the validity and equality of all religious approaches were in general either feeble or overly simplified. But the precritical period of historical studies of religion was independent of any ecclesiastical encumbrance, a state that was congenial to the general temper of the Enlightenment.

Both in the precritical period of the history of religions and in the later efforts of Max Müller, one notes the growing skills and capacities of the interpreters, particularly the presence of sufficient language ability and study to cope with alien cultures. Somewhat prior to this development was the parallel growth of biblical and exegetical studies with their need for adequate language and literary training to cope with the environment in which the biblical literature had its origin. The historical-critical method, now common to both the history of religions and biblical interpretation, is generally agreed to have had its origin in Richard Simon (1638–1712). The stormy history of Simon, whose *Critical History of the Old Testament* of 1678 led to its proscription by Bossuet and his dismissal from the Oratorians, indicates that the historical-critical method was not readily accepted by authorities within certain religious communities, a fact that was to lead to an increasing distance between the history of religions and theology as well as an uneasy tension between biblical studies and theology. With Robert Lowth's introduction of literary criticism to the study of the Old Testament in his well-known *De sacra Poesi Hebraeorum praelectiones* of 1753, the movement was established in Britain. And with the German translation and annotations by J. D. Michaelis in 1758, the historical-critical method was established on the Continent and was to exercise a profound influence on scholars like Heyne, Eichhorn, and Gabler. The field of hermeneutics was implicitly operative in Lowth's assertion that to understand the ancient Hebrews one must think and feel exactly as they did, a principle adopted concretely by Herder in his own great capacity to experience and reproduce the sentiments found in ancient literature.

If we seek a common ground between the history of religions and theology, it will first be mediated by the historical-critical method developed in biblical studies, inherited from classical research, and shared by both the history of religions and biblical inquiry. The historical-critical method, however, exercised at first a very uncertain influence on theology, where it was greeted with emotions ranging from suspicion to outright hostility. Theology had an existence of its own in the Western world, either because of church formulations and needs or because of the sway of the classical culture in which theology reflected a world in which truth was timeless and universal. This tension between the historical-critical method of biblical studies and theology has remained to the present day. It is the most significant factor in the decline of theological force and in the uncertainty felt by religious believers within liberal traditions.

It was inevitable that the same malaise should be present between theology and the history of religions, which was dominated by the historical-critical method. No better example of the antagonism of the critical method to theology can be found than in the resignation of Wellhausen from his position as professor of theology at Greifswald in 1882 and in the reason he gave: historical and exegetical work was "incapacitating my hearers for their office."[9] An instance of longer duration appears in the pronouncements of the Roman Catholic biblical commission from the early twentieth century to the encyclical of Pius XII in 1943 in which the historical-critical method was resolutely accepted. Nonetheless, one could perceive a certain backtracking in the encyclical of the same pontiff in "Humani Generis" of 1950. The firm acceptance in theory was unaccompanied by any mention of the revolution that the historical-critical method would cause both for theology and belief.

Tension between theology and the history of religions was exacerbated by the contributions of Tylor, who sought the origin of religion in animism; by Frazer, who outlined stages of magic, religion, and science, and by Durkheim, who saw totemism as the most elementary form of religious life. At the same time the history of religions was assuming a definitive context by subjecting its hypotheses only to the critical norms of academic approbation, within which one could propound hypotheses with little or no deterring sanction from extraneous sources. Thus hypotheses underwent continual revision in terms appropriate to their adequacy or inadequacy. No one thought of suggesting that theology and religious belief might prosper in the same context.

Nor was it helpful that the history of religions did not make too many pronouncements about the truth or value of religions. An unusual convergence solidified the gap between the history of religions and theology, while at the same time offering some hope for the future. By 1876, there were four chairs in comparative religion in Holland and the historical-critical method was well enough developed in biblical studies to anticipate the works of Wellhausen, Gunkel, and Bousset.

It was perhaps W. Schmidt (1868–1954) whose work most strongly contradicted theories of animism, preanimism, and others tied to developmental presuppositions in the study of religions. Though his conclusions were by no means unanimously accepted, his historical approach was to be not only influential but decisive in the methodology of the history of religions. By the time of such moderns as Van der Leeuw, Wach, and Eliade, the legitimacy and productivity of the historical-critical method was assumed and the study moved into contentual, structural, typological, and phenomenological constructs. The history of religions as practiced today, a subject to which we now briefly turn, bears the imprints of its origins and development.

History of Religions Today

Intellectual patterns and presuppositions of the past, suitably modified in the course of time, constitute productive dialectical tensions within the study of religion. These current tensions are inseparably bound up with the work of early historians of religion. When historical studies, coupled with the work and reports of missionaries, disclosed the varied shapes of religion and of religious discourse, investigators such as Wilhelm Schmidt, Rudolf Otto, Erwin R. Goodenough, James

Frazer, and Emile Durkheim introduced conceptual unity by postulating either a first principle, an elementary form, or a basic mentality from which religions evolved. Details may be found in the very useful contribution of Walter H. Capps, in *Ways of Understanding Religion.*[10] By the time of Lucien Levy-Bruhl's death in March, 1939, the search for either a fundamental or foundational principle, mentality, attitude, or form of religious life had been largely abandoned, though the questions of where and why religion begins still shadow the investigator.

Dissipation of the hope to find origins led to more attainable goals— the phenomena, the structure, and the perceptible features of religion. Influenced by Husserl and Merleau-Ponty, writers such as George Dumézil moved beyond Müller's etymological method by describing and comparing historically related religious phenomena.[11] He reached a "mythological tripartition," "a habit of thought ... an ideology."[12] Historical and comparative methodology were clearly ascertainable. Meanwhile, Mircea Eliade, in a still larger context, proceeded from his distinctions between sacred and profane to the minute study of "every rite, every myth, every belief or divine figure,"[13] in so far as this was attainable.

To this historical and comparative goal was added the nuance of attending to the personal confession of individual men and women. Wilfrid Cantwell Smith proposed that "attention be given ... to two fundamental factors, the historico-cultural 'cumulative tradition,' and the personal faith of men and women."[14] This, of course, widened the parameters of historical concern. Hence, sociologists such as Bellah and O'Dea turned to what I would call the relation of religious forms to culture—Bellah discovering what he called a civil religion, and O'Dea uncovering the conservative influence of institutional forms on religious traditions.

Occasionally theologians intruded into this large field, particularly those whose textual training and interests involved them in the historical-critical method and therefore, as I have already mentioned, involved them in the study of other religions. But by and large, the historian of religion considered theology to be a normative study and hence in basic conflict with the scientific study of religion. Theologians, as we shall see more specifically in the following chapter, frequently gave good cause for this turn of events by assuming one or other hierophany to be privileged or by attempting to give some theoretical justification for the normal historical devaluation of earlier hierophanies by later hierophanies.[15] The point relevant here is not the rejection of a theological approach as once manifested, but rather that this summary exclusion of the theologian slowly called attention to the evident presence of theology in all religions and later to the role that preunderstanding plays in all interpretation. Accompanying this peculiar constellation of events was the rise of an almost all-comprehensive field, that of hermeneutics.

It would take us too far afield to discuss the works of psychologists such as William James and Allport, not to mention psychoanalysts such as Freud and Jung, or anthropologists such as Radin and Malinowski.[16] But one cannot neglect mention of what Capps has called "modal parsing,"[17] which focused first on the nature of religious language, then on symbolism, and finally moved into its current configuration, which is shaped by comparative symbolic studies, archetypal criticism, and the activity of coherent literary analysis. "By literary analysis I mean the manifold varieties of minutely discriminating attention to the artful use of language, to the shifting play of ideas, conventions, tone, sound, imagery, syntax, narrative viewpoint, compositional units, and much else. . . ."[18] While this new dimension is still in its infancy, its influence is already palpable in the study of religions and literary analysis is gently modifying the methods of studying religion.

This diachronic historical movement, with its synchronic accompaniment, suggests that the history of religions has refined itself and artfully implied a conjunction with other mental operations such as the theological, the literary, and the comparative. Such, in schematic form, is the present shape of the history of religions, with any of its archaeological forms capable of emerging and changing this description.

Despite what the cultured student would recognize as growth in scientific procedure, one cannot ignore what Marcel Simon, in his presidential address to the International Association for the History of Religions in 1975 at Lancaster called a widespread suspicion that the IAHR is a group of "religious propagandists,"[19] or is perhaps undermining the foundations "of religion in general, or of that precise religion which prevails in a given country."[20] The latter fear, is, of course, not unfounded since all new epigenetic differentiations within critical consciousness alter past perspectives and eventually modify the status quo.

Hence it is safe to say that the history of religions is a complex study, one that demands a concurrence of discrete activities and operations that I will describe later. This summary of the context of contemporary comparative religious studies leads to the final aspect of our current consideration, pluralism, or the issue of unity and diversity, the variety of heuristic visions. Before one can suitably distinguish operations adequate for the study of religion, one must deal with the absolute claims of religious traditions, the very variety of which seem to contradict the claim.

The Unity and Diversity of Religion

Perhaps the most provocative theory to explain and maintain the unity and diversity of religion, to support the simultaneous coexistence of an absolute claim made by seemingly relative pluralisms, is that of Frithjof Schuon in *The Transcendent Unity of Religion,*[21] a 1975 translation of the 1948 French work. Unless one establishes a foundation for the unity of religions, then theology must inevitably be a completely different enterprise from the history of religions, and the history of religions will continue to denote an atmosphere rather than a precise operation studying coherent data. If one identifies the unity of religions in common themes, motifs, and areas of interest or concern, the unity of religions would seem to be extrinsic and accidental. If religions are totally diverse, admirable, perhaps, but contradicting each other, then religions appear as arbitrary, accidental, compulsive postulates assuming the cultural garb of particular times and places.

Schuon's thesis in *The Transcendent Unity of Religion* maintains the absolute nature of unity and the absolute necessity of diversity—not an easy balance. Motion toward transcendence is the reality common to all religions and does not imply that either the motion or its term is univocal. Historically conditioned cultural forms are the basis of the diversity. But diversity of cultural forms is not simply equivocal so that the forms would suggest mutual antinomies or direct contradictions. The effort of appropriate transcendence, so to speak, occurs in the world of intentionality and meaning; it admits degrees. The closer to the transcendent believers within one religious tradition come, the nearer they move to believers in another religion in which the same degree of proximity to the transcendent is evident even though the transcendent is not univocally conceived.

The spatial metaphor should not, however, suggest that all believers are moving to one and the same transcendence. This would be to oversimplify the activity and to define transcendence as a reality that can be domesticated. Motion toward transcendence allows one to leave behind the culturally determined symbolic forms that were at first absolutely necessary for the appropriation of the religious tradition. This is clear among religious mystics of diverse traditions. The common denominator in religions is the transcendent dimension and the intentionality directed to transcendence. The absolute and necessary varieties of religion are grounded in historicity and the symbolic variations imposed by diversified cultures. In relation to each other, the traditions or codes of cultures are relative. In relation to the individual within a particular tradition, the code of the culture and the religious tradition is absolute. It is not necessary for one to be born into the Buddhist or Hindu tradition, but it is absolutely necessary that one so born obtain religious identity by that particular tradition. In pluralistic cultures also, this is true. The difference, however, is that would-be believers have more options: they may indeed abandon, change, or maintain the original tradition or lack of tradition that has first conferred identity on them.

In the course of human history symbolic consciousness has created worlds of extraordinary significance and force. The horizons of these worlds are unlimited. Meaning in these worlds is ultimate and provides answers to questions that have beset the human race from its beginnings, such as, What is the ultimate meaning of my existence? Such worlds perennially answer the Kantian question: What may I know? and What may I hope? The symbols of such universes of discourse are understood first on the exoteric level and then on the esoteric.

In the introduction to Schuon's book, Huston Smith presents an illuminative diagram. Above a line horizontally bisecting a pyramid, one finds what Schuon calls the esoteric appropriation and practice of religion. Here the forms of religion "are to be transcended by fathoming their depths and discerning their universal content, not by circumventing them."[22] The forms, of course, are the symbols by which the religious tradition is mediated in particular cultures. These forms are absolutely necessary for individual and collective identity, as I have noted in the discussion of tradition. They are relative only when compared to other cultures and symbolic universes; they are absolute in the meaning that they mediate. On the esoteric level, above the line horizontally passing through the pyramid, the forms become more and more negotiable because the believer is closer, to continue the spatial metaphor, to the transcendent. This figure of speech, however, is meant to be illuminative and not to confine meaning or transcendence to spatial referrents. In the ascending motion to the transcendent, believers from diverse traditions come closer to each other not because they participate in the same forms, but rather because they share in some common intentionalities to which the forms point. They are participating now in a more common world of meaning. That is to say that unity is now more evident than is diversity. It is not to imply that a transcendent entity is regarded as a univocal point at which all roads converge. Such an oversimplification would annihilate the mysterious nature of the transcendent. The transcendent, by definition, always remains on the outer edge of all horizons.

Below a certain point, beneath the horizontal line Smith uses, is the exoteric level in which most believers in religions are to be found. Here the diverse symbolic forms are indispensable. At the beginning the form is grasped before its meaning. Only through the particular historical and cultural symbolic form can the reality of the religion begin to be mediated to the believer. The forms are beginning points, absolutely necessary footholds in a symbolically constructed universe. This is the case with regard to language, which is absolutely necessary for speech; but the particular form of language, as compared to other languages, is only relatively necessary. The power and force of the elementary forms and symbols is clearly manifested in their opposition to the developed stage of consciousness disclosed in a method like the historical-critical method.

On the level of the exoteric the diversity of religions is most striking. Here likewise is the source of the tenacity with which the believer holds on to the forms and derives religious meaning. On this level any development is seen as challenging, threatening, destructive, deadly. The exoteric level casts so strong a spell in history that racks, censures, excommunications, and even wars have been its protector. Here the forms are not negotiable. While the exoteric level is not known for broad-mindedness, its instinct is sociologically sound. Mahayanistic Buddhists, for example, cannot move to another form or symbol since the historicity of their existence and therefore their own identity depends totally on the forms mediated to them by the tradition. The subject is at an elementary level of differentiation of consciousness. Form and meaning are absolutely identified, even though one admits that the form points, in the intentional realm, to transcendence and involves ever higher differentiations of consciousness. (The rich Hindu vocabulary for states of consciousness is a good illustration of this.)

At the exoteric level, believers exhibit a fear when the symbols and their usually univocal meaning is expanded. For this elementary stage of appropriation demands acceptance of the symbols in a univocal, simple, straightforward fashion. Believers may at a later date question their earlier understanding of the symbols. And this examination is generally accompanied by fear and anxiety. The symbols may not mean what they were once understood to mean. That which for didactic purposes was presented as a steno-symbol begins now to be seen for what it really is, a tensive symbol. There is then the possibility or need that believers invest the symbol with a new meaning and purify the old understanding. They then stand face to face with freedom and with the choices and anxieties it imposes. They are at a new stage in the differentiation of consciousness. If they reject the freedom, they will generally assume that if the symbol does not have their meaning, it has no meaning. Thus they will go to extravagant lengths to attempt to escape the anxiety that the new stages of self-development generate. The emphasis in a developed exoterism of this sort is to restrict freedom, to remain where one is, to hope that anxiety will be removed by continually reiterated confessions of the exoteric symbolism and by the exclusion of any dissidents. So does the tensive symbol become the steno-symbol. And the believer remains at the elementary exoteric stage.

Schuon's distinction between esoteric and exoteric is based on the nature of the symbol as well as on the capacity of religious subjects for continuous differentiation within their consciousness in the appropriation of meaning. Thus both the unity and diversity of religions are ultimately grounded on the internal human world. The religious symbol mediates reality under the form of meaning. But all symbols are necessarily relative—relative to the reality they symbolize, relative to the society in which the symbol is found and develops, and also relative to the believer's capacity to appropriate the *existentiell* significance of the symbols. Symbols are therefore capable of various levels of understanding and interpretation according to the historical situation of the one utilizing the symbol and according to the intrinsic capacity of the individual to develop as a religious subject in the technical sense of the terms as described in the introduction. Development as a religious subject means evolution in the imaginative understanding and grasp of tensive symbols.

It is therefore clear that esoterism, particularly on the higher ranges, will be the prerogative of a relatively small group within any religious tradition. And it is they, the holy ones, the ones grasped by imaginative vision, who give vitality time after time to a religious tradition. The symbolic codes at the disposal of a Zen Buddhist and a Sufi are quite diverse. But if the two are in the domain of esoteric symbolism the nonverbal similarities of human semiosis are strikingly similar. On this level there is little to distinguish the Franciscan mendicant from the saffron-robed Buddhist.

But exoterism is the prerogative of the majority of people. It is the only vehicle by which an individual can first enter the religious world, and, seemingly, the rather permanent and constant possession of most believers after accepting a religious tradition. The exoteric is in no way to be demeaned. At the beginning it is of absolute necessity. And for many, it remains so during later periods. But exoterism, not at all blameworthy in itself, becomes dangerous by "its all-invading autocracy,"[23] that is, when it claims to be the only way of understanding a religion. It is, of course, the only way for the beginner. While the exoteric level is relative among all forms of religion, in a sense it is absolutely necessary in all its formal and symbolic aspects as a starting point.

Using exoteric criteria one can make no absolute claim for a particular religion. Such a claim is simply too confused and indeterminate to be of any significance.

> An absolute requirement to believe in one particular religion and not in another cannot in fact be justified save by eminently relative means, as, for example, by attempted philosophical, theological, historical, or sentimental proofs; in reality, however, no proofs exist in support of such claims to the unique and exclusive truth, and any attempt so made can only concern the individual dispositions of men, which, being ultimately reducible to a question of credulity, are as relative as can be. Every exoteric perspective claims, by definition, to be the one true and legitimate one. This is because the exoteric point of view, being concerned only with an individual interest, namely, salvation, has no advantage to gain from knowledge of the truth of other religious forms. Being uninterested as to its own deepest truth, it is even less interested in the truth of other religions, or rather it denies this truth, since the idea of a plurality of religious forms might be prejudicial to the exclusive pursuit of individual salvation.[24]

Nor can the transcendent be identified with any expressions about it, with any symbols which represent, or any judgments which seek to explain.

The foregoing can be summed up in the following formula: pure and absolute Truth can only be found beyond all its possible expressions; these expressions, as such, cannot claim the attributes of this Truth; their relative remoteness from it is expressed by their differentiation and multiplicity, by which they are strictly limited.[25]

It is important to keep this distinction in mind lest one bring transcendence into the world as immanent and reduce the transcendent to an object over which one can have control and power and mastery. If this becomes the case, either in study or religious practice, we are no longer speaking of transcendence.

If we accept Schuon's hypothesis, and it makes more sense than any other with which I am acquainted, then what is at work in diverse religions are symbolic forms that are more or less adequte to express some religious intentionality to point to transcendence. But symbols are meaningful only in the context of subjects who appropriate the symbols. And the subjects in this case are capable of continuing development in their conscious and unconscious appropriation and understanding of the symbol and the transcendent referrent. The subjects are capable of some degree of participation in the intentionality and meaning that the symbol discloses. At the exoteric level, however, believers are tied to the symbolic form as form; they constrain the symbol. In contrast, at the esoteric level, believers gradually release themselves from the symbolic form in the appropriation of the meaning for which the form exists; they allow the symbol or form to liberate them.

But Schuon's hypothesis can be augmented and clarified by considering what the believing subject contributes to the vitality of symbols, primarily on the esoteric and secondarily on the exoteric level.

We have already indicated in proposing a cognitional paradigm that individuals as such are oriented to "an other" in whom they can believe and hope, and whom they can love. These dynamisms are dispositions of the healthy human person. We may then suppose that the religious symbols accepted by a believer are not simply culturally conditioned but likewise invested with meaning by the threefold disposition of the believer. These dispositions, as in other areas of human living, are creative in the religious area, they transform the believer and they create the reality to which the symbols now point. Creative imagination bestows meaning on the symbol. But this meaning is anything but arbitrary precisely because there is a linguistic and literary universe as objectively palpable as any other universe, a point developed more fully in chapter 7.

The symbols may be diverse in the varying religious traditions, though there will obviously be a common fund of archetypal symbols. The apprehension on delineation of the transcendent may likewise be quite different. But what is similar in the human personality is the threefold disposition of belief, hope, and love which operates dialectically with the symbols—creating meaning and receiving meaning. Thus one must avoid the absolutizing temptation that affirms one transcendent reality that must be conceived in one particular fashion.

Analogous to this dialectic is the love one has for one's mother and father. It is belief, hope, and love, in varying degrees of intensity and configuration, which bestow on this set of parents a unique and absolute love. But the love for this particular mother and father is not paradigmatic for anyone outside the family. Nonetheless, one may speak of qualities that should be found in good parents and that will generate love as such.

The matter may be illustrated more concretely. What invests reality with diverse meanings even where symbols may range from the same to the similar to the diverse? What explains the situation wherein a Muslim can say, "I can understand Judaism, but could never become a Jew," or when a Buddhist says, "I can understand the claims of Hinduism, but could not become a Hindu," or when an agnostic claims, "I understand Christianity but could not become a Christian"? It is obvious that personal decision plays a decisive role. But why was the decision taken?

On this uncertain terrain one can only suggest a tentative answer. What seems to be at work here is the acts of believing, hoping, and loving that generally issue from a wishing and then a subsequent trusting in the symbolic mediation that is chosen. If symbols, particularly those with a second intentionality are evocative, then they evoke responses within the horizon of the believer. The imagination, within the scope of a particular horizon, constructs a whole symbolic universe and establishes a particular religion (or nonreligion) as true in quite the same way that individuals and their historicity construct a world in which they love only this particular mother and father. But, as in the case of a mother or father, it is nonetheless possible that this or that religion may be so at variance with what the religion should be that one can choose another or strongly affirm a disbelief in any religion.

Now while we may seek a certain unity among religions in their esoteric dimension, both revelation and religious wisdom, as the content of religious communication, are nonetheless potentially intolerant. Revelation's historical location and its claim to represent adequately if not totally the transcendent for the individual suggests a vertical intolerance. This intolerance of other vertical transactions is necessary to establish the moral certitude of the claim laid upon the individual, who is free to assent or not. This assent, after some form of intellectual appropriation, is a matter of individual decision and responsibility that involves the elimination of other claims for this believer. This we may term the vertical level of assent.

On the horizontal level, the religious assent can only be tolerant of individuals and groups who, for one reason or another, make a different choice. The certitude provided by the individual's vertical religious experience cannot, in the present state of the world at least, be transferred to the horizontal level. Nor can any form of pressure or solicitation substitute for the individual's personal and responsible transaction with transcendent meaning mediated in one particular symbolic system. So must religions be tolerant on the horizontal level. Such tolerance can very likely be defended by the fact that no individuals nor any particular group can assert or defend the proposition that they possess all transcendent meaning, what the medievals called *totum et totaliter*.

This assertion, of course, brings up the larger question of the relationship of religion to truth—a question that demands realism and delicacy. One might of course consign religious assent totally to individual choice and leave it at that. But such an answer is incomplete and suggests that perhaps religion is a matter of taste or even caprice. We have made some attempt to provide a coherent explanation of both the absolute and relative aspects of diverse religious symbolic systems. Given the state of a pluralistic world today and the apprehension of this pluralism, this answer is temporarily satisfactory. But the question still remains: is religion a matter that has to do with truth or with taste? Before attempting an answer to this question one must accept the symmetry of religious systems and the distinction between the exoteric and esoteric levels and their relationship to symbolic presentation. That will mean that our present position respects differences and hints at similarities in presentations of transcendence. But because there has been no long and large-scale meeting of religious symbolic systems or of their cultural counterparts, we are not yet prepared to perform a full-scale comparison of religions and of their symbolic systems. Instead of cultural unity we exist in a world of diversity that continually sets up poles of opposition. And this world is hardened particularly by the adherence of believers to symbolic forms on the exoteric level. And, unfortunately, believers on the exoteric level not only must manifest a certain intransigence but also seem to find strong institutional forms suitable to diffuse and at times impose their own intransigence. But religion at the exoteric level remains relatively primitive in terms of religious differentiation, just as the endless repetition of "Twinkle, twinkle little star" is primitive for the beginning musician. One's development, of course, may be arrested at the primitive stage. But the question of truth is proposed primarily to maturity, to development on the esoteric level, although it would seem that religious organizations as such tend to promote the status quo. Can we, though, say anything about the larger question of the truth of religious symbolic systems? Or better, can we at least develop the state of the question as this problem meets the historian of religion?

Mortimer Adler has presented the question from a Western perspective.[26] He notes that cultural unity is lacking and therefore it is quite difficult to find convincing points of agreement on the nature of what is true. Nonetheless, one may maintain in principle the unity of truth, the unity of mind, and the unity of humanity. So may one assert also the existence of reality independent of the mind. In some areas, criteria of truth and of falsity are irrelevant: cuisine is a matter of taste, not of truth, and so in matters of cuisine we expect and are not at all troubled by cultural diversity."[27] But mathematical theorems and demonstrations "command an assent that transcends all national and cultural divisions."[28] So too does the agreement on truth in mathematics, the experimental sciences, and technological implementation constitute areas in which there is a large measure of "doctrinal agreement."[29] "Wherever the fruits of technology are used or enjoyed, the truth of science and mathematics is acknowledged. The fruits of technology are now used all over the world—in the East as well as in the West."[30] Are religions to be classified as systems that have a cognitive value comparable to the empirical sciences and therefore to be subject to the same criteria of truth and falsity? Or are religious matters comparable to those of taste? Or is there another option?

If religion does not claim to involve knowledge comparable to any knowledge currently available by normal means, then there is no problem. But Judaism, Christianity, and Islam "all claim to be knowledge based on divine revelation and all promise God's help in achieving salvation."[31] Here there is a claim to truth. But the principles by which truth is adjudicated in mathematics, science, and philosophy are transcended and adherence to the religions is based on a special revelation. Therefore, by definition these "dogmatic differences will not yield to adjudication by any of the logical means that are available to us in the spheres of mathematics, science and philosophy."[32]

Here Adler sees an obstacle which he feels is insuperable. If, however, historicity is taken seriously, and if the double intentionality of the symbol, particularly on the esoteric level, is developed, then there is at least the hope that one might see more clearly exactly where the similarities and differences among these religions really reside. Basically Adler supposes that there is one kind of truth—that which is exemplified by the empirical sciences, where the symbols used are always steno-symbols, that is, a world of language closed by consent. But the stock-in-trade of religions is the tensive symbol, that is, the symbol that stands "for some larger meaning or set of meanings which cannot be given, or fully given, in perceptual experience itself."[33] This is similar to the world of poetry and art. It is the world in which a symbol has at least a second intentionality. This type of symbolic language, used by everyone, is best exemplified by the use of metaphor, which, on the face of it, is absolutely illogical and therefore totally different from the steno-language of the natural sciences. For in metaphor one asserts the illogical: "this is that." But of course this is really never that, but rather somehow like that. The metaphor says one thing but means something else.

The symbols in religions therefore intend to stimulate the imaginative vision, and their semantic action, as Wheelwright calls it, intends to raise the reader to the level of the language that is created to communicate an original religious vision. At the exoteric level one is dealing with the elements of perception; at the esoteric level one actually begins to see. Thus if one compares the writings of John of the Cross to the Upanishads, the reality to which the tensive symbols point does not seem discrepant. What seems clear is that the symbols are never identified with the transcendent but are rather evocative pointers. Thus if one is to speak of the truth of religion, that truth is not the same as the truth found in knowledge mediated by steno-symbols but rather the truth found in tensive language or the truth found in art rather than science. Nor does this suggest Adler's option that religious truth is simply a matter of taste.

Moreover the question of truth is not one decided at the level of exoteric symbolism, which is by definition the beginning of the learning process. Rather, the question of truth is here, as in every cognitive process, a late question, depending on the long procedure of experience, understanding, and judgment. Judgments about truth made on the basis of elementary and primitive experiences will be as erroneous as they are in every such instance of human learning. To clarify the question of truth one must turn to the mediators of religious tradition.

The subject matter of religious tradition is mediated by five generic categories. First of all there is a body of literature, either potential (oral forms) or actually written—words consigned to the memory or to the eye. This comprehensive corpus may be accepted as constitutive, that is normative or foundational, or as consequent, that is, literature emerging after and from the foundational literature. Lines of distinction here are not as clear as frequently assumed, even when authority attempts to close a canon. Second, there is the mediation of religion through visual art forms such as painting, sculpture, and architecture. Third, there is the aural art form, usually some type of sacred music. The music may stand alone or be accompanied by the dance or by some other form of mimetic activity. Fourth, religion is mediated through historical formulations that are distinct from the literature, the visual art forms, and the aural genres. These historical formulations and monuments may include correspondence, protocols, popular forms of devotion, religious attire and gesture, and the development of institutions and professional custodians of the tradition. Finally, each religious tradition maintains itself by theological formulations that may be implicitly present in the story, the song, the myth, popular wisdom, the legend, the saga, or in more developed systematic formulations that are modes of transmitting the initial vision in concrete forms. From these five forms of mediation emerges the cultural code that we call religious tradition. Therefore it is quite clear that one does not do justice to the complexity of a religious tradition by asking whether religion deals with truth or taste in a univocal sense. Religious traditions propose visions and mediate these visions in polymorphic fashion. Canons of discrimination must be proportionate to the mediators of the religious vision. And apart from simple systematic theologies and elementary creedal or catechetical formulas, the mediators of religious meaning are primarily art forms. Proportionate to the forms are modes of understanding, which are themselves art forms.

Proportionate to the first mediator of religion, literary and oral transmission, is the operation of literary criticism in the broadest sense of the term. Proportionate to the second and third mediators, visual and aural art forms, is an aesthetic operation. Proportionate to the fourth mediator, the historical, is an historical operation. And finally, congruent to the fifth mediator, the theological, will be a theological operation.

It is quite obvious that the five proposed operations have their own canons of procedure. In fact, any one of these operations is a specialty in its own right and generally forms an identifiable institution or guild. Each operation has its own genesis, its proper and discernible evolution, its own critical development culminating in thematized reflections and highly differentiated procedures.

Basically the operations are divisions of labor, both for the individual and community. The operations should be both complementary and dialectically related. Overemphasis on one or another operation or sub-operation will inevitably produce a limited or one-sided view of religion. Distortion may also occur when procedures successful in other fields of study, for instance the natural sciences, are assumed to be valid procedures when applied unequivocally to all the mediators of a religious tradition. So too is it inaccurate and deceptive to suppose that the basic research required to begin the study of religion is anything more than a preliminary step to the five operations. From the variety of the mediators and their proportionate operations arises an appropriate series of questions that are not at all adequately included under the rubric of the truth of the religion, if truth be understood here as truth found within the closed systems of steno-symbolism.

One might rather suggest that the proper question is whether a religious vision enables the individual to see all that is to be seen and hear all that is to be heard. Is the religious vision one of compelling and constructive power? What we are here proposing is similar to the approach suggested by Michael Polanyi.[34] He sees religion as a "heuristic vision" and therefore aligns religion "with the great intellectual systems, such as mathematics, fiction and the fine arts, which are validated by becoming happy dwelling places of the human mind."[35] Therefore to speak of the truth of religion against a correspondence theory of truth (and this seems to be Adler's presupposition) or to assume that the truth of religion must be like the truth of the natural sciences and their derived technologies is to ignore the fact that religious belief is a "passionate heuristic impulse which has no prospect of consummation."[36] And even the formulted systematic theology to which the term truth is frequently applied "can be said to be true or false, but only as regards its adequacy in formulating and purifying a pre-existing religious faith."[37]

Thus, in religions are heuristic visions; their diversity will be manifest at the level of exoteric symbolism, their unity at the level of esoteric symbolism. Elementary historical study will primarily indicate the diversity. But as there are diverse mediators of a religious tradition, so too must there be diverse operations corresponding to the polymorphic mediators. It is to these operations, and the particular history of one, the theological, that I now turn.

·6·

THEOLOGY AND
THE CONSTITUTIVE OPERATIONS
IN RELIGIOUS STUDIES

An ill-defined theology finds itself something of an orphan. Within the field of religious studies the history of religions has been accorded a primacy because of its seeming proximity in methodology and presuppositions to traditional university disciplines. But the exclusion of theology from the broad field of religious studies is as much due to theology's self-portrait as to competition from other disciplines studying religion. The estrangement of theology from the field of religious studies and its very uneasy alliance with the history of religions originates proximately in the Enlightenment and in a procedure in which theologians themselves attempted to distinguish theology from all other forms of knowledge. The story is too long to allow more than a brief sketch.

Shortly after comparative religion, as it was then called, became a relatively clearly defined zone and about the same time that comparative mythology turned into a field of serious study, Schleiermacher (1768–1834) had affirmed experience and feeling (*Erlebnis* and *Gefühle*) as the basis of religion.[1] The relation of his Moravian background to this assertion is clear. Then Ritschl (1822–1889) "and other nineteenth-century theologians could develop an antimetaphysical theology faithful to Kant's first critique and a theological account of man's moral experience faithful to the second critique. Theology thus found a secure niche for faith, far from the onslaught of critical reason and science, in the depths and mystery of man's experience as a moral creature."[2] Wilhelm Herrmann, a strong influence in continental theology, emphasized that "Christian faith does not fall within the sphere of world knowledge."[3] Nor does religious knowledge—both that of actual religious practice and that of theological reflection on that practice—come in any other way than through relevation. In fact, where reason or any other objective type of thinking operates, there God cannot be.[4] The individuality and incommunicability of the religious experience included reflection on that religious experience. So it would be assumed that only in and from faith could a person properly do theology. This presupposition was often defended as typical of all intellectual process by comparing it to the presuppositions of the empirical scientist, who assumes the capacity of the mind to attain truth, presupposes the existence of data, and relies on the validity of a particular method.

The neo-Kantian school moved further by hardening the distinctions among faith, religious knowledge as such, and reason (*Geist*). The role of the intellect as *Geist* was to objectify the contents of consciousness and to manifest "the self-enduring forms," to move "toward externality."[5] And externality as such is one step removed from *Erlebnis* plus *Gefühle*. The dynamism of reason (*Geist*) and the term toward which it tended were opposed to the concept of the individual who becomes individual and whose self-manifestation is only "in the immediacy of the moment."[6] The seeming objectivity of *Geist* and its term is opposed to the truly individuated person, who becomes such by "the interior, subject side of conscience, present only in the mode of *Gefühle* or *Erlebnis.*"[7] Thus knowledge, objectified in science, morality, or even art, and quite obviously in any established metaphysics, are all produced by the intellect (*Geist*). It is this concept of intellect that "appears initially in Greece, becomes dormant, and is reborn in the Enlightenment and mathematical science of modernity."[8] The broad world of what we call culture is distinguished from the religious experience itself and from the study of that religious experience—the realm that is broadly described as theological. This radical dualism becomes intensified, justified, and seemingly irrefutable when mind and its products are identified with works (of the Law).[9] The intention of distinguishing contents of revelation from products of human ingenuity was partially achieved, but not without cost. Lacking the contributions of historicity, hermeneutic, and understanding, theology gradually increased its distance from objectifying forms of thought. Paradoxically enough, despite all the efforts to restrain the inevitable workings of the human mind, the Enlightenment and post-Enlightment periods produced systematic and speculative theologies that did indeed resemble systems produced by philosophy or other anthropological disciplines.

Whatever the later theoretical conflict, the intention to promote theology as a unique intellectual enterprise gave to the academic world grounds to consider theology a subject quite distinct from university disciplines—particularly when comparative religion found itself at home under the rule of objectifying reason. German, Swiss, and the older British universities had no practical problems of importance since theological faculties or divinity schools had long been an established part of the university system. Elsewhere theology was confined to seminaries and to schools with strong confessional associations, where, presumably, students would encounter the proper experience (*Erlebnis*) and its individuating effects (*Gefühle*). At the same time the administrative arms of churches exercised a controlling influence.

In the late nineteenth and early twentieth centuries, by way of a mild and unintended countermove, theology occasionally came to mean *any* understanding of religion. This stance later posed the question of whether theology required a predisposition of faith and sometimes involved the even more nebulous issue of whether one who "did not practice the faith" could study theology. Could one, for example, whose allegiance to a church seemed minimal or nonexistent study its theology? In general, the conventional wisdom that theology required faith as a beginning point prevailed.

A new dimension gradually intruded: the use of the historical-critical method by scriptural scholars in the last quarter of the nineteenth and beginning of the twentieth centuries. Among these scholars may be listed Bousset, Reitzenstein, Eichhorn, Gunkel, J. Weiss, Wernle, Heitmüller, Grossman, Troeltsch, Dibelius, Bultmann, and earlier, J. Wellhausen. Basically, what these scholars pursued was a literary, historical, and comparative methodology that placed the revelation of both Old and New Testament in the broader spectrum of religious studies. Scriptural studies used a method and an approach common to those used by anyone who would study religions. There then slowly developed a separation of scriptural studies from what were assumed to be the traditional forms of theology, a separation that still exists today. It is still not uncommon for official and professional religious authorities to caution students who would pursue scriptural studies in a university context. In most cases, whether in seminaries or elsewhere, the last thirty years have witnessed an attempt to reconcile the findings of scriptural interpretation both with traditional theologies and with any church that has sanctioned, governed, or controlled theological thinking. Gradually scriptural interpretation moved inevitably out of the church and more toward the field of the history of religions. Major forces in this movement have already been mentioned. Where the results of the historical-critical method were taken seriously by people, such as Harnack, Herrmann, and Troeltsch, whose interests were historical, theological, or social,[10] there was a perceived need to reorganize theology in such a fashion as to be compatible with new truths. Forces had been set in motion, the full influence of which are only being realized today.

The complete history of the attempts by churches and theologians to deal with the new perspective remains to be written. In any case, one of the effects of the historical-critical method and its accompanying literary activities was to move the study of Scripture, and hence, of religion, into a broader intellectual arena. In practice, if not in theory, one could study a religion without being hampered by either religious presuppositions or firm adherence to a church context. Mostly for this reason practitioners of the historical-critical method were suspect by members of both the intellectual community and the religious community. The former could not forget the confessional past; the latter, on sound sociological grounds, feared ecclesiastical and theological modifications vast in scope if not in intention.

The history of religions, on the other hand, never had either epistemological or social problems of quite the same scope. The discipline gained almost immediate acceptance. And it is very likely for this reason, unconscious though it may be, that historians of religion who venture into methodological reflections nearly always describe theology as a discipline practiced by committed believers who accept and promulgate a normative approach within a community normatively constituted. Though such historians of religions have ignored the strides of history, theologians themselves have given good ground to those outside the field of theology to consider theology a vastly different type of study from both the nonnormative discipline of the history of religions and the other disciplines that may be gathered together under the rubric of religious studies.[11] Given the development of historicity, hermeneutic, and understanding, such oversimplifications deserve reconsideration.

There are immediate and self-evident similarities between the history of religions and the work of theology. The history of religions and comparative religion directly involve historical study and a comparison of traditions. But historical and comparative work involve literary activities (or comparable archaeological activity in the case of nonliterate religions). There is little dispute about the historical and the literary activities. But the term *comparative,* when applied to the comparison of religions, frequently bears an overtone of objectivity, of distance from the object of study, as well as an implication that such studies are rather easily accomplished by the truly objective scholar, who is unhampered by any religious or theological presuppositions. This notion is highly questionable insofar as the material for comparison has first to be assembled, completed, compared, reduced, classified, and thematized,[12] and then at each stage of research the data must be understood and judged. Since we are dealing with a complex body of symbols, the second intentionality of the symbol must not only be interpreted but also postulates the act of interpreting the interpreter, if the interpreter is really to come into contact with the subject matter. But the subject matter of religions is mediated by a symbolic system that has been generated, expressed, and articulated theologically. Any type of comparison must be accompanied not only by the activities mentioned above but also by an operation that can only be called theological. Surely no one would seriously maintain that comparisons can be made between religious traditions without studying the theologically constructed meanings. No one would seriously attempt a comparative history of music without the competence and experience proper to music. Thus both the historian of religion and the theologian deal in principle with the same symbolic systems. One therefore cannot use comparative activity as such as constitutive of an approach or field thoroughly different from that of theology.

It is worthwhile to recall that Luther exercised a comparative activity, as did al-Ghazzali and Maimonides. So too did the developers of Theravada and Mahayana in Buddhism, not to mention the contributors to the Islamic schools of theology. Nor has theological comparison been as limited as sometimes assumed. For at least in the field of classical Protestant theology, comparison is not confined to historical comparison within the same tradition but extends to any religious tradition that is tangential to the understanding of the written scriptures. Here one need only refer to Old Testament studies, which routinely refer to

Babylonian, Assyrian, Egyptian, and Canaanite traditions. Comparisons are made within the biblical religion as the interpreter seeks to distinguish authentic Israelite tradition from inauthentic tradition. And the comparisons pertain not only to the historical development and thought progression—what occurred, what happened, what was said, what was meant—but also to the theological contrasts and similarities. One speaks quite properly of a theology of the Deuteronomist, a theology of P, of E, and of J. The legitimacy of the comparison can only be called into question when the one comparing knows and accepts a result before engaging in the comparison or if the interpreter simply does not understand or is unsympathetic to one of the terms of the comparison. Error is also possible if the interpreter imposes alien categories on the material to be compared.

This is particularly clear in Old Testament studies, where the matter is broader than it is in the New. The theologian and the biblical scholar are subject to the same criteria for truth as are the historians of religion, for they are all dealing with the same subject matter mediated by particular symbolic systems. Once this principle is established, there is no intrinsic reason why the theologian of one tradition cannot understand and compare theologies of other traditions. Such comparisons will be fruitful to the extent that the theologian is capable of grasping the convictions and forces at work in another religion. In itself, orientation to a particular faith and belief system does not invalidate either historical or comparative study. If the interpreters have made an existential analysis they will know the absolute necessity of differing religious symbolic forms as well as the impossibility of value judgments over matters of individual decision. Furthermore, if theologians understand the differences between esoterism and exoterism, particularly in their own religious tradition, they will avoid the common error of comparing two completely different terms. And in all instances they will be aware of the subject matter of religion, which is ultimate intentionality directed to transcendence. Confusion here can be a de facto problem but it surely is not de jure. The most common cause of error on the part of theologians is the influence of exoterism on them. This can be seen in even the best intentioned theological works when they turn to the delicate subject of "other religions."[13]

But a word remains to be said about the historical activity. Comparison as such may be made within a religion or among religions. In either case a prior historical activity is necessitated. But the history itself is in all cases constituted by the various intentionalities at work and by those unforeseen and unintended outcomes that become a part of history, occurrences that go beyond the conscious intentionality of any one or of any group. But where does one find the intentionalities, both intended and unintended, except in those symbols which constitute the religion and its interpretation? The actual experiences of history are only available via the symbols and by something comparable to the sympathetic reenactment of the past, of which Ricoeur writes. What produced the symbolic systems in the first place? Quite clearly an operation that can be called theological in the same sense that operations which produce political systems may be called political. One does speak of political history, social history, or economic history. This indicates quite clearly that a single reality provides a variety of aspects under which it may be studied. It would be naive to suggest that one aspect—be it the historical or theological dimension—exhausts the intelligibility of religious reality. It is quite proper therefore to speak to a theological history that is available and intelligible to theological study. And since intentionalities directed to ultimate transcendence occur in time and space, the theological history becomes accessible through a concomitant historical operation.

The historical operation as such—considered in the minimal sense as the reconstruction of the past events, the recounting of what was said, done, and meant—is completed by an operation proportionate to the subject matter and the symbolic systems mediating the subject matter. Were this not the case one would not write from a sociological, anthropological, economic, literary, psychological, or linguistic viewpoint. The dimension of study must be proportioned by the aspect that generates the symbols mediating the subject matter. By strict historical means, it is fully possible to reconstruct the role of oral tradition in Amerindian religious life without at all grasping the immediacy and ultimacy of the oral situation in which writing or transcription of any sort violates the sacred situation in which the Great Spirit operates. The ultimacy and immediacy of the intentionality at work is not a simple datum of history but of the religious meaning with which the Amerindian invests the situation. Both the history of religions and theology inform us that it is possible to reconstruct a religion in which "pagans worship images" and miss the theological aspect that suggests that the worship is actually directed to that which the image represents.

One may obviously object that the historical operation so pursued is inadequate not because it does not comprehend the specifically religious dimension but rather because the historical operation itself has been inadequately performed. The objection is serious indeed and not altogether without foundation. An example may clarify the issue.

If a nonmusician, unskilled in performance and theoretical understanding, writes a history of music, it is conceivable that such a history might catalog rather accurately the development of music and the external aspects of what was done and what was said. A good deal of what passes for history consists of such external cataloging. In one sense the history would be adequate, particularly if it unwittingly included the crucial external events in which the musician could find key transitions and meanings. In quite another sense, however, the history is inadequate. Examples of such histories abound. But where is the inadequacy to be discerned? Certainly not in the recounting of the past events, which by definition might be satisfactory. Rather the inadequacy is to be sought within the interpreter's inadequate relationship to the subject matter. The flaw need not be in the historian's lack of the skill and craftmanship required for the general study of history. The defect lies in an undeveloped dimension within the interpreter. That dimension is broadly described as musical appreciation and understanding. Since vital transitions, almost immediately perceptible to the musician, correspond to nothing within the historian's experience, the historian will obviously bypass the specifically musical dimension, however that dimension be defined. The same situation occurs when a reader returns to a classic book that he once had read either out of external compulsion or the feeling that such reading is necessary for the cultured. A rereading at a later date brings a new understanding and appreciation of that classic. Again what has changed lies within the interpreter: the literature now corresponds to something within the experience of the reader. The horizon of the reader has expanded to include a relationship to the subject matter of the classic.

The case is quite the same for the historian of religion who lacks theological sophistication. Ample testimony to this may be found in textbooks introducing the study of world religions. One cannot fault the cataloging technique. Everything seems to be there except the meaning of religion and its development in various religious traditions. Again, the defect seems to be in the lack of a relationship to the subject matter and the exoteric and esoteric dimensions of the symbolic systems, which seek to mediate this meaning. Were this not so one would not so often see in views of sociology and anthropology books the observation that the authors miss the specifically religious dimension. It is not generally the historical presentation that is called into question but rather the fact that the authors have not done justice to the subject matter and its theological mediation. I will return to the vexing point of why such criticisms occur.

As it would be impossible for a nonmathematician to write a history of mathematics, so too it would be impossible for a nontheologian to write a history of religion. It is the theological dimension that differentiates the work of a historian of religion from that of the anthropologist, the sociologist and the philosopher. It is utterly impossible to understand the sun dance of the Wind River Shoshones without grasping the theological intentionality evident in the belief system of the Shoshones. It is by understanding the religious beliefs articulated in a symbolic realm of discourse that one comes to some understanding of the faith behind the religion in question.[14] The symbolic systems have both a historical and theological dimension. The perspectives present in the symbols must likewise reside within the interpreter. The theological dimension is the intentionality directed to ultimate transcendence. This intentionality is accepted by faith and articulated in a tensive symbolic system proportionate to the intentionality. This holds true whether one speaks of the theology of the Mu'tazila in Islam, or of a dependent origination functioning in the temporal modalities of past, present, and future in Theravada. The specific intentionality will be understood by an interpreter whose consciousness is sufficiently differentiated to apprehend the theological dimension.

The theological dimension is characterized moreover by immediacy and ultimacy. Immediacy means that the reader or investigator—and therefore all intrepreters—is directly addressed by the text (oral or written). Ultimacy means that the texts are conceived to have an absolute validity and unconditioned transcendence. An interpreter therefore must have an understanding of the forces and the convictions that this meaning generates in human life. The force and conviction is bred by the experience and posture of faith; both are articulated by a theological symbolic system. In the intellectual realm the theological operation is characterized by a differentiation in the symbolic consciousness of the interpreter. If the interpreter's consciousness is not sufficiently differentiated then everything that does not fall into the realm of personal experience may be easily denied, as for example, the musically unsophisticated person may not notice realities immediately perceptible to the musically differentiated consciousness.

It should be evident that the theological operation and the historical operation should occur in close conjunction. "History, therefore, is the field in which these manifestations (full of aim and meaning) take shape in the works of culture, in social and political orders as well as in philosophy, religion, world-views (Weltanschauung), and in art and poetry. Every work is a manifestation of physical life."[15] Physical life is the source of the intentionalities intelligible in themselves and available within the field of history. Neither a true theology nor an accurate historical study of religions can prescind from the study of the intentionalities manifest in the language, myth, ritual, and creeds of religions, and from the more externalized and objectified manifestations of the religious intentionalities. The presence of an internal and external world of religious experience demands the two operations for adequate comprehension of any religious phenomenon.

What comes into history in the case of religions is some perceptible symbolic articulation that attempts to express a meaning and intentionality directed to transcendence and proposed with immediacy and ultimacy. Since the symbolic construction exists in time and space and produces tangible effects, there is likewise a historical dimension comprising what is said and what is done. The criticism of the subject matter that discovers what is meant and what is intended is constitutive rather of the theological operation. There is no such thing as a theology that is totally removed from history because the experience of intentionality directed to transcendence occurs in the concrete encounters of the individuals. If theology withdraws from history, as indeed it has in many instances, then it loses its hold on the people who sense instinctively the distance of what is really a properly philosophical speculation from the concrete circumstances of their own historical existence.

The great temptation of theology has been to remove itself from the seeming contingency of history and historicity, more by presupposition than actual intent. Thus the continuity of theology, particularly in the West, has been sought from within propositions formulated in the past. The propositions may be understood in a new fashion. But the propositions, particularly if they articulate a dogma, remain the same. Thus theology finds itself in a static problematic characteristic of the now virtually defunct classical culture.[16] But the inroads of historical consciousness begin to be felt when one places a particular religion directly within the field of historical investigation. Wrede's suggestion that Christianity be described as the religious history of primitive Christianity or the history of the religion and the theology of primitive Christianity, is gradually finding acceptance not because the proposal was correct but rather because the influence of historical consciousness is inevitable and relentless. The medieval synthesis is as irretrievably past as the world view of Ptolemy; there is no return. Only that which can survive the newer methods of rational scrutiny and the atmosphere of historical consciousness deserves retention: it is like moving to a new home and being forced to part with some beloved but unnecessary possessions. But the discarding of what is deemed unnecessary or useless should not proceed by arbitrary or capricious elimination as, for example, is done by some modern theologians.[17]

To place religion and its theology in the context of historicity seems to lead at first glance to absolute relativity. Hence the importance of developed notions of historicity, hermeneutic, and understanding, as well as an evolved notion of coping with the unity and diversity of religions and their absolute and relative aspects. The conflict within theology is not from the power of historical consciousness as such but rather from historical consciousness as it is concretely manifested in the historical-critical method, particularly as this method is applied to the Bible and to authoritative texts in all religious traditions. Nor is the tension between a dogmatic or systematic theology and historical methodology a new phenomenon, as appears from the already cited example of Wellhausen, who, in 1882, resigned from the theological faculty at Greifswald and assumed the post of professor of Semitic languages at Halle. His reasons for the transfer are informative:

> I became a theologian because I was interested in the scientific treatment of the Bible; it has only gradually dawned upon me that a professor of theology has the practical task of preparing students for service in the Evangelical Church and that I was not fulfilling this practical task, but rather, in spite of all reserve on my part, was incapacitating my hearers for their office.[18]

But theology may be removed from its historicity and hence from any direct need to integrate itself with the historical-critical method by a much more subtle procedure: here the theologian postulates mental laws at work in the transition from what he calls the intersubjective categories of Scripture to the objective language of authoritative bodies such as church councils. This transition from the so-called intersubjective language of the authoritative texts to the more objective language of technical theology is mainly described as a transition from rather elementary categories—the reality of the authoritative texts as related to me—to the more profound categories in which the mind asks, "What is this reality described in the authoritative texts *in itself?*" The example often cited is the transition from the common-sense categories of compounds to the more objective presentation found in the periodic chart of the elements.

This so-called transition from intersubjective categories to the more objectifying role of intellect and reason is frequently identified as a new stage of meaning, an advance upon the so-called intersubjective relationships that are found, for example, in religious literature. The technical definitions such as the *homoousios* of Nicaea, the two natures and the one person of Chalcedon, or the two wills of Constantinople represent the transition from scriptural categories to conciliar definitions. One moves, so it is said, from the *causae cognoscendi* to the *causae essendi,* from the *priora quoad nos* to the *priora quoad se.* As the periodic chart of the elements represents progress and allows for later systematization, it is likewise assumed that the so-called transition from simple scriptural categories to conciliar definitions and to the speculative theology emerging therefrom also represents inevitable intellectual progress, the manifestation and development of mind. This position has found a wide following, particularly in Roman Catholic circles.[19]

The proposal and its implementation possesses the allure of unity and offers the hope that theology may be a science in virtually the same sense as the empirical sciences. So too this procedure hints at a theological continuity and progression which would somehow incorporate aspects of the historical-critical method and at the same time transcend it. So, unconsciously, would the classical culture intrude itself and allow the mind freedom from the unsettling results of the more plodding historical-critical method.[20] Despite the undeniable charm of such assumptions, the position contains a number of highly suspect suppositions, only some of which can be mentioned here.

First of all, if one turns to the early church councils in which the supposed transition from the intersubjective to the objective takes place, one will note that the church councils intended to find a terminology that would clarify seeming scriptural antinomies while at the same time remaining as close to Scripture as possible. The intention of Nicaea, for example, was not to shift into new categories of thinking, but rather to preserve "the soteriological and liturgical concerns of the Church, for which it was mandatory that Christ be divine."[21] The term *homoousios* (consubstantial) intended to show that it was God, not a messenger or an angel, that redeemed.[22] The decree attempted to reconcile a theological position with a liturgical status.[23] In other words the attempt was not to move to a new realm of discourse but rather to restate the reality maintained in Scripture in a language congruent with the historical situation of the believer. The function of the different wording was to validate the liturgical rubric or to support the intersubjective relationship of the believer to the object of worship. And this indeed is the true role of theology, however much later theological speculation was to remove itself from this aim. The council is really a scriptural commentary, an effort to translate the meaning of Christ for human existence in categories appropriate to a world three centuries removed from the primal events. The language, therefore, is as close to Scripture as possible and ultimately derived from the historical culture to which the council wishes to speak. As such, the terms are clothed in the historicity of the age. The movement here is not parallel to what Snell calls the discovery of mind, much less to the later discovery of the periodic chart of elements.

If there were some inevitable intellectual laws at work, if Nicaea, and later Ephesus and Chalcedon, were all instances of a new shift in thinking, of a kind of intellectual determinism, then it is quite difficult to account for the dissidents of the Eastern churches who opposed the outcome of this intellectual transit and who today remain separated from the group in which this technical language developed. Surely at some point the Eastern churches would have caught up with what is conceived of as a new stage of meaning, a new intellectual development parallel to that manifested in the periodic table of elements. But the thrust of the councils was not in the arena of the unthematic to the thematic, from the unsystematized to the systematic. The councils sought to find an appropriate and suitable language to express the meaning of Christ to the contemporary age. To see more than this intention at work and to build a speculative system comparable to those of the empirical sciences is flattering to the empirical sciences but totally inappropriate both to the realities of Scripture and of historical consciousness. What the Eastern churches objected to was not the so-called step forward in human consciousness, but the more jejune matter of appropriate terminology.

The so-called transit from intersubjective to objective categories not only ignores the position of the Eastern churches and ascribes to them an intellectual backwardness but also, as the Protestant Reformation should have proven, minimizes Scripture. It is even today a vast over-simplification to say that Scripture speaks primarily of events,[24] imply-ing thereby that the meaning of revelation is better mediated by an or-ganized system that proceeds from primitive terms to univocal definitions and an overall speculative coherence and symmetry.

One may suggest that there is every bit as much speculation and sys-tem, if at times implicit, in Scripture as in the most elaborate specula-tive systems of later thought. For example, passages such as Prov. 8:22–31, Prov. 3:19–20, and Isa. 63:9 (LXX) played a significant role in the Logos doctrine as well as in definitions of Jesus as the Son of God. These passages are not adequately described as events. The tie beween Nicaea and Prov. 8 is much closer than that of an event which is then transcended by the abstraction indigenous to theological systematiza-tion. These same passages played a profound role even in the articula-tion of Arian formulas. Both sides used the same passage: Arians relying on the "creation" of wisdom, anti-Arians invoking Prov. 8:23 as indi-cating that the existence of wisdom as anterior to "the age."[25] The forces at work were, as Pelikan notes, "late Jewish and early Christian apocalypticism,"[26] and the "new Hellenized Christianity."[27] There is no possible way of abstracting from the details of Scripture without reduc-ing the richness of Scripture. Nor is there another mode of presenting the wealth of scriptural language apart from commenting on it by using the historical-critical method. That is to say that one may have a systematic approach to religious literature if this approach is consonant with the tensive language used to express religious experience. But sys-tematic theology that reduces tensive symbols to steno-symbols needs overhauling.

A theology therefore that removes itself from its historicity by one of the ways described above or by any other way runs the risk of becoming immediately obsolete. Such a theology will lead to divisions among be-lievers—some of whom band together to restore the certainties of the past (usually based on exoteric symbolism) while others pursue a reli-gious life even where the exoteric forms of the religion are sterile and void. A removal from historicity is a removal from life. Nor can a sys-tem so built ensure the rational consistency of consciousness. Conflicts and deteriorization have occurred concretely because the historical-criti-cal method is a new differentiation of consciousness and a signpost that a new stage of meaning has been reached. This is always disturbing to prior states of consciousness and their assumed meanings. The reconciliation of the historical-critical method with the theologies of particular belief systems can only take place when a new context is established. The new context is determined by evolved development of history, hermeneutic, and understanding.

If there is a specifically theological operation required for the interpretation of religions, this does not mean that such an operation is first in the temporal order. The interpreter of religion faces a hermeneutic field. This field is the horizon in the radical sense of the term, that is, the field includes everything that is to be understood from a particular perspective. This field in general consists of elements, subject matter, and operations. The elements for the interpreter are usually whatever mediates the religion in question, the interpreter's own consciousness, the religious community, and the world or culture in which the religious tradition exists or existed. The subject matter is humanity's persistent search for ultimate meaning or the ultimate questions that beset human existence. Proportionate to this field and heuristic to the elements and the subject matter are four hermeneutical operations: the literary (or its corresponding archaeological and field-work operations), the historical, the comparative, and the theological. I turn now to these latter operations and leave the hermeneutic field for the final chapter.

The Literary Operation

Classical world religions exist not only in the lives of those committed to particular religious traditions but also in religious texts that, in varying degrees, are considered to be normative texts. In contrast to the tradition incarnated by believers, the texts and their interpretations are both record and direct address. Interpretative operations must do justice to both dimensions of the text. The first operation proper to authoritative written and oral documents is a polymorphic literary operation. In most instances, the first act of literary criticism, the establishment of the text, has been effectively enough accomplished, though new discoveries may continue to modify the text and alter its understanding as, for example, is the case with the Nag Hammadi texts, the Qumran discoveries, and the Ebla documents. An outline of how religious texts come into existence is reasonably well established: oral tradition in a variety of forms, compilation of the oral tradition into written forms, revision of the written form into cycles or groups, redaction by editors, final formation, and acceptance of the writings as normative. The Aristotelian canons of literary criticism are both useful and necessary. The interpreter proceeds through a formal analysis of structure, style, and content.[28]

Because the entire text to be interpreted is understood through its parts and the parts through the whole, the literary operation proceeds as a hermeneutic circle. The text is analyzed in terms of grammar, syntax, word usage, and the employment of terms and forms in the contemporary environment. The literary operation must also tend to recover the force of religious texts, not simply the lexicographical definitions. The text demands the study of appropriate languages and the compilation and use of lexica, monographs, and philological analysis, which then make possible stylistic criticism, genre criticism, source criticism, form criticism, and redaction criticism. The procedure must include the actual structure of the text, the origin of the text, developments and modifications of the text, traditions behind the text, and the intentions of both tradition and text. The literary procedure advances from the assimilation of data, to the suggestion of hypotheses and conjectures, to judgments that range from certitude to probability, doubt, opinion, and nescience. This operation, with its complementary historical and comparative operations, is an essential part of the historical-critical method or, more simply, scientific exegesis.

For purposes of clarity and simplicity, the term literary operation is employed here in as broad a sense as possible. There is no suggestion that the literary operation is simple nor that it is easily learned or transmitted. Nor does the operation exclude any of the suboperations that are more and more important to the delicate task of literary criticism. The literary operation is that activity which understands a text by any operation proportionate to the object. This operation, however, is contrasted to any type of interpretation that would base itself in charism, authority, spiritual power, inheritance, institution, or the so-called conversion. Each of these realities may be considered in the context of literary interpretation but as such they do not at all seem proportioned to religious texts or religious traditions.

The point of the literary operation, and whatever operation corresponds to this in the case of dominantly oral traditions, is not simply the accumulation and development of an enormous amount of specialized information, though this will be a by-product. The intention of the operation is understanding of the body of religious literature in question. For this understanding there is required an exact textual knowledge, a sensibility for the historical and social setting and environment, an ear attuned to the life of language, and a driving concern that the intention of the author be preserved. A religious text comes to life only when the interpreter "gives it voice."[29] This procedure can only take place when the reader moves from naive to critical reading. The role of religious imagination in the literary operation cannot be overestimated. Although one cannot provide a handbook to generate religious imagination, familiarity with classic literature does provide the interpreter with a mental atmosphere and climate quite different from that acquired through an organized systematic theology, which claims, at least, to have its beginnings in the religious text.[30]

The ultimate aim of the literary operation is to play its proper role in the total, integrated, and comprehensive understanding of the texts in question. The soundness of the literary operation is manifested by its role in generating an overall understanding of the tradition in question. The literary operation is integrated with the historical, comparative, and theological operations; it moves through ancient traditions about the text, and into the complexes of tradition in the text itself to the actual subject matter of the text. The effectiveness of the operation is judged by the simple analysis of whether the operation successfully mediates the subject matter of the religious texts.

The literary operation is distinguished from the theological operation in that the former deals with transcendent, immediate, and ultimate intentionality only implicitly, whereas the theological operation understands transcendent, immediate, and ultimate meaning as actual possibility and a demand made upon interpreters and readers of the text. The distinctions here are fine. For the literary operation may well include the question of how religious texts understood and applied ultimate meaning to their own contemporary situation. As such, however, the literary operation can keep the text and its demands at a distance, which is an actual requirement at times for sound interpretation. The theological operation, on the other hand, always seeks to overcome the aesthetic distance and preserves the text as a form of address directed to the interpreter and reader or hearer. Therefore, the theological operation demands a self-interpretation by the interpreter. The remote foundation of the interpretation will be the generic relation of the interpreter to the subject matter mediated by all religious texts; the proximate foundation will be the relationship of the interpreter to the specific way in which this particular text mediates the subject matter.

One peculiarly modern difficulty, very likely more pertinent to the theological than to the literary operation, deserves mention. The hermeneutic field as here described does not confront the ordinary person as much as those with a professional interest in the phenomenon of religion. The operations within the hermeneutic field are necessarily attainable by a small number, that is, people whose talent, skill, and desire have placed them in a world in which a classical education, foreign-language study, and the subsequent breadth of reading play an inordinately large role. That this training seems to be diminishing can hardly be questioned. This does not necessarily mean that there is today a smaller number of people with the talents and skills and training required for the study of religions than there was a hundred years ago. Rather, a decline has taken place in public literacy. The causes of this decline are multiple and sometimes controversial. At best there is a chasm between two cultures; to which Snow referred. At worst there is the gulf between true literacy and functional illiteracy. It cannot be denied that, in the West at least, the study of literature has become almost an esoteric luxury, especially when compared with the electronic means of mass communication. And even in the developing nations it seems likely that indigenous cultures, dependent as they are upon the science and technology of the West, may pass into the age of electronic media with little or no time dedicated to the reading characteristic of society after the invention of the printing press. That is to say that what took place gradually in the Western world may take place with undue rapidity in the developing world.

This suggests that the literary operation based on careful introduction to the alphabet, to writing, and to the interpretation of words in their secondary medium of space may become the possession of a smaller number of people. Hence the actual teaching of religious traditions and the appropriate methods of study will have to take cognizance to the fact that students are more and more formed by the mass media than by any type of humanistic tradition based on reading. So the teaching and study of religious traditions will have to find a propaedeutic for modern students than can prepare them for the operations needed to study a religious tradition. Very likely the propaedeutic will consist of placing the religious tradition in the larger arena of communication, a point to which I will return. Certainly part of the literary and of the theological operation will have to concern itself with how a religious tradition becomes accessible to the sensorium and the psyche formed primarily by these new means of communication. But this is to recall the importance of historicity and hermeneutics and to provide a concrete illustration of their importance in all religious interpretation.

Because I am suggesting that literary criticism should be accorded an unusual primacy in the hierarchy of operations designed to understand religious traditions, it is necessary to justify and amplify this emphasis in more detail and to contrast literary criticism with what is commonly called theological discourse. To achieve this, I will begin by borrowing a widespread religious symbol, that of the center, and examine the emergence of literary criticism and theological discourse from the center, which is religious literature.[31]

In the history of religions, the center is the zone of the sacred and centering is the bestowal of meaning from which all other meaning derives. Thus to consider religious literature as a center is not an arbitrary or artificial choice but one suggested by the simple fact that all religions have at their origin a literature, potential or actual, that may be called foundational, manifesting the primitive experiences from which the religion issues. All foundational religious literature exhibits a will to communicate a significant religious experience. This will to communicate is confirmed by forms of institutional approval that put books into our hands and confides to our memories oral forms that determine the nature of a religious tradition. It is no hyperbole, therefore, to conceive this body of literature as a center, for from it comes our knowledge of religious experience.

This institutionally approved and transmitted literature is part of a broader literary world. There is such a phenomenon as a literary universe, a world of literature whose reach and dimension is easily illustrated by a single work such as Dante's *Divine Comedy,* which incorporates genres and conventions common to other works, pursues its own poetic development, and at the same time utilizes in unique fashion symbols, images, and metaphors that belong to a wider constituency. This world of semantic autonomy is quite independent of an author's intent, desire, or feeling, as may easily be illustrated by the multiple meanings of "So should the lines of life that repair . . ." in Shakespeare's sixteenth sonnet.[32] The beginning of this world according to Northrop Frye is very likely found in mythical discourse, stories about the gods that later developed into sagas and legends about heroes to whom is ascribed either some forward leap in culture or whose activities are somehow larger than life. Sophisticated plots of tragedy and comedy developed later and merged more or less into fictional forms.[33] All the original forms may be simultaneously present in one instance of literary discourse.

Because this literary universe exists and exercises its influence in both conscious and unconscious ways, Frye notes, the experience of literature is associative and allusive, that is, the readers or hearers associate what they are hearing or reading with what they have previously heard or read. So when one hears the word injustice or justification, one's understanding of the term will be associated with how one has previously heard and understood the term. Because the images, symbols, and metaphors of literature are drawn from human experience this world of meaning is of potential concern to all people. Moreover, the creative imagination manifest in literature is likewise present in the imaginative uses of language by every child beginning to enter the world of words and discourse. The creative transformations employed by every child, apparently not learned from experience or social training and seemingly derived from innate powers, are but the beginning of the flights of imagination that constitute literature. Potentially, therefore, every human being inhabits the formal literary universe. Grimms' fairy tales, for example, are really just a collection of stories that were already in existence in the communal consciousness. But the use of the imagination, so clear in children, is really a form of life and therefore depends on continual nourishment for its sustenance, a critical development of prethematic activities.

A characteristic, therefore, of the creative imagination that generates literature is that *non stat in indivisibili,* i.e., either you have it totally or not at all, either you are Shakespeare or you are totally unable to use language creatively. Thus the attempt to catalog literature with exactitude is not always successful. But one thing the history of religions teaches us is that the world of oral and written literature is larger and more comprehensive than we were once inclined to believe. The study of the classics of Greece and Rome, augmented by the investigation of Near Eastern literature in which the Bible plays an important role, and completed by the study of English literature with an occasional nod toward literature of one or other European country (usually in translation) is still but a small aspect of a larger literary universe.

The extent and scope of this literary universe, its presence through-out the entire human race as well as within each untutored child, and its impetus and origins in a common imaginative procedure seem to have been first seriously grasped by Giovanni Battista Vico (1668–1744) and Johann Gottfried von Herder (1744–1803). And no one who reads *Conversations with Ogotemmeli,* a member of the Dogon tribe in present-day Mali, recorded by Marcel Griaule, will long hold that the imaginative and creative capacity of human consciousness is confined either exclusively or primarily to one or other culturally and scientifically advanced society. It would therefore be naive to demand of all literature, either oral or written, that it conform to certain predeter-mined cultural categories or conventions, as, for example, is frequently done implicitly when one rigorously demands that religious literature conform to recently established canons of historiography and give the facts as they actually were. So too is the Enlightenment's emphasis on a common unchangeable human nature, which is the same at all times and places and which exhibits a single unified structure, misleading.[34] Such a mentality would restrict the world of literature to arbitrary and deceptive a priori categories. So too is it a destructive mentality, with clear roots in the Enlightenment period, that would approach the Bible, the Koran, the Avesta, and Analects, and the Vedas with the intention of extracting from these pieces of imaginative literature a systematic theology that, by virtue of its arranging and organizational principles and their resultant aesthetic symmetry, would purport to represent a positive forward motion of human thought domesticating and tran-scending the literature. Nor is this movement to a supposedly higher form of system legitimated by appealing, as is often done, to Bruno Snell's *The Discovery of the Mind.*[35] For this work has precisely as its the-sis the development of literary expression. Nor does the metaphor fre-quently adduced by Western theologians, "the road to Nicaea," that is the so-called transit from the supposedly benighted intersubjective cate-gories of the New Testament to the purportedly more esoteric world of theory and the world of objects as they are in themselves—the move-ment from *causae cognoscendi* to *causae essendi*—do anything to justify completely unwarranted evolutionist assumptions or to conceal the fact that there is here an effort to reduce plurality to unity, to reconcile di-versity by a subtle form of omission. The literary universe still remains what it is: the creative imaginative effort to confer meaning on human existence in imaginative and rhetorical fashion, intractable in any terms but its own. This literary universe is not a passing stage on the road to something higher. It is an autonomous world allowing of no substitutes.

Literary Criticism

Given, then, the existence of a literary universe, the task of literary criticism is clear. Literary criticism should enable the reader or hearer to enter the literary universe and to establish step by step a communion with the texts, the personnel, the imagery that constitute the literary world. The function of literary criticism is to explain and thus to facilitate the literary experience. But since literary criticism depends on prior stages and capacities it may be well to distinguish earlier levels of procedure and understanding.

There is first the supposition that texts are available and that these texts have been critically established. On the part of the potential reader, there is the requirement to be acquainted with the alphabet and its combination into phonemes, words, sentences, verses, and discourse. Thus, a certain precritical semiotic and semantic level is required. This, of course, assumes a certain lexical knowledge as well as a working acquaintance with grammar, syntax, and rhetoric. Accompanying the general requirements for literacy (except in the cases of oral literature) is some acquaintance with imaginative symbolism, usually to be found in conjunction with an implicit knowledge of literary forms, conventions, and genres that are incorporated into every cultural code or tradition. So too must one have a feel for language. This prethematic and preconceptual orientation to literary criticism requires moreover an acquaintance with free narrative. It is clear that the requisites for entrance into the formal literary world may demand propaedeutic preparation in certain instances. But it is likewise clear that the capacity to exercise the imagination is inherent in every human mind and develops through the mysterious power of creating a world through language.[36]

It must be briefly noted that the propaedeutic task anterior to literary criticism may be larger than we are to admit. In the absence of the professional storyteller found in all oral societies, the one who fostered the imaginative and intellectual capacities of the listeners, the need for development of the imagination is pressing. Our age still carries its Enlightenment presuppositions, complemented by a certain cult of ignorance. Competence, learning, and skill, as Asimov pointed out,[37] is called elitist and those preserving the intellectual heritage of the human race are often poorly remunerated.[38]

Whatever the needs of propaedeutic activity, literary criticism begins to take place when one thematizes the world of symbolic discourse that constitutes the literary universe, that is, when one exercises "a criticism which studies literature through its organizing patterns of convention, genre and archetype."[39] So the literary critic considers one piece of literature in its triple context: its meaning in the text, in the total works of the author, and in broader literary experience of world literature. The concern is with genre and convention, symbol, image, metaphor, and all the rhetorical modes of expression and persuasion. If then religious traditions are mediated in large part by literature it will be clear that an understanding of a religious tradition cannot be mediated exclusively by purely historical study, by systematic theological formulation, or by any procedures extrinsic to literature. Much less will ethical codes or simple catechetics substitute for literary criticism.

The critical operations requisite for understanding religious literature are really divisions of labor.[40] And departments in universities are concrete manifestations of these divisions. Each critical operation has its own specific aim and intention. The goal of literary criticism is participation in the literature: "The end of criticism and teaching, in any case, is not an aesthetic but an ethical and participatory end: for it, ultimately works of literature are not things to be contemplated but powers to be absorbed."[41] Following distinctions made by Plato, literary criticism intends a type of knowledge ascribed to *nous* (knowledge of things), as opposed to *dianoia* (knowledge about things). The knowledge of things "implies some identification or essential unity of subject and object,"[42] whereas knowledge about things essentially suggests a dichotomy of subject and object. This Platonic observation, elaborated by Frye, has been expressed by other distinctions, such as *existential* (abstract, theoretical) versus *existenziell* (concrete, intersubjective), and is mirrored in the terminology of some theologians who speak of theology and praxis. So too writers such as Bultmann have emphasized that religious literature is always a form of direct address. *"Tua res agitur"* he was fond of repeating—"At issue is your life." One then understood the literature in response to it. So literary criticism is the critical operation that should bear the reader to the threshold of participation. Actually dwelling within the literary universe on the thematic level is the business and choice of the reader. Frye is quite correct in saying, "it is impossible to teach or learn literature: what one teaches and learns is criticism."[43]

It is here worthwhile to note that the literary universe is a real world and not an addition or appendage to the supposedly more real worlds of politics and economics, or the world of making a living, or even the intellectual world of the empirical sciences, which has so palpable a connection with technological implementation. There is a widespread assumption that the world of literature is a kind of luxury indulged in by impractical minds incapable of pumping gasoline, selling insurance, or making the cash register ring. So students of literature are described as living in an ivory tower. This philistine approach to reality is not at all borne out by the facts. As Frye noted,

> When the students of today were babies, the King of England was Emperor of India, China was a bourgeois friend, Japan a totalitarian enemy, and Nazi Germany was ruling as powerful an empire as the world had ever seen. It is clear that what we think of as real society is not that at all, but only a transient appearance of society. A society in which the presidency of the United States can be changed by one psychotic with a rifle is not sufficiently real for any thoughtful person to want to live wholly within it. What real society is, is indicated by the structure of the arts and sciences in a university.[44]

What we therefore have in the world literature, and particularly in the universe of religious literature, are visions of the real world, panoramas of meaning that give some permanence to the more fleeting, transient, and apparent worlds of politics, economics, and practice. The literary world represents the permanent and real world, whose almost illusory and certainly fleeting foreground is in a consistent state of metamorphosis and is therefore really quite comparable to the evanescent world that Plato contrasted to the more substantial universe of eternal forms. Frye, following Blake, saw that it is apocalyptic reality that constitutes "reality in is highest form."[45] So there is good reason to distinguish the phenomenal world, that which is immediately perceptible to the senses and which intrudes itself by kinesthesia, from the world that is apprehended and constituted by the "reach of the imagination."[46] This imagination creates the theater of human existence, where the serious realities are rooted in myths of freedom and concern.[47] Yeats has expressed it more simply: "The only two powers that trouble the deeps are religion and love, the others make a little trouble upon the surface."[48] These are the powers that religious literature evokes.

Religious Literature

By religious literature I mean directly that body of specifically religious writings which religious traditions consider to be foundational, normative, or canonical, of particular moment in establishing the religious tradition. Such literature has an institutional approbation and acceptance. I am not including all literature that has religious themes or motivation, although my discussion could be applied to a broader field than I wish to cover here. This wider use of the term is valid because even the canonizing of religious literature or the official closing of a canon by an authoritative body does not remove other literature from the historical process. This is to say that religious literature in the broad sense tends to leap over any arbitrary decisions as, for example, can easily be illustrated from Christian teaching about angels and a primeval battle which owes much more to extracanonical literature, particularly Anglo-Saxon writing, than it does to the canonical books. Literary parameters of ancient religions are clear, if somewhat fortuitous. For example, the literary inheritance of Mesopotamia indicates as definitive Enuma Elish, the Gilgamesh Epic, and the Descent of Ishtar. For Egypt one may single out the Book of the Dead, the Memphite Theology of Creation, the Deliverance of Mankind from Destruction, and the Story of Sinue, along with other prophecies, songs, and poems. One can isolate a body of foundational literature in every religious tradition. Either it is foundational by some form of self-definition or by some vehicle or institutional approbation.

The literature, both oral and written, is characterized by a narrative and mythological form and content. The structure is permeated by what Wheelwright calls tensive symbols,[49] that is, the opposite of the steno-symbol, the one-to-one correspondence. The semantic tension of the tensive symbol reflects the problem of human existence and what Leonard Bernstein in his Norton Lectures[50] has called the ambiguity at the heart of human existence. This tensive language is visible and operative in imagery, symbol, and metaphor so that one can properly speak of an iconography of the imagination that attempts to express the inexpressible and allow the reader access to reality by symbolic presentation.

Wheelwright acceptably defines the symbol as "a relatively stable and repeatable element of perceptual experience, standing for some larger meaning or set of meanings, which cannot be given, or freely given, in perceptual experience."[51] Metaphor is the most striking instance of symbolic usage and has occupied commentators from Aristotle to Ricoeur.[52] Recent works on the parables in New Testament studies, the appearance of the journal *Semeia,* and a book such as *Jesus and the Language of the Kingdom*[53] devoted to the analysis of a single metaphor, are recent manifestations of concern with the exemplary symbolic instance of the metaphor. At work in the metaphor is a semantic transformation where two seemingly disparate objects are identified: "This is that." The repeatable element of perceptual experience stands for something else that cannot easily be given in perceptual experience. So we have in metaphor, as in all figures of speech, not an adornment of language but rather the effort to bring order into what is potentially a chaotic and overwhelming universe. The figures, particularly metaphor, are an attempt to keep the universe in a human measure.

It is no accident that literary discussions of symbols, images, and metaphors, even when done by literary critics whose area of specialization is not directly the history of religions, focus on the use of symbols, images, and metaphors in the classic religious literature. This is clear in writings of Wheelwright and in all the works of Frye. Concern with religious symbolism is understandable, for no other writings are faced in principle with the enormous task of expressing the inexpressible and must therefore search the imagination for semantic identities that are expressed in symbols, images, and especially in metaphor. So one finds in all foundational religious literature the transcendent identified as light, or as a being on high, or as a center, or as the equivalent of water or Mother Earth. This religious use of imagery, symbolism, and metaphor has its root in the belief in the creative and generative power of the word, its capacity to create experience, to evoke from hearers a wide range of imaginative response. So do symbols create the only world we really know, the world of language. And this insight is every bit as present in what some authors call primitive religion as in classically developed religions. In *Conversations with Ogotemmeli* we read, "The voice of man can arouse God and extend divine action."[54] This observation is not difficult from Gunkel's statement that "poetic narrative is much better qualified than prose to be the medium of religious thought."[55] It is but a development of Ogotemmeli's assumption when Gunkel goes on to say that the reader must "have some aesthetic faculty, to catch in the telling of a story what it is and what it purports to be."[56] So too can

Gunkel say that one "must feel irritated by the barbarian—for there are pious barbarians—who thinks he is putting true value upon these narratives (old legends) only when he treats them as prose and history."[57] And not too far removed from these observations is the remark of F. R. Leavis quoted by Nathan Scott:

> There is no reason to suppose that those trained in theology, or philosophy for that matter, are likely to possess what is essential to the practice of literary criticism, that 'sensitiveness of the intelligence' described by Matthew Arnold as equivalent to conscience in moral matters. A theological training seems to have a disabling effect and has subsequently to be struggled against when literary criticism is the concern.[58]

And this observation brings our reflections to the distinct field of theology, a field that has historically emerged from the center, which is religious literature, and become a mode of discourse that at times has set itself up as a center.

Theology

It is, I think, quite clear that there is a theological dimension to all foundational or primal religious literature. For this religious literature, and the images, symbols, and metaphors that constitute its fabric, intend to portray the transcendent and ultimate dimension of human existence, that is, some relationship of man to ultimate meaning, to what Tillich has called ultimate concern. This intention is clear even in the case of Buddhism, where the use of the term theology is at first glance inappropriate, and likewise clear in the case of Hinduism, where there is no word for theology but where *darshana* expresses a comparable idea.

It is likewise certain that the theological dimension of religious literature is one aspect of the literature, one level, albeit central, of meaning. This same literature, for example, may be examined in terms of linguistics—the phoneme, the morpheme, the word, discourse, and so on. Within linguistic units, new levels of meaning, greater than the sum of the parts, are discernible.[59] So too classic foundational literature reflects history and is itself part of the larger historical process. Because literature is a part of the historical process it offers extensive opportunities for historical comparisons in language, imagery, ideology, and culture. Historically there have been systematic theologies that isolate one dimension of the literature and attempt to organize this aspect in conceptually tractable fashion. This world of systematic theological discourse is one potential level of meaning within a larger constellation of denotation and connotation that is really only found in the literature in its constitutive and integral form. Systematic forms of theology are always consequent to the original religious experience and the narration of this experience through myth. Regardless of the claims of institutional authorities, systematic theologies cannot historically be proven to be constitutive of religious traditions but are rather consequent to the experiences and the narrations. The very effort to create a systematic theology, however legitimate as an intellectual enterprise, cannot conceal the fact that the reduction of the tensive symbol to the steno-symbol virtually eliminates imaginative scope and tends to domesticate an intractable transcendence. Such diminution is evident even where the imaginative vision behind the system, as is the case in the *Summa Theologica* of Aquinas, is indeed breathtaking. So a systematic theology can never be a substitute for religious literature and can never assume that its simplicity, clarity, symmetry, and elegance place it in a higher domain of intellectual discourse. Religious literature will always retain is primacy as a mediator of religious tradition.[60]

But what exactly is this world of systematic theological discourse? Certainly in its Western forms, especially as exemplified by the systematic and speculative theologies of the medievals and their jejune continuation in theological manuals and catechisms and forms of catechetical expression, systematic theological discourse falls into the area of *dianoia*—knowledge about things rather than knowledge of things. As knowledge about things, systematic theology is quite similar to the natural sciences, which proceed from the established distance between subject and object. In fact distance is required if one is to attempt the peculiar type thinking characteristic of the empirical sciences, the perspective that attempts to dominate the subject it studies. In fact the legitimacy of the theological enterprise is frequently based on this alleged and hallowed claim to objectivity, which is founded on distance and distinction between the observer and the observed. This claim of systematic theology to objectivity has made it as much a prisoner of events as of theory, for the claim of systematic theology to be a science, perhaps quite legitimate, has canonized its status as a knowledge about things. Yet, not thoroughly satisfied with this status, systematic theologians speak of theology and praxis, or postulate communication as a functional specialty within systematic theology, as if wistfully attempting to bridge the gap between system (knowledge about things) and participation (knowledge of things).[61] So too is there occasional use of almost incantatory formulas.[62] Thus does theology in its systematic aspirations manifest the tension between its ideals and pragmatic demands. Systematic theology's search for a congenial homeland is perhaps an unconscious sign that theology has not yet adjusted to the primacy of literary criticism as the critical operation best suited to understand religious literature.

One of the major obstacles encountered by systematic theology arises precisely because of its seemingly successful organization principles. Because of theology's systematic arrangement, it can be learned and transmitted rather easily; nor is great imagination needed. While the old thesis method is not a totally fair presentation of systematic theology, its procedures are representative. The structure—stating the question; definition of terms; proofs from Scripture, councils, history, and natural reason, and the systematic answering of objections—offers a form that is logical and coherent. So can the prospective theologian be examined quite the same way the student of medicine is examined on *Gray's Anatomy*. Therefore it is difficult for theology to be so systematic and speculative that it lose this historical advantage of easy transmission and so continue to provide a poor substitute for the more arduous procedure of literary criticism. And at the same time systematic theology has thus far not been speculative enough to provide a genuine theology that embraces all religions. For what we are accustomed to call theology is not that at all, but rather simply one or other form or type of theology. To my knowledge we do not yet have a theology of religion but rather theologies of particular religions. And of course it is this vacuum that has been temporarily filled by the history of religions. Hence the history of religions and literary criticism must be the foundation and basis of any genuine theology.

The intention here is not to demean an enterprise that has occupied great minds for generations nor to imply the total futility of constructing a systematic theology. But the literary experience suggests that there is a plurality of irreconcilable human ends. Frequently enough systematic theology has too easily adopted the methods of the natural sciences and consequently assumed that the sphere of moral development is susceptible to the same procedures that have disclosed a certain regularity of nature. The history of religions has uncovered a plurality of modes of conceiving of the transcendent. It is now, therefore, difficult to conceive of a systematic Christian theology, for example, that would ignore or confine to footnotes the Buddhistic, Islamic, Chinese or even atheistic visions of the world—all of which are available to us in literary form. In conjunction with the basic research required to study the history of religious literary criticism offers meaningful structures that can disclose the literary and religious universes of all people. If there is to be a large systematic theology in the future it will have to be congruent with the data disclosed by the critical operation of literary criticism. And the task of theological interpreters is to ensure that their vision of the theological world be at least as broad as the literary universe.

That which troubles systematic and speculative theology as an intellectual discipline may be summarized: first, its supposition of an unchangeable human nature everywhere fundamentally the same; second, the immediate consequence that theology study religion in a fashion similar to the study of nature—the assimilation of theology to the natural sciences, and third, its supposition that the world of theological theory and system represents an intellectual evolution transcending or supplanting literary criticism. While these generalizations may be true, the most critical problem for Western theology has an exact historical location where one may establish the origin of the unresolved conflict between the aims of systematic theology and the more recently defined discipline of literary criticism. I refer, of course, to the allusions in the New Testament where myth is contrasted to the true doctrine about God.[63] This distinction between myth and truth, found fleetingly in the New Testament, was taken up by Clement of Alexandria in his *Stromata* where he "contrasted Christian *theologia* with the *mythologia* of the pagan poets: just as the maenads in the story of Dionysius tore the god in pieces, so the truth of the imperishable Logos (*theologia*) had been fragmented by the philosophers."[64]

This contrast between theology and myth, really an antithesis between truth and falsity, was farther amplified in the thirteenth century when theology was described as a science. This was in striking contrast to Augustine's thesis that science dealt with the temporal and the transitory whereas wisdom (*sapientia*) "was devoted to the Eternal, that is to God as the highest good."[65] It was only a question of time until theology was virtually assimilated to the later definitions of science that were canonized in the natural sciences.

With the growing acknowledgment that myth is a universal and necessary carrier of meaning in all cultures and at all times—a notion promoted by Vico and Herder,[66] and not easily accepted by members of the scientific establishment—the initial contrast between theology and myth was shattered. This was a fact of monumental importance and one whose implications we are still experiencing. Without a drastic rearrangement of concepts, vision, and heuristic structure, theology, in its Western forms at least, has been incapable of dealing with the new historical climate. Patchwork modifications cannot conceal the central problem. So it is that productive work in theology today is found not among systematic and speculative theologians but rather among those who concern themselves with the large area of language and of literary criticism and among historians of religion. One need only call to mind scholars such as Levi-Strauss, Paul Ricoeur, and the recently acknowledged pioneer in literary studies of the New Testament, Amos Wilder.

It is not unreasonable to conclude that systematic theology has experienced a tide that rolled in while no one noticed. Religious expression, oral and written literature, has reasserted its role as a center.

The Historical Operation

The second operation proportionate to religious texts that speak of events, persons, periods, and beliefs within the world of time and space, and which direct themselves to men determined by their historicity, is the historical operation. It is obvious that the historical operation is not separate from the literary operation but is, however, distinct from it, as studies in poetry and drama clearly indicate. Analysis of the historical operation still suffers from the obscurity of the canons of historical method, no less than from disagreement of historians about the more recondite matter of cognitional procedure as such. We cannot here attempt to resolve the disagreements except to refer back to what has been said about the unity of cognitional structure and the influence of historicity on hermeneutical procedure as such. Whatever the disagreements about the method, there is surely agreement that a thing cannot be understood outside of its development in a particular time and space sequence. This historical operation is the attempt to understand via the temporal and spatial sequence. But because the interpreter cannot stand apart from history, the engagement of the interpreter here is somewhat different from that of the empirical scientist, even though we are now learning that the perspective of the empirical scientist too determines the nature of what is studied. Hence the necessity of what I have called an existential analysis on the part of the interpreter—an apprehension of what precisely are the dimensions of the subject matter and its mediation which the interpreter brings to the text. In a sense therefore this existential analysis is part of the historical operation, for it is the historicity of the interpreter as this historicity mediates historical understanding or renders the interpreter capable of entering into a dialectic with events of the past. The procedure is amply illustrated by a work such as Edwin Hatch's *The Influence of Greek Ideas on Christianity*.[67] Thus the object of the historical operation is the subject matter mediated in texts insofar as the subject matter and the texts are determined by times and places and have their effects in the world of time and space. Concretely the historical operation has for its term the subject matter of the texts, the elements of the text, the authors, the determinants of the subject matter or its matrix, and the interpreters themselves, insofar as all of these elements are determined by historicity.

I am inclined to agree with Bultmann's description of history and the historical procedure. Historical study utilizes objectifying thought for reconstructive purposes and an approach to the past as *Historie*. What is objective, certain facts and various interpretations of these facts, can be objectively known. The role of intellect here is primary. But in addition to pure intellectual apprehension of history (*Historie*), there is the establishment of history as direct concern to me (*Geschichte*), that is, as a series of possibilities for understanding my own existence, the existence of the community, or human existence in general. To intellectual apprehension is added volitional apprehension. The objectifying procedure, typical in the study of nature, is supplemented by historical understanding (*geschichtliches Verstehen*) in which the human factor—what the interpreter makes of the situation—is added. The diversity of approach does not constitute two different realms of being but two different aspects of one and the same reality. What Marx makes of history is quite different from what Augustine sees in human history, as what Churchill made of human history was diverse from that of Mao.

The view of history as the field of human decisions, and therefore as a series of possibilities for understanding human existence today, is opposed to a study of nature wherein one studies with the hope of finding comprehensible and immanent laws. History is not a development according to inevitable and fixed laws that imprison humanity so that the human essence can only be perfected by an escape to a heavenly world

of some sort, even though this approach, particularly in religious traditions, has a long genealogy.[68] Nor is history the Stoic realm of God's
rule, where all is mysteriously brought to a destined end by an inscruta-
ble providence. The subject matter of history is the decisions of people
and their consequences apprehended as possibilities for present existence.

Thus in history of religions, the intention of the historical operation
is the objective reconstruction of the religious past (*Historie*) and the
subjective dimension of understanding the past in such a way that the
full potentialities of the human race will be disclosed (*Geschichte*).[69]
Thus, all historical study in the history of religions will be both idealistic and pragmatic. When the study of history justifies itself simply on
grounds of antiquarian interest or the satisfaction of curiosity or as
something that somehow or another should fit into all education and
be a part of the cultured person, then surely the serious study of history
will disappear and become a matter for dilletantes. This has become the
case in secondary education in North America, where the new category
social studies seeks to supplant what used to be called history and likewise suggests that the serious study of history must relate to the present
possibilities of humanity. But the new category conceals rather than
solves the problem The simple fact is that the time, energy, and resources of the individual and of the community are limited. While the
entire past of the world may be broadly described as constituting history, an indiscriminate reconstruction of this past (all the events constituting *Historie*) is neither desirable, necessary, nor possible. What
one seeks is enough understanding of a field that discloses the potentialities of man, without predetermining beforehand what these potentialities are. Hence the statement that the historical operation is idealistic
in its aims and intentions, and pragmatic in its selection and execution.
An example may be illustrative.

What does the historian as such do with the synoptic Gospels' peculiar use of historical material? Is, for example, redactional criticism a
tool of literary criticism, of historical criticism, or more proper to the
act of comparison? Redaction seems to belong more to the act of comparison and to the literary operation than to the historical operation.
But certainly the process of redaction is an historical phenomenon and
has theological purposes. In this sense one process is open to diverse
modes of approach. Redactors construct the material so that its meaning is ultimate, its demand urgent in the sense that it calls for a decision

and transcendent in that it goes beyond all other claims. This is the tyranny of which Auerbach spoke. One may indeed freely deny ultimacy, urgency, and transcendence, but one cannot deny that the authors believed their claims to be ultimate, urgent, and transcendent. The operations used to understand the subject matter and its mediation will have to make clear and persuasive why the writers made the claims they did. If the historical operation directs itself to history as the field of human decisions insofar as these decisions disclose human potentialities, then the historical operation will not stop at the simple disclosure of what have traditionally been called the facts. Here, of course, the historical and theological operations are closely and dialectically connected.

Paradoxically enough theology, particularly theology in its apologetic form derived from Descartes, actually deviated from its religious context and sought to approach the method of a detached history. The assumption was that a detached historical operation could disclose the ultimacy, urgency, and transcendence of the Gospel. This was done in a variety of ways, through arguments such as: Reliable and truthful eyewitnesses wrote the Gospels; they had no reason to deceive, therefore the Gospels are credible. Or, Jesus Christ was a legate, one sent from God; only a divine being could perform miracles; therefore this legate is divine and must be believed by anyone of good will. This type of apologetic has not been dislodged by the fact that the historical-critical method has overthrown the assumptions on which such an apologetic was built, for one could indeed build such a type of apologetic in modern times by using the results of biblical criticism. What has ultimately led to the demise of such an apologetic is the fact that the apologetic ignores that which is central, the appeal that the religious literature makes to the human will as a possible way of understanding human existence at all times. As pure possibility, this appeal is disclosed by the fullness of the historical operation; as actual possibility, by the theological operation.

In interpreting religious literature there is no way in which we can legislate a series of mechanical operations requisite for understanding—operations that would be the equivalent of the way in which one builds a house or removes an appendix or even swings a golf club. We can, however, propose operations that are found in the interpreting subject and that correspond to dimensions of the subject matter as this subject matter is mediated. This subject matter is transmitted by language, by symbols, by concrete forms of historicity, by a cultural context, by the intentions of writers, and by the force they attribute to what they experience as the theophanic. It is these dimensions which suggest the four operations proportionate to the subject matter. Since the dimensions of the subject matter are distinct, the operations too can be at the very least mentally distinguished and are at the same time mutually complementary in the complex activity required for the understanding of religion. (It may be added that religions such as Shintoism, which have no authoritative books and are thus folk or state religions, are accessible by operations that may be broadly classified as historical and which are complemented by anthropological, sociological, and linguistic operations. Here the interpreter will have to experience the oral forms, the shrines, the rituals, the household festivals, the acts of purification through fire, water, and the dance. It is not my intention here to specify all the operations necessary to comprehend a folk religion, but the operations, both constitutive and nonconstitutive of religious studies, will be proportionate to the modes in which the subject of the tradition is mediated.)

If we earlier attributed an unusual primacy to the literary operation, as much emphasis must be bestowed on the historical operation. In fact, if one were to choose the operation most basic to the study of religions, he would have to select the historical operation. For the history of religions, at least in theory, omits nothing. And it is from the historical operation that all other operations become possible and then proceed.

The bipolar concept of revelation—whether revelation be conceived as proceeding from a divine impetus or, as in Buddhism, Taoism, and Confucianism, be conceived as taking place through powers, or nature—directly involves a religious experience, some relationship to transcendent meaning, to an encounter with some force that is conceived by its very ultimacy to be sacred. This personal disclosure or enlightenment and its subsequent transmission takes place in time and space and thus is itself a history.

It is clear that one must distinguish in the study of religions between history and historiography. While history is long and complicated, historiography is shorter. History is what has actually occurred. Historiography is a selective account of what has taken place. History is the total process while historiography is the selection and study of determinative events, movements, and decisions within the total process. While history extends to the presently evanescent moment, historiography is inevitably a bit behind the historical process not only because of the diagnostic and selective nature of historiography but also because the intended and unintended effects and forces of events are not immediately operative and because there is frequently a temporal distance from cause and effect. So the fecundity and productivity of historical events and forces can only be determined from a distance.

If history is the long process of decisions, events, and currents, and historiography is a selection from this virtually incomprehensible complex, then historiography will be the "particularly significant incidents in which historical decisions are, as it were, concentrated."[70] One may say that in the life of either an individual, a community, or the world, there are decisions and events and influences that have a peculiar power. This was certainly one of the findings that assured Freud a permanent place in history. These decisions, events, and influences, particularly when seen from a distance, have a generative force that not only distinguishes them from routine decisions, events and influences but also manifests a power that constitutes an epoch, a generation, a century, a culture. "We call such moments, in which a freely chosen action has a decisive effect on history, epoch-making moments or crises, and the individuals whose actions have this effect can be called, to use Hegel's phrase, 'historic individuals.' "[71] Whatever continuity exists in history arises from its decisive moments. Whether it is the length of Cleopatra's nose, the invention of the alphabet, the Prussian troops appearing on the horizon at Waterloo, the Balfour declaration, the events have a determinative power and force and can be recognized as such. The history of religions constitutes a field from which the historiographer must select decisive forces, decisions, and influences, for not only does the historical operation include the history of the mediators of religious tradition (oral, literary, aural, visual, sensory) but also the cultural matrices from which religion appears.

Significant here is that the study of a religion is not to be identified with the study of one aspect of the tradition, with, for example, its theological dimension or its doctrinal articulation: the oral and literary dimensions, the theological aspects, the ritual and ethical shapes are but significant parts of the whole. A religious tradition normally includes and comprehends music, art, theology, sociology, anthropology, philosophy, and the interactions of all these with the personal and communal consciousness of particular individuals and societies in particular times and places. In theory, then, the historical operation is all comprehensive.

Because it might seem that the task of the historian of religion, indeed the work of the historian of ideas, is virtually impossible, I would like to suggest a distinction. A dimension of historiography that pertains to the first state of the historical operation is the accumulation of data and information. Because this first stage of the historical operation includes prior interpretations of data, the first stage actually becomes potentially infinite. At some stage in this preliminary procedure the historians of religion must come to a decision that they have enough representative data from which they will then proceed to suggest the decisive forces that constitute an historical period. Without this synthetic effort there will not be historiography in the true sense, but rather the accumulation of data from which perhaps someone may later write a real history.

But more must be said to clarify this matter. The elementary stage of the historical operation, which I have described as the accumulation of data and which occupies historians of all dimensions and hues, has a concrete origin similar to that of the division of critical operations required to understand literature. That principle, of course, is the division of labor.[72] The structure of universities, with faculties, schools, and departments, reflects this division of labor, as do monographs and articles in specialized journals. As Toynbee has noted, the principle of "divisions of labor has its origins in the industrial system which exercises a great hold on our imaginations."[73] So we have in the large field of historiography a massive series of specialized studies of which learned monographs and technical articles in scientific journals are the visible sign. This Toynbee calls the " 'assemblage' of raw materials—inscriptions, documents, and the like—in 'corpus'es' and periodicals; and, when they have attempted to 'work' these materials 'up' into 'manufactured' or 'semi-manufactured' articles, they have had recourse once again, to the division of labour and have produced synthetic histories like the several series of volumes published in successive versions by the Cambridge University Press. Such series are monuments of the labouriousness, the 'factual' knowledge, the mechanical skill, and the organizing power of our society."[74] All of this might be classified under what we have earlier called *Sachexegese*.

But the overall meaning of history, like literature, does not emerge from *Sachexegese* alone but rather from *Sachkritik*. All of the monumental work described by Toynbee is as a matter of fact preliminary research and in no way guarantees that the historian is actually in touch with the historical moments that constitute an era as historically significant. In fact, work with the raw materials from which history may be meaningfully reconstructed is dependent on the historical accident of how much raw material, to use Toynbee's phrase, particular societies have left for the investigator. Thus, as Toynbee points out, early Egyptian society has left an enormous amount of raw material for investigators. Seleucid society, on the other hand, has left a smaller amount of data. Scholars "have tended to measure the historical importance of the Ptolemaic Monarchy by the amount of raw material accessible for the reconstruction of its history and by the intensity of the labour which they themselves have devoted to this reconstructive work."[75] Examples such as these abound.

To extricate oneself from the preliminary operations pertinent to historiography, one might suggest that the essence of the historical operation does not reside in the division of labor that generates what is called hard research. For the meaning of history does not appear automatically from the preliminary dimension of historiography, which is basic research. Nor does this stage of the historical operation suggest the relationship of past to present or distinguish historiography from what would have to be called antiquarianism.

In the history of religions, therefore, one might suggest that what is required on the part of the historian and what seems itself to be constitutive of the historical operation in the phases beyond the accumulation of data is historical imagination. Hugh Trevor-Roper notes that "it is the imagination of the historian not his scholarship or his method (necessary though these are), which will discern the hidden forces of change."[76] This reflects what "Mommsen meant when he spoke of the divinatory gift of the historian, and ... Burckhardt meant when he spoke of *Ahnung,* contemplation, the capacity 'to see the present lying in the past.' "[77]

This emphasis on a central phase of the historical operation that accompanies, proceeds from, and follows the significant reconstruction of the past is of peculiar moment in the study of religions because their stock-in-trade is an imaginative vision—a background from which the visible and perceptible data emerges. The historian of religion is faced with the anomaly that both history and the ultimate meaning and transcendence that religions seek to represent are beyond our knowledge and assuredly beyond the direct control that one can exercise via the empirical sciences on nature. Thus imagination is the only means of coping with the mysterious texture of religious meaning and the symbolic universes that each religious tradition creates. So the historical operation must be characterized by imaginative and divinatory powers that perceive the strands of intelligibility permeating the great religions. Only imagination will enable the historians of religion to overcome their tribal mentality whereby they hold that the religious tradition best known to them is really representative of all religions. And historical imagination may farther suggest that the question of the truth of religions may be more profitably moved to the higher realm of the truth of religion. One may then conclude by suggesting that the historian of religion inhabit the larger historical universe where religion has always been a constitutive element and where individual religions are but concrete manifestations of the broader religious universe.

And so we are led to the next operation constitutive of religious studies, the comparative operation that is demanded by the fact that each religious tradition has a history and religious traditions together have another history.

The Comparative Operation

The third operation constitutive of religious studies is the activity of comparison, about which one finds very little theoretical elaboration. It is not necessary to give here a psychological description of the process or a philosophical analysis of how comparison may or should take place. It will therefore suffice to locate the act of comparison in the circular hermeneutical procedure requisite for the understanding of a religious tradition or of religious traditions.

"To compare can be to hold two things together in order to let them act together; it can also mean perceiving their resemblance; or, again, it can mean apprehending certain aspects of one thing through the copresence of the other."[78] The act of comparison is implicitly present in the historical, literary, and theological operations where the gathering and collection of data brings "things together" and almost necessarily suggests that they "act together."

A classic instance of the perception of dissimilarities, resemblances, and occasional genetic relationships occurred in the work of the history of religions school at the turn of the century. The study of comparative mythology, with its origin in Vico and Herder, not only disclosed myth as a universal and necessary carrier of meaning, but led to the structural studies of Levi-Strauss. And the study of comparative mythology, to stay with one example, has entered the fabric of literary criticism. So a literary critic such as Northrop Frye can present an essay on archetypal criticism in which the varied myths can be classified according to apocalyptic, demonic, and analogical imagery and can be farther divided into myths of the four seasons. What we have here, therefore, is a transit from the prethematic to the thematic. It is clear that the comparison supposes the gathering of discrete data, an art that pertains primarily to the historical operation.[79] The prethematic, both in the historical and literary operation, is basically the ordering and establishing of the evidence.[80]

This ordering and establishing of evidence must be as comprehensive and universal as possible. This again suggests that the student of religion begin with the ordering and assembling of data within one religious tradition. Hence the required existential analysis that has been discussed will include the explicit intellectual assimilation of the tradition closest to the interpreter. So will the interpreter be involved in what I have called criticism of the subject matter, that is, the activity of examining whether the developers and transmitters of a religious tradition as a matter of fact actually did transmit the subject matter. Here the interpreter criticizes and judges the adequacy of symbols to their intended subject matter, the relation of desire to actual execution. But criticism of the subject matter always involves the act of comparison, so much so that the two activities seem almost to be only notionally and not really distinct activities.

Thus one of the more significant roles of comparison is its potential for establishing what an authentic tradition is, what is constitutive for a religion or for its sects. So comparison is part of a larger learning process.[81] Is every movement that terms itself Buddhist authentic Buddhism? If not, what is the criterion of judgment? How does one arrive at norms that may be said to indicate what is constitutive of Buddhism and not merely consequent to it? Who are the true followers of Muhammad—the Kharijites or the Umayyads? Or, is the religious distinction of the Murji'ites correct, namely, that God alone can judge who is an authentic Muslim and who is not? Can the scholar judge whether a monarchical episcopate, first hinted at in the Ignatian letters, is regulative for the church but not constitutive? Is it possible in any religion that the so-called tertiary symbolism of speculative theology occasionally distorts the intention of the primary and secondary (the story and myth) symbolism?[82] Historiography, which proceeds from the historical operation, theoretically includes everything that has determined the religious tradition. Comparison, holding two things together in order to let them act together, leads not only to thematization but also may disclose progression or regression and possibly deviation. So comparison exercised within one religious tradition may at least lead to the question of the authenticity of the tradition.

We are here, of course, on delicate ground. It is all too easy to assert that the role of historiography is to present an intelligible account of what happened and to restrict the comparative operation to the activities necessary to write the history of a religion. But I am here suggesting that comparison, in addition to providing thematic similarities (the patterns that emerge in the now traditional presentations of comparative religion),[83] can also play a more positive role. Within the study of one religious tradition, comparison can suggest the possibility of deviation, of distortion—and this by criticism of the subject matter. Comparison can suggest that there have been misunderstandings of the subject matter. And while the historical operation includes both understandings and misunderstandings as these constitute history, the comparative operation can tend in the direction of establishing an authentic religious tradition. And at this point the comparative operation informs or shapes the theological operation.

The possibility of so elaborating the comparative operation, and thus relating it not only to theology but also to actual life of religious tradition, can be corroborated by a concrete illustration. It is safe to say that the literary, historical, and comparative operations are roughly equivalent to what has been called the historical-critical method. It is not unreasonable to assert that the historical-critical method is a Western invention and has been more massively employed in the study of the Bible than elsewhere. Nor is it rash to assert that the theologies of the West have not come to grips with all the implications of the historical-critical method.[84] This affirmation does not mean that the problems raised by the historical-critical method are confined to the religions emerging from the Bible. The power and prevalence of the historical-critical method will inevitably bring to the theologies and proclamations of the East the same problems that characterize the study of Western religions. Ebeling's observation that there is a "fatal isolation of the historical disciplines from systematic theology and from the life of the

Church,"[85] may therefore be extended to include a real problem that pertains to the life of all religious traditions. If one insists that study is divorced from life, then the problem may be relegated to that category of problems which go away if ignored. But since the literary, historical, and particularly the theological operations should have a direct influence on minds, it would seem more realistic to suggest that the work of study be connected with the life of practice, however slowly the accommodation takes place. Still it is clear that the "critical-historical method is certainly recognized in principle ... [while] in practice it is widely felt in ecclesiastical and theological circles to be really a tedious nuisance. Its results may perhaps be noted, but then they are left aside after all instead of being worked through."[86]

It would seem that the ultimate reason that the history of religions has a favored position in the modern academic context, particularly in contrast to theology, is that the history of religions is committed, in principle at least, to the historical-critical method. In varying degrees, both the religious community and theology have only reluctantly yielded ground where the historical-critical method has presented incontrovertible evidence suggesting some alteration in an either ecclesiastical or theological posture or position. But reluctant submission is no substitute for integration and development. Hence the modern theological period is reminiscent of the Greek period when a general disaffiliation from the Homeric gods yielded to an allegorical interpretation that would make the chasm less profound—but a chasm it was, nonetheless. "The chasm between the older religion which was embodied in the poets, and the new ideas which were marching in steady progress away from the Homeric world, was widening day by day."[87] It is no accident therefore that whatever official theology remains as an authoritative teaching body, be this in Islam, Judaism, or Christianity, it stands somewhat officially opposed to the theologian who makes some small attempts to substitute the personalistic categories of thought that result from historical consciousness for the more metaphysical categories of classical consciousness and of ancient ecclesiastical definitions or tradition.[88]

A concrete function of the comparative operation is its ability to correct theological misunderstandings. The first three operations in concert have established, for instance, that the New Testament and its sources do not provide material for a psychological analysis of Jesus, just as the same methodology has reached the identical conclusion when applied to Buddha and Muhammad. So one can attribute to pious but fertile imagination the hagiographical works that played some role in determining religious attitudes of past generations: thus the comparative operation is capable of correcting theology. As the comparative study of religious myths established that myth is a valid, necessary, and universal category of meaning, it reversed the assumptions of an earlier generation.[89] Hence one cannot long use a distinction between myth and truth to distinguish religions, much less to establish the superiority of one over another. Comparative studies have indicated moreover that all religions are faced with the one central problem of explaining how the transcendent, the eternal, and the infinite makes itself present in an immanent, temporal, and finite world.[90] We owe such widely accepted conclusions to the act of comparison in religious studies. In these instances the comparative operation can protect piety and declare what is authentic and unauthentic tradition. Such definition nourishes the integrity of symbolic consciousness and plays no small role in protecting religion from the projections of unbridled imagination.

One more example illustrates the role of comparison. The Old Testament critic can make a comparison of great extent when he classifies and compares the evolution of covenantal development. This historical operation discloses the patriarchal covenant, the Sinai covenant, the covenant with David, and the establishment of Zion and its own tradition. Each of these central traditions is established and understood differently by the historical writers who formed the tradition. Each of the prophets interprets the traditions in a unique fashion. The common element—interpretation according to the needs of the times—cannot conceal the differences in the development of the tradition.[91] The forms or elements of the literature both within and outside of the tradition are compared. Apocalyptic is contrasted to prophetic and related more directly to wisdom literature. The traditions are compared and contrasted in their historical context; the vehicles of tradition are minutely differentiated. If one studies apothegms, prophetic and apocalyptic sayings, wisdom logia, similitudes, miracle stories, historical stories, legends and saga, the intention is to understand the peculiar character of religious literature, to comprehend the *Sitz-im-Leben* of the forms, to establish the motive forces behind the literature and thus to come to an understanding of the intentionalities behind and in the literature. From elements, configurations emerge. Configurations undergo metamorphosis. But the configurations of meaning can yield patterns and types. Such is the outcome of comparison.

Comparative work demands extensive competencies. It likewise demands that the comparatist be able to correlate and evaluate the work of specialists. So too must comparison include the cultural components that are the matrices of religion and thus the background of comparison is always the larger environment of religions.[92] Included in this background is a study of the human psyche as it proceeds from the aural-oral stage to the chirographic to printing to electronic modes of communication.[93] Thus the field of comparison is larger than was originally suggested by historians of religion.

There is broad agreement that comparison is an integral part of the historical and literary operations. It is worthwhile pointing out here, however, that two mediators of religious traditions have received comparatively little attention within the history of religions or have existed on the periphery of specific attention. I refer to music and art. These are part of the large system of signification that we call religion. The act of comparison is here of peculiar importance by virtue of its unitive function. For not only is the comparative operation to be employed in what I would call doctrinal development or in establishing the relationships between archaeological discoveries and literary studies but also in the more recondite area of the development of symbolism in art, including here both music and visual arts. A simple example of this technique would be the combination of historical and literary analysis with art-historical analysis in asking why the patriarch Joseph is carved on the episcopal throne of Archbishop Maximianus in Ravenna.[94] In this case comparison yields more firm conclusions if the religious symbolism is studied not only in its literary forms but also in its visual or aural forms. The same might be said of music, which offers similarities to the current structural studies of myth and poetry and which also suggests parallels to the imagery and metaphors used in literature. Comparison allows one, for example, to enter the fascinating world of the relations between architecture and music theory in the Renaissance period.[95] This incursion into the comparison of symbols mediating religious traditions suggests that comparison will first begin with elements, proceed to configurations of the elements, then analyze metamorphoses of the elements and configurations, and finally arrive at patterns and types.

The historical-critical method, which I have broken down into four distinct yet dialectically complementary operations, approaches the mediators of religious tradition with appropriately proportioned activities.

Therefore this method does not seek to distill meaning nor to present meaning in categories alien to the nature of the mediators. Nor do I suggest that the historical-critical method evolve into a sort of system that would be supposed to represent an advance on the four suggested operations.

Theology has not yet adjusted to the new realities. The task for theology is not the construction of new systems but the development of a conceptuality equal to the new world disclosed by the historical-critical method. It has been supposed that the historical-critical method demands some casual adjustments in the theological enterprise, a sort of updating or footnoting. Nothing is farther from the truth. The historical-critical method represents an onslaught on the theologies formed in an era anterior to that of historical consciousness. Nor is the problem rightly conceived if one asserts that speculative and systematic theologies of the past were even inadequate in their own environment. Indeed, at their highpoint, they represent magnificent constructions of the human mind. Rich in conception, suggestive in inference, productive in exhortation, they were a synthesis that we are unlikely to see again. But like most human products they are a testimony to their own historicity and thereby become a challenge for those who would rise to similar heights but by different vehicles. The problem and task was pointed out by Bultmann as early as 1928.[96]

Relevent for the thesis of this book is that a theology that resists the historical-critical method will obviously be out of place in a university. Such a theology must ultimately be reduced to paranesis, exhortation, or simple apologetic; and the reduction of theology to such a state will affect the development of religious studies.

Historians of religion have almost routinely objected to theology being considered as a constitutive element of religious studies for two reasons: first, because of the frequently parochial orientation of theology, and second, because the history of religions encounters religions that are not theistic, as, for instance, Buddhism or Confucianism, and to which the term theology is inappropriately applied. While I have already suggested a response to the first objection, I will turn momentarily to the second objection.

Obviously the term theology suffers from the ambience of a simpler time in which it was assumed that God was the object of theology as stars are the object of astronomy. But classic theologies have always maintained that positive statements about God are virtually impossible except under the rubric of metaphor and in the light of faith. In their better moments even those who have strongly maintained the scientific nature of theology were fully aware of the fact that the manipulative form of thought that enables man to attain a certain mastery of objects in the empirical sciences is not reproduced in theology. With the expansion of historical consciousness and the increased knowledge of other religions introduced by the history of religions, one can now assert that the object of theology, or any other word that can take its place, is the religious experience of the human race. Theology is the methodical study of intentionalities directed to ultimate meaning and immediate transcendence. So one affirms a transcendent and ultimate in Buddhism, for example, though that transcendence is nontheistic. In contrast to the discursive forms of thought used to articulate systematic theologies stands the Buddhist approach to transcendence and ultimate meaning, which is basically silence before the emptiness of the transcendent.[97] In Buddhism what we call the theological operation will have to focus more on liturgical and cultic elements because it is in these elements that the religious intentionality discloses itself. If theology is conceived of in the large sense of the study of all intentionalities directed to the sacred, the holy, the ultimate, and the transcendent, then it will automatically include all religions, and the three operations—historical, literary, and comparative—required to study all of human religious experience will be complemented by the one operation that specifically centers on the element of belief and commitment that is central to all religions. I would think too that even particular forms or uses of theologies dedicated to the understanding and maintenance of one belief system will also prosper if they proceed in the larger theological context of the religious experience of the whole human race. (The work of Friedrich Heiler is instructive here.)

The notion of theology here proposed—the theology of world religions as such or the form of theology developed in particular confessions—means that theology cannot be subjected to any control or authority outside of itself. For any external authority that seeks to preserve theological orthodoxy seeks to remove the possibility of making errors. But only if theology—in both senses of the term—has the freedom, like all other intellectual disciplines, to make errors will it be capable of arriving at truth. Theology has for its aim the understanding of ultimate meaning and immediate transcendence. A scientific theology becomes a contradiction if it is to be controlled by an outside authority. In fact, any alien authoritative body controlling theology leads directly to a contradiction (unless one bypasses the problem by postulating a charismatic controlling office, but this then leads to another contradiction, one that takes theology out of the intellectual arena and hence out of the university). For any authoritative office would assuredly have to employ theological criteria to distinguish between theological truth and falsity. Since an adminstrative power would judge theology through theology, there would then be two sources of theology. The administrative body then inherits the very possibility of error it seeks to curb. The supposed need for one controlling body suggests in theory the need for another controlling body, and so on ad infinitum. Though this theoretical possibility would not occur in practice, what would occur is equally pernicious: administrative bodies would simply apply the theology of the past to judge present theology. This would lead not only to the demise of a serious scientific theology but likewise to the ultimate incapacity of symbolic consciousness to integrate itself coherently.[98] Then, slowly but surely, the practice of religion becomes difficult or fraught with anomalies. In the end authority would destroy what it sought to preserve.[99] Realistically theology can only exist in a large and self-correcting hermeneutic field, to which I now turn.

·7·

THE THEOLOGICAL OPERATION
AND THE HERMENEUTIC FIELD

"How can we know the dancer from the dance?" asks W. B. Yeats.[1] Paul Cézanne, who could well become the patron of theologians as well as of those dedicated to semiotics, dismantled to reconstruct.[2] He painted nature "so as to reveal its basic structures."[3] And Eliade notes of Dumézil's *Archaic Roman Religion:* "This vast, superb work is not a textbook, nor is it a collection of monographs, loosely integrated. The author insists on the central place to be given to what he rightly considers the most important element in the understanding of any type of religion, that is, its ideas and representations of divinity: in sum its theology."[4] The dance behind the dancers, the structure behind the transient forms, the transcendent behind the representations of divinity: this is what the theological operation seeks to disclose. And its disclosures will be creative transformations. For behind particular heuristic visions and their cultural mediation, is the one heuristic vision. Behind the many theological representations is potentially one theology.

At the outset it is useful to distinguish this one theology from apologetic searches that seek to describe and define to local communities the logical coherence of one particular set of exoteric symbols, the gestures and rites of one particular dance, the structure of one particular vision. Such apologetics is a valid introduction to esoteric symbolism, whereby the theologian begins to feel at home with music of the dance, with the holy ones of a religious tradition. But if a genuine spiritual and intellectual life, characterized by growth in religious and spiritual metabolism, is to emerge, the believer and the theologian must move beyond a single group of dancers and transcend the elementary apologetics and catechetical forms of religious expression and instruction. This is a genuine theological necessity not simply because no one dance, to stay with this metaphor, encompasses all possibilities, but because no one religious tradition represents the total range of experience or expression. So too in every religious tradition one finds what von Grunebaum has called "untouchable subjects" and "spheres of disinterest."[5] While the theologian must begin with one tradition, the historical, comparative, and literary operations will begin to make clear that the search for a theology, even one within one's own tradition, cannot be fruitful until it includes the esoteric symbols of other religious traditions. Even the attempt to formulate the theology of one particular tradition will fail unless it accounts for other traditions, as would a literary criticism that confined itself to limited specimens, or a political science that limited itself to one or other particular society or culture. The limited forms of theologies, usually found within particular religious traditions and better called catechetical and apologetic formulations, are the first stages of self-appropriation and the beginnings of a movement toward the one theology.

The nature of the theological operation and its creative implications are seen in the theologians who initially establish religions. This is true whether we speak of Hinduism, Zoroastrianism, Buddhism, or Shintoism; whether we consider religions where the founders are clearly discernible or not; whether we speak of folk or popular religions. From all of these, as well as from theologians such as the Yahwist, Jeremiah, or Mark we see what can be called a theological activity. I have already mentioned that every religious expression emerges in three stages: an original experience (a theophany or experience of enlightenment), a subsequent will to communicate, and then in an actual communication. The attempt to communicate the experience, whatever the vehicle, is not the experience itself but rather a creative transformation of the experience, usually into poetic discourse that the writer or speaker hopes will transmit something like the original vision. The communication therefore is a new creation arising out of what is best called poetic vision.

This foundational procedure is suggestive for the work of the modern theologian. The first phase of the theological act will be to understand the three stages above—at first in one tradition, then in others.

This the theological interpreter does in concert with literary, historical, and comparative studies. The four operations are dialectically related and constitute a continuing self-revising hermeneutic circle. At a certain level of theological interpretation "everything in the hermeneutic circle, and not just the reader, is in motion at the same time."[6] The historical operation not only studies the past but also, by posing new questions, uncovering new data, and modifying past assumptions, actually changes the past. The literary operation, by changing its focus from text, to reader, to conventions, to the horizon of expectations, continually revises and expands its scope and creates new meanings. So comparison, letting two things act together, continually changes. It may then be expected that the theological operation, informed and transformed by the other three operations, will be moved by different impulses and energies as it continues its quest for that which lies beyond and behind the esoteric symbols. Thus, the theological operation will have to be similar to that of foundational theological procedure, creative transformations. But this is basically the second phase of the operation.

The first phase of the theological act will be the critical state of mind called by Ricoeur a "second naivete."[7] The critical equipment provided by modern scholarship leads the theologian back to the communications of primal experiences where the interpreter is asked to *reenact,* a term reminiscent of both Schleiermacher and Collingwood. Actually this latter injunction can be made more specific by suggesting that the interpreter "identify the conventions and operations by which any signifying practice (such as literature) produces its observable effects of meaning."[8] The first phase of the theological operation, in the context of the other three activities, is to uncover meaning in the past. This complex semiotic activity focuses on what has been called the eidetic understanding of the symbols, the underlying conventions, the interpretative codes of the past with all of their presuppositions. Without the equipment provided by literary, historical, and comparative criticism theologians would soon be lost in a minefield.

While the first phase of the theological operation is complex, particularly if it is repeated in diverse religious traditions, the second phase of the theological operation encounters difficulties of a different order. Here theologians are to make the transit from the *was* of the past to the *will be* of the future. Here theologians, determined by the conscious appropriation of their own tradition (or its rejection) and by the hermeneutic of their own historicity centers on what *was not* previously apparent. Their effort is to unleash forces inherent in a tradition, a movement from *was once* to the *is not yet but may be*. Or, in the words of Thomas R. Martland, the theologian, like the artist, "raids the inarticulate,"[9] a procedure for which there are no rules. This second phase of the theological operation may be compared to the work of Cézanne who gave to the modern mind "a new frame of perception."[10] Or, in the words of Proust, cited by Martland, "Women pass in the street, different from what they used to be, because they are Renoirs. . . . The carriages, too, are Renoirs, and the water, and the sky. . . . Such is the new and perishable universe which has just been created."[11] So does the theologian in the second phase of the theological operation provide the necessary equipment to move into a new future,[12] a new way of seeing. So does a theologian like Paul, by creative transformations that virtually escape systematization, move through two perceptible phases of the theological operation, as do the authors of the Upanishads.

The basis of the creative transformation is the continuum of concern existing between the past and the present so that the elements which express concern in the past may be situated in the human quest for meaning. The theologian, therefore, seeks to release and therefore to express anew the concern and thus to generate a new psychic energy. This note of concern, once expressed in the past, is typical of all religious traditions and characterizes religious traditions as directed to the future. Canonical religious literature, for example, is not, as is the case in fiction, history, and biography, finished. Religious expression is directed to the future, at what is not yet but may be. Thus there is a peculiar type of apocalyptic present in all religious expression, particularly in its poetics.[13] The postulate of a second theological phase not only arises from the procedure of the founders of religious traditions but also from the futurity of the tradition, its direct address to all potential readers. The second phase is a talisman and a bridge.

A clear instance of a second phase manifesting a creative transformation is typological interpretation, particularly Paul's usage. This ingenious transformation, finding its roots in the Old Testament reinterpretation of past traditions, "changed the Old Testament from a book of laws and a history of the people of Israel into a series of figures of Christ and the Redemption, such as we later find in the procession of prophets in the medieval theatre and in the cyclic representations of medieval sculpture."[14] The first phase of the theological operation grasped the note of promise inherent in the Old Testament authors' reinterpretation of an old tradition. In the second phase, what Auerbach has called "poetic vision,"[15] and Frye called "faith, hope and vision,"[16] transformed a past *was* to a future *will be.* Like all new translations, this interpretation toppled a stable past world, put a past interpretation in peril, and moved to a new transformation of consciousness. Like all new hermeneutic acts, the second phase of the theological operation usually engenders division; former insiders now become outsiders.[17] Once again appears the conflict between Apollo and Dionysius.

Whatever the risk, it is the task of theological criticism in its second phase to disclose future possibilities for experiencing the numinous, to lay open "the attitude peculiar to the consciousness which has been altered by the experience of the numinosum."[18] If the theologian cannot proceed through two phases, something incomparably rich in human experience gradually will begin to disappear. Darker realities assert themselves with results that are as evident as they are disheartening. The elimination of the numinous as present and future possibility suggests not a return to Apollo but to chaos. For man is an inveterate symbol maker, and the symbols created are not only carriers of meaning but also protectors from the unknown and from the meaninglessness that is more surely destructive than any atomic arsenal. "At our peril we look behind the symbol, for it is the symbol which finally stands between us and the meaningless."[19] The theological operation in its two phases deals not simply with recondite modes of thought nor with systems of aesthetic symmetry but rather with "the human meaning of being-religious in the lives of ordinary folk, not only virtuosi."[20]

It is clear then that the theological operation should not be confused with apologetic operations destined to articulate, explain, and maintain particular belief systems. These are largely catechetical structures, either elementary or advanced, theology *in fieri,* a state of becoming.

Beyond the potential tension generated by the fact that the catechetical understanding of any one religion is theology in its formative stage, there is still another tension—that introduced into individual traditions by the interactions among traditions and particularly highlighted by the literary, historical, and comparative operations. The continually moving hermeneutic circle discloses new meanings for the future and, like art, actually changes "what is."[21] It expresses a reality that will be, adds "what does not exist."[22] This is the tension between Apollo, the conservative impulse, the stability of the past, and Dionysius, the creative impulse, the uncertainty of what is to be; the tension between the consoling present foothold and the challenge to an Abraham, who goes out "not knowing where he was to go."[23] How well the theologian performs the work of Dionysius largely determines whether Mithras and Isis will become curiosities of the past, whether Demeter will be a reminder of antique beliefs and agricultural connections, or whether the creative transformations of the Yahwist, of Shankara, of Fa-tsung, of Hirata Atsutone, of 'Abd al Qādir al-Gilani will find modern counterparts. In short, the theologian traffics in effective heuristic visions.

From this structuring of the theological operation, we may now move to placing this operation within the larger hermeneutic horizon.

The large hermeneutic field we have been analyzing is the horizon of understanding pertinent to the study of religion. This field is permeated by intentionalities directed to final transcendence and by the concrete and palpable monuments created by the intentionalities. The mediating symbols exist in individualized cultural matrices. Symbolic differences are most evident at the exoteric level, similarities at the esoteric level.

The field is constituted by subject matter, elements, and operations proportionate to the subject matter and the elements. The subject matter of religions, about which enough has been said, is the human search for ultimate meaning. The elements are all religious traditions, the interpreters themselves, the intellectual and spiritual communities, and finally the all-embracing world. The subject matter and the operations proportionate to the subject matter and its mediators have been discussed. It remains simply to outline the other elements of the hermeneutic field and thus arrive at a coherent structure of religious studies. Thus we turn to the interpreter, the community, the world.

The Interpreter

As an element in the hermeneutic field, the interpreter is subject to a twofold interpretation that effects the transit from the naive and precritical to thematic and critical consciousness. There is first the self-interpretation of the interpreter, which is in general the accompaniment of every existence. This is the self-understanding of the individual. It is the role of an existential self-analysis to raise this implicit understanding to the level of the conscious and explicit. In the case of a religious interpreter part of this process will be the articulation of the interpreter's relation to the subject matter of religious traditions—intentionality directed to ultimate meaning and transcendence. The procedure and its outcome play a large role in constituting the person as an autonomous subject, indeed in establishing the individual as a truly human being who is self-aware of capacities and limitations and who can exercise some choice and control over his or her own human destiny. The complex procedure by which this self-interpretation is to take place cannot be developed here, except by the suggestion that such self-analysis is found in all the classic religious traditions and it is difficult to conceive of an interpreter of religious traditions who does not reflect the analysis that is immediately at hand in the traditions studied.

In addition to the disclosure of the actual self-interpretation possessed by the interpreter there is the more specific demand raised by the futurity of all religious texts as forms of direct address. As I have earlier suggested, the religious word places the interpreter in the position of one who must decide, for only through decision can the word become event and hence real communication. The modalities of the religious word as this word is mediated in diverse traditions are different. Islam and Judaism are not identical, and yet both deal with ultimate transcendence. In each individual tradition interpreters must somehow decide whether their religious tradition is a possible understanding of existence in the particular case of the interpreter. To make such a decision, of course, is to suggest a thorough grasp on the part of the interpreters of themselves and of the tradition; otherwise such a decision is precipitous. In any case, the orientation of the interpreter to such a position will eliminate for the interpreter the temptation to do what Goethe claimed the churches had done to religion—to trivialize it. The proposed bipolar self-interpretation is a requisite for a genuine theological interpretation.

In recent times it has become almost trite to assert that all interpreters have some sort of self-interpretation, understand themselves in a particular fashion. This self-interpretation is transmitted by family, society, and the general process of socialization. Obviously, in many instances this self-interpretation is really a misnomer since the interpretation is really done by others rather than by a genuinely autonomous or inner-directed self. But this normally unconscious self-acceptance or understanding is of enormous importance because it determines what the interpreter shall hear and understand when confronted with other interpretations incarnated in religious traditions. And it is safe to say that the more unconscious the self-interpretation, the more powerful and all pervasive it is. For an inherited tradition literally forms the individual. It is that tradition which confers identity on the interpreter. And that tradition is supported not simply by conscious presuppositions but also, and perhaps more importantly, by an elaborate and obscure unconscious that buttresses and defends the interpreter's self image and makes any new interpretations or possible personality revisions enter on terms acceptable to the already existing self-interpretation. The difficulty of self-revision or of a change in what is best called temperament cannot be overestimated. I am not interested here in what some writers have called conversion or radical change in consciousness but rather in the general awareness on the part of the interpreter that the issue in encountering religious studies is the existing self-interpretation and the role it plays in attempting to understand religious traditions. The widespread discussion of presuppositions, which assumes that interpreters can simply take a close look at their presuppositions and then move on to the important issues, totally confuses the profundity and power of the presuppositions, which are ultimately identified with the very being of the interpreter.

Thus the existential self-analysis that we suggest is a demanding process that is largely characterized by a genuine encounter with the self. This lifelong attempt at self-appropriation is the necessary condition for a genuine encounter with religious traditions. Nor need it be said that the encounter will assist the interpreters to find their own location in the spectrum of exoteric and esoteric within their own tradition, or may even disclose that at a deep level the interpreter has never seriously raised the question of the meaning of human existence. In either case, interpreters are engaged in a continuing conversation with themselves and are thereby exposed at least to the possibility of genuine conversation with the great religious traditions.

Concretely, the preunderstanding or the presupposition is constituted by whatever relationship the interpreting subject has to the subject matter of the texts. A crucial point here is that the preunderstanding is composed of whatever relationship the interpreter has to the polymorphic mediators of religious traditions. An underdeveloped imagination, for example, will find itself shipwrecked in the presence of the religious myths that have enriched civilization. An underdeveloped appreciation of language renders the classic religious texts mute. A literalist mentality, so effective in many fields, leaves the interpreter lost among the

Vedas. As in language learning, if a new linguistic mediation stands for nothing within the hearer's experience or preunderstanding, the mediatorial form will mean nothing to the interpreter. Meaning becomes possible when something new finds a point of contact in the learner's consciousness. In fact the proximate point of contact with the subject matter of religions may even be positive antipathy. But more generally it would seem that the point of contact between the interpreter and the religious tradition will be the preunderstanding of life and death, of what constitutes good and bad, of what differentiates authentic from inauthentic existence, of what indeed is the meaning of human existence and what is the relation of expressive symbols to these larger realities. Every religious tradition, and indeed in modern times, all world-encompassing ideologies, address these concerns and mediate their answers in some form of language. Concretely, then, the relationship of the interpreter to the subject matter of religion is determined by the presence of ultimate questions and by the capacity of the interpreter to enter into the world of language in which possible answers are proposed.

The particularized preunderstanding and interest in the subject matter of religious traditions may be contoured as historical or psychological, or as "the interest may be the knowledge of man.... In this case the interpreter, reflecting on history, reflects at the same time on his own possibilities and endeavors to gain self-knowledge.... This questioning is only possible if the interpreter himself is moved by the question about his own existence."[24] Interests, talent, sensitivity, spiritual capacity, and the level at which the interpreters find their epigenetically differentiated self-consciousness—all these influence the seriousness with which the interpreters confront both themselves and the texts. In proportion to the vitality of the questioning relationship, both of self and text, will interpretation of religious texts provide new insights. The questions the interpreter brings to the texts may be modified, corrected, redirected, enlarged, and opened up to the unexpected by the reciprocal questions the text suggests to the interpreter. Here begins dialogue, which is essentially a procedure in which two discussants enter upon a theme to which each has answers but find out that a genuine dialogue produces an unforeseen outcome—otherwise we have a confrontation and not a dialogue. The analysis of this process, involving as it does the interaction of the interpreters with themselves, with the text, with the interpreting community, and with competing secular and religious viewpoints, is an intriguing topic worthy of more careful development than is possible here. Suffice it to say that the fecundity of a religious tradition depends mainly on the vitality of the questioning relationship the interpreter brings to texts. The role of the interpreter is therefore of paramount importance, as may be confirmed by the history of hermeneutics, which may be briefly summarized as a history of moving from the object of interpretation to the world of the interpreter.

To summarize: in the interpretation of religious forms of communication, the interpreter approaches the forms with an organized and differentiated consciousness that is both presupposition and horizon. Serious interpretation postulates an explicit and developed relationship to the subject matter or referrents of the tradition. Preceding the interpretative arts is an aesthetic and discriminating sense that enables the interpreter to distinguish the forms in which a religious tradition is mediated. The interpreter must acquire or develop the skills necessary to understand poetic, literary, and discursive forms of language; to understand and appreciate the visual and aural arts; to grasp the diversity of forms used to mediate the subject matter of religious traditions, and to appreciate that not only is a serious relationship to the subject matter indispensable, but likewise must the presuppositions and horizon of the interpreter include the ability to differentiate the forms, to understand them, and to integrate them. So each of the principal operations—literary, historical, comparative, and theological—rises out of the way in which the subject matter is mediated and is proportioned to a particular dimension of the mediated religious subject matter. But the operations themselves demand particular talents and training. Ultimately, the unity of religious studies resides in the epigenetically differentiated consciousness of the interpreter.

But since no interpreter, and in particular, no theological interpreter, exists as a totally unique or isolated phenomenon, it is necessary to discuss the next element of the hermeneutical field—the interpreting community.

The Community

A community is normally constituted by temperament, shared presuppositions, common modes of interpretation and understanding, and by a common meaning that unites all the members of the group. Maintenance of community depends on the protraction of common meaning, on genuine communication; it is theoretically developed, understood and integrated by some form of metacommunication.[25]

The purpose here is not to analyze or even to suggest the roles that differing communities play in the formation of either the individual or the society. But something must be said about the role of community in the intellectual life of the theologian.

If it is correct to say that the theological operation performed in the field of religious studies is that operation which seeks to understand and translate intentionalities directed to ultimate transcendence, and to comprehend their consequent polymorphic differentiations of consciousness and the effects of these differentiations, then it is true to say that there is an identifiable group engaged in this theological activity, as there is, for example, a recognizable group of musicians, artists, or sociologists. In general, members of this aggregation perform historical, literary, comparative, and theological operations. But this constituency can hardly be called a community, except potentially, because there is not only vagueness but dispute about the nature of the four operations, their context, and their purpose.

I have earlier attempted to point out that categories such as "the believer" or "the man of faith" are heuristically feeble and do not match the realities of human existence where experience indicates that people are moved by the question of ultimate meaning, however they concretely come to terms with it. But it is precisely with the question of ultimate meaning that religions concern themselves. The explanation of this ultimate meaning is theological. Hence the theological enterprise as such is as universal as the search for ultimate meaning and as broad as the varying languages used to express ultimate concern. That traditional theologies have been somewhat more parochial than this ideal simply indicates the contingencies of history and suggests that the human attempt to match efforts to visions is frequently unsuccessful. But if a larger vision of the human search can be envisioned as an ideal at least, then there can be sufficient common meaning to begin to unite a heterogeneous mass into a genuine theological community. And if the theological operation can be placed within the broader context of the other three intellectual operations, then there is the foundation of a genuinely intellectual and spiritual community capable of making intelligible the unity of the religious search and ultimately of formulating a theology of religions. Then one could hope to make some sense of the harsh historical realities that indicate to the innocent observer a series of incompatible and normative theologies and communities that oppose and contradict each other in the name of transcendence and ultimate meaning. One could hope for a universal grammar of theology that would replace the limited systematic theologies used to buttress one particular form of faith.

If we turn to history, it would seem that theology has developed within three possible configurations and has grouped itself according to the contours of the chosen constellation of meaning. First theology develops in a context where there is no official authoritative body to distinguish orthodox from unorthodox teaching, incorrect from correct theology. In this instance whatever authority exists in the religion comes from the persuasiveness of the gifted, either in thought, spirituality, or persuasive power. Perhaps one can locate Jewish, Hindu, and Chinese Buddhist forms of religion here, as well as early religions whose almost exclusive vehicle of transmission is myth. Folk religions, though governed by the canons of a much more social dimension, can also be practically included here. I have in mind, for example, Shintoism and forms of Buddhism as propagated by Ashoka.

Second, there is a type of theology in which the actual religious life of the community is the ultimate ground for theological thought. This, of course, is rarely found in pure form. In general the assumption in such instances is that a revelation has been made and accepted. A transcendent force, generally named God, nourishes and stimulates the religious tradition. Authority is not discriminative but declaratory and is conceived to be primarily a sociological characteristic; it exists to administer but should abstain from declarations about orthodoxy. The ultimate authority is some form of the working of the spirit of God.

A third type of theology occurs in religious bodies where there is at least tacit acknowledgment that a particular authoritative body within the community judges on orthodoxy in matters of teaching, belief, and religious practice. This authority generally has the power to legislate in matters of faith and morals. Instances of this would be Roman Catholicism, Anglicanism, certain Protestant sects, as well as some Islamic sects where the mullahs are authoritative. One might also suspect that forms of Theravada Buddhism could be here included.

It is clear that in all three groups the weight of tradition and the interpretation of canonical scriptures exercise a conservative and hence judicial function. But only in the third group is there a reasonably clearly defined authority capable of judging between true and false teaching. And in all three constellations, the effort to establish a universal grammar and syntax of theology is not a prominent feature, for there is inherent in all the assumption, varying in intensity and presupposition, that one theology is normative.

There is no major difficulty in allowing the theologies of the first two divisions to be disciplines within the university, at least in theory. In varying degrees the theologies are subject immediately to evident academic canons. One can quite easily employ the literary, historical, comparative, sociological, and anthropological operations and likewise admit that these operations are not basically determined by nonacademic criteria. One might quibble about including the study of Evangelical continental theology because of its supposition of a divine intrusion. But the beliefs of these groups are fairly immediately accessible to intellectual operations. In each of the first two groups one might speak of a theological operation that can be pursued in a fashion similar to the study of languages, natural sciences or the humanities. The operation itself is not subject directly to any authoritative body considered as normative.

It is, however, in the third instance that there has traditionally been a difficulty with legitimating the study of religion within the university context, if this study is to include a theological dimension. For in the third instance theology not only seems to be defined by its relation to an external authority but also by its use to support a particular faith posture and belief system. In the last resort an authority external to purely scientific canons can intervene and determine what is true or false. In this climate theology must tend to become a dignified form of catechetics. And in many instances the general result of such a structure is the preservation of and emphasis on the exoteric symbolism of the religious tradition, as the history of the mystics within such traditions clearly indicates. The legitimation of the authority takes place through the postulation of a charism with which the authority is then endowed. Such endowment suggests that the literary, historical, comparative, and theological operations—operations in principle open to any and all who would take the time to acquire the appropriate skills and who are concerned with the subject matter and its mediation—are allowable and effective only within certain limitations. Under such conditions it is quite clear that theology would have something of a problem with the context in which university studies operate.

Whether one agrees with these overly simplified divisions, the broad histories of the development of religious traditions and their postures towards theology exercise a certain determinism upon what theology actually is, as opposed to what it might be. It is this concrete reality with which one must deal if one is to suggest an expansion of the theological horizon.

Now since theologies are human creations, it is quite clear that a theology can choose to operate in any of the above contexts. Surely a theology can be formed along the lines of an ideology to serve one limited function. And such constructs, comparable to Marxist-Leninist ideologies, will have definite sociological and psychological advantages. Nonetheless it would seem that sooner or later such limited applications of theology will present a problem in a world where only armed force can pretend that one world view has a monopoly on truth. Only as long as a theology can exist in a nonpluralistic society, or manage to protect and insulate itself from a pluralistic environment, will such a theology remain relatively untouched by competing viewpoints, either religious or secular. But so too will such a theology inevitably end up confined to enclaves and be excluded from the interests and concerns of humanity as such.

So the danger of a parochial theology is not so much that such a theology must ultimately founder, but rather that such a theology removes itself almost on principle from the efficacy of the first three operations in religious studies, and separates itself from the open investigation of the search for ultimate meaning and transcendence. Even if a theology does not remove itself from the first three operations of religious studies but allows the three operations a restricted influence, extent, or validity, there too must the theology be inefficacious as a potentially universal concern because it still subjects itself to impertinent extrinsic control. The theory of such a theology, no matter how skillfully articulated, is simply not equipped to deal with pragmatic reality. Nor can one adopt the canons of the historical-critical method only where that procedure is congenial to restrictive presuppositions. As is evident from nineteenth-century European thought once one accepts the realities of scientific procedure the direction of the procedures is not at the disgression of control external to the procedures.

But if theology, on the other hand, is ultimately grounded in a relation to the transcendent that all people experience, and if theology is proximately located in the mediation of this transcendent by a historically conditioned symbolism, then the theological operation has for its proper object a reality seemingly shared by all people and a symbolism potentially intelligible to all. So conceived, theology deals with a universal concern and focuses on the symbolic expression of shared universals. Thus one emphasizes what unites rather than what divides the human race.

Still it is obvious that the theological operation can, given its general horizon, have other functions or uses. Particularly in the second phase of the theological operation, where it is metacommunication, theology can have the function of articulating the historically conditioned symbolism of a particular faith posture. This is what formerly was called the apologetic dimension of theology or, in Aristotelian terms, the use of the habit of theology. Thus will the individual religious traditions continue to define themselves and articulate precisely what they are in concrete circumstances. But even in this necessary use of the habit of theology, if we may so speak, there is present the constant larger horizon, the relation of all people to ultimate meaning and final transcendence. So conceived, theology has no method of its own. There is simply a theological operation whose object differentiates it from other intellectual activities.[26] Thus, theology is not controlled by any authority external to intellectual procedures as such, for external authority is consequent to the formation of community not constitutive of the community. The coexistence of the sociological phenomenon of authority in a religious community with intellectual procedures available to all and with practices that at times necessarily challenge the authority is subject to the rules that are valid for any society that must ultimately have an authority. The alternative to this is some form of totalitarian control; there is hardly a middle ground. So the problem of authority and freedom is not peculiar to religious groups. But if the authority which is ultimate is the authority of the discipline and its procedures, then the basis for a theological community becomes reasonably clear. The theological community is formed by those who officially dedicate themselves to the study of intentionalities directed to ultimate transcendence and to the study of the symbols used to mediate this transcendence. Thus, Muslim, Zen, Hindu, and Anglican theologians are all members of one community united by shared presuppositions and a common meaning. Their local mediatorial functions should not obfuscate their common search and shared presuppositions. The only controlling authority in such a concept or image of theology will be the intentionalities directed to ultimate transcendence, their consequent polymorphic differentiations in consciousness, and the concrete effects of the intentionalities and differentiations. The only operative presupposition is the existence of an articulated relationship to the subject matter of the intentionalities.

It is not pertinent here to develop further the multiple functions or uses of the theological operation. Certainly one of the necessary functions of the operation will be to indicate how the culturally determined symbolism of one religious tradition can impose absolute obligations on the members of that religious tradition, how, in fact, that one religious tradition is true. Theological literature has dedicated almost no attention to this problem or has included the solution to the difficulty among its unspoken assumptions. Moreover, the use of the theological operation within a particular tradition will clarify the concrete possibilities and responsibilities of the believers in particular situations. These two aspects of theology are equivalent to the theoretical and practical discourse of theology as metacommunication. An illustration of the second aspect is the effort of some theologians to clarify the responsibilities of believers in Germany during the Nazi period. This clarifying role of the theologian, that is, the attempt at metacommunication on the level of theoretical and practical discourse, can be achieved on the intellectual level as well as on the level of worship. Here the theologian does not establish the communication—the religious tradition itself does that— but clears the ground so that the message of the tradition is audible in concrete circumstances. What the hearers then do is their privilege and responsibility. The theologian works in the large theological community. With this environment as the context the theologian pursues intentionalities directed to transcendence beginning within the microcosm of one tradition and moving beyond to the larger horizon where the lights and shadows of varied symbolic usage are mutually illuminative.

While being a member of the smaller and larger theological communities, the theologian continues to exist in the total human community, what we commonly call the world, the final element or dimension of the hermeneutic field.

The World

I have hitherto analyzed discrete perspectives and realities, conceptual entities leading to some intellectual control over the field of religious studies. In distinguishing subject matter, elements, and operations proportionate to each, a hermeneutic field is outlined. But this field exists within the larger reality of the world. In some ways the field is almost identified with the world, at least in the material sense. But the field is basically all that is to be interpreted from a certain perspective and thus is distinguishable from the larger concept of the world. World, therefore, is the context of the hermeneutic field, its ecology. The term world denotes something larger than the individual, a state of being that is independent of the individual, an objectively existing reality, one that has its existence independent of the wishes, desires, study, or control either of individuals or particular communities. Whether one speak of the world of nature, of politics, of history, of religion, of culture, of science, of law, of morality, of art, of childhood, of adolescence, of adulthood, of scholarship, of business, or of technology, one is always speaking of a conglomeration or constellation, a totality that has a certain palpable and undeniable objectivity. It exists independently of any one individual, has its own inexorable laws of development, its own forms of evolution, and is at the same time an ordered set of relationships. It is to this totality, to this set of relationships that I wish to apply the term world. And I am here suggesting that this world be explicitly included in the hermeneutic field in which the theologian operates. All attempts to limit world to a particular world view will lead to an impoverishment of theology.

It is clear that world may mean all the entities present within the physically constituted natural world. It may also mean the natural world and all worlds of meaning created within this natural world taken together. The world thus is the physically constituted place, a world of nature modified by human activities. So the world is a state of being, an environment of intellectual, moral, and social actualities and potentialities. Hence world comes to mean the constantly evolving place and state or condition in which the individual and a variety of communities exercise endless possibilities for interaction on all human levels. This world is both external and internal; external in the sense that the world, as a totality of interrelationships, has an existence and motion independent of any individual or group; internal in the sense that the individual and community appropriate the world, are socialized by it, become capable of a creative response to the independent movement of the world. This larger notion of world, together with its modifications by individuals and communities, a world shaped by history, politics, and religion, is the inevitable context in which the theological operation should be exercised.

History indicates that how one views this world determines both the nature of religion and the study of religion. The Stoics, for example, considered the world as a cosmos into which one inserts oneself by intellectual understanding and in which one becomes a citizen by constructing the city ruled by the law of the gods. Moral orientation is effected by an intellectual apprehension of the ordered whole and by an act of the will following the intellectual perception. Aspects of this hierarchically constructed cosmos penetrated deeply into Christianity. Gnostic forms of religion see the world as an imposing power from which humanity must be liberated by an esoteric form of knowledge. Gnostic forms of understanding have grasped the objectivity of the world and the force it exercises on the individual. So one finds strains of gnosticism in Buddhism, Hinduism, the dualism of Mani and in any form of Christianity wherein the world is governed by a beneficent Providence, whose workings are apprehended by faith. In its original meaning gnosticism was an attempt to release humanity from the reign of evil, an effort at inner transcendence. The movement seems to have been widespread and to have penetrated Judaism, Neoplatonism, Christianity, and the mystery religions. Parallel to a Gnostic understanding of the world is the assumption that the scientific thought procedure is the most valid mode of thought, the method of obtaining dominion over the world, a transcendence of its own genre.

Confucianism contrasts with all forms of gnosticism in its insistence on the apprehension and constitution of the world as an ordered and harmonious series of social relationships. The intellectual component and stress is high, and thus Confucianism has similarities to forms of gnosticism but stands in clear contrast by its implication that the liberating principle is human reason. Taoism, in contrast, focuses more on the world of nature and sees the world as a series of interconnected laws that are better understood by intersubjectivity than by intellect. So Taoism suggests that the vegetative, sentient, and rational human life be assimilated into a larger cosmic harmony that constitutes the world. One cannot mistake here a similarity between Taoism and the forms of Christian philosophy that saw as the ultimate norm of morality human nature conceived in a sufficiently broad and comprehensive fashion (*humana natura adaequate spectata*). The contrast, of course, came in the more restricted definition of world. A different view of the world emerges in the Hindu tradition, particularly in the Upanishads, which do not stress the world as a natural or social phenomenon or even as the basis for ethical behavior, but rather emphasize the internal psychological development of the individual believer who seeks deliverance from the temporal vicissitudes and appearances behind which stands the one all embracing reality, the Brahman. So the dominant world is the internal world of assimilation and appropriation to the one ultimate reality.

One finds in Judaism, Christianity, and sometimes in Islam a high regard for the world of matter, that world in which the Gnostic seeks either liberation or dominion. So these views contrast with some Chinese traditions where world is primarily the world of social relationships and social ethics. This contrast explains why Christianity has not been notably successful in creating one worldwide community and yet has been very capable of relating itself to the general world of science and culture in which high respect is accorded to the world of matter and human manipulation of the material world. Contrasts among religious views of world and the consequences of such positions are striking and have not escaped the attention of the historians of religion.[27]

These observations are significant for several reasons. First of all, these views of the world are intentional entities, spiritual perspectives, categories of religious meaning and value. Second, these diverse perspectives and the means by which they are propagated form a significant part of the world that I am here considering as an element in the total hermeneutic field. Theology, therefore, cannot ignore other intentional worlds modulated to one and the same subject matter. Nor can theology prescind from the totality of relationships that constitute the world in which it operates. Third, the very diversity of perspective and the simultaneous coexistence of diversified constellations of religious meanings give rise to what I shall term the problem of ambiguity.

The problem of ambiguity arises when two or more meanings are given to the same subject matter. In this instance the subject matter is ultimate transcendence and the human relationship to this transcendence. One may attempt to resolve the consequent ambiguity by suggesting that religious meaning exists in the world of intentionality and meaning, and that religions are similar in the very fact that each postulates a transcendent and a relation to that transcendent. And this, of course, is a similarity of structure but certainly not of conception and content. The intellectual articulation of transcendence and of the human relationship to transcendence are mainly diverse and at times contradictory. And since there has not yet been a massive confrontation among the classic world religions, there is no immediate possibility of resolving the state of ambiguity arising from the existing plurality in the world of religious meaning.

Thus, the concrete resolution of ambiguity lies squarely in the hands of the individual. The individual who yearns for absolutes cannot transfer the burden of responsibility to any monolithic entity or to any institution that claims a certainty it cannot yet possess. No institution, whether established by religious revelation or metaphysical speculation, can provide the total answer of how one should conduct one's life. What the institution can provide is a possibility for understanding human existence. In the face of differing possibilities potential believers are required to make a decision, to assume responsibility for their own life and choices, and to diminish the anxiety of ambiguity by a positive choice and a responsible decision. This state of ambiguity and the proposed resolution suggest not only that individual theologians take more seriously other theologies but also that they be seriously concerned with what constitutes their own religious tradition, the one with which they presumably will be best acquainted. This bipolar orientation and perspective should lead to the possibility, at least, of reasonably clear choices—hence the four operations constitutive of religious studies.

To return directly to the point: to speak of world as an element in the hermeneutic field is to speak about the inherited totality of meanings ascribed to the multiple dimensions of human existence, the alteration of this totality by choice, by circumstance, by the tides of history, as well as the consequent ambiguity that results from plurality of meaning and interpretation. More than any of the other elements within the hermeneutic field, world specifies ambiguity and thus proposes not only the context of theology but also its theoretical and practical procedure. The work of Roberto de Nobili and Mattheo Ricci in its intellectual dimensions are as yet the beginning of unfulfilled promises. Nor have the insights of Ramakrishna Paramahamsa found successors among many of the world's classic religions. Each of these individuals was primarily engaged in establishing the consistency of rational and intellectual consciousness in the world of intentionality. Theology, therefore, still stands before unfulfilled promises.

If I have thus far spoken of heterogeneity in the world and therefore of a consequent state of ambiguity in the world of assertion, there is nonetheless an underlying world structure that is quite constant beneath the variety of surface structures. I refer, of course to the fact that the world is linguistic in nature.[28] This world has, as we have noted, an existence independent of the individual because of its linguistic constitution.[29] In a certain sense, therefore, the experience of the world by any individual or community is an absolute.[30] So, at a very basic level, there is a unity to both human experience and to the formation and framing of this experience. The establishment of reality by language is an exclusively human attribute and frees humanity from habitat and environment in a way totally different from anything found in the animal world.

While it is true that there is a diversity of languge and therefore a diversity of symbols, it is precisely the diversity, as Gadamer notes, that is illustrative of man's freedom. Even in this diversity, the constant is the fact that through language and speech human beings create their world.

The significance of this point for the interpreter of religions, as opposed, for example, to the sociologist, is the evident fact that the primary habitat of language, and therefore of the linguistic phenomenon as such, is conversation, discussion, the encounter of language between persons. In the large world of understanding and interpretation, the primary analogue is the understanding that takes place among persons. This quite ordinary phenomenon of human life[31] becomes the common ground in which different religious traditions become capable of encountering each other. So the language of conversation, if it is about a common subject matter, gains its reality or becomes itself in the process of genuine communication. Communication is not something added to language but rather is the reality of the language of conversation. Thus the theological operation in its first and second phases intends to make conversation a living reality, whether this conversation be with the self of the interpreter, with a text and its referrent, with another tradition, or with an interpreter of another tradition. It would be futile to think that the act of communication is something that one adds on to the theological operation, or to presume that communication and hence conversation is something quite distinct and different from the theological operation. That there are levels of conversation is evident from one's own experience with differing age groups. But to assume that communication is something added on to the act of theological understanding, or that communication is a functional specialty following upon theological understanding, misconceives the linguistic constitution of reality. One either understands in conversation or one does not. The potential remedy for the latter state is not the introduction of some new methodology or novel procedure but rather the continuation of the same linguistic phenomenon that we call conversation.

As there are differences among individuals, so too there are differences in cultures and in cultural expression. And even in one culture there are differences from one time period to another. But, as I have indicated in the chapter on tradition, the structure of the tradition, the structure of consciousness, the role of tradition, and its linguistic constitution are constants. One is not floating about in a sea of relativity. Thus, as Gadamer notes, "Every such world, as linguistically constituted, is always open to itself, to every possible insight and hence for every expression of its own world picture, and accordingly available to others."[32] But nonetheless the very existence of differences in the linguistic constitution of worlds reaffirms what I have said earlier in this section and in the discussion of the relative and absolute nature of symbols. There is a fundamental contingency to all linguistic expression. This quite obviously makes it difficult, if not fallacious, for one religious tradition to claim a universalism or absolutism that can be imposed on every other linguistic world. In other words, in the present state of human existence it is not at all clear that there has been enough conversation among traditions to yield any type of linguistically expressed religious tradition that would be equally persuasive to all. Hence the role of individual theological and any missionary efforts that emerge from these theologies should not seek to make up by force what they cannot supply by argument, but rather should try to establish conversation and communication within and among traditions. The theological operation is identified with the conversation and the communication. It is not satisfactory to bypass the theological operation and to substitute in its stead a catechetical form of indoctrination, which essentially vitiates genuine conversation.

As it is true that there are differences in culture and cultural expression, so is it likewise true that the linguistic universe is constituted by different forms of world construction, that is, by diverse thought modalities. Ultimately these variously constituted linguistic worlds depend on a diversity of intention, different ontological modes of perception, and the susceptibility of reality to varying modes of access. So we have a common-sense way of experiencing, conceiving, and defining the linguistic world. And there is an inter-subjective way of experiencing and constituting the linguistic world in which the sun still rises and sets. And finally there is the mode of world creation best exemplified in the procedure of the natural sciences. This coexistence of diverse modes of perception and cognition suggests a dialectical relationship among the thought modalities, complementarity, and a grounding in the diverse living relationships that the individual and community have to the world as habitat. It is pointless to speak of one mode of constituting the linguistic world as absolutely superior to another, as it would be futile to suggest that Stravinsky is superior to Mozart, or vice versa. On the other hand, it is quite to the point to indicate their common use of a twelve-note chromatic scale. It would be pretentious and naive for the scientific thought mode to hold that it encompasses all reality and thus deserves a preeminence denied to common sense or intersubjectivity. Few would think of claiming for one national form of music a superiority over another national form. The scientific mode of thought, for example, does not include as its object the one doing the research nor does it explicitly include value judgments. Nor does the scientific mode of thought prescind from the supposition that the work at hand is worthwhile and should yield results. So the ideal in theological thinking cannot be a form of thought that would leave behind the more jejune procedure of conversation.

In fact it may be affirmed that the intention common to scientific procedures is at odds with the thrust of genuine conversation. That intention, of course, is to establish a methodological procedure intended to achieve dominion over a certain defined area of reality. This intention, if exclusive, completely violates the nature of conversation and limits the freedom of at least one of the participants.

It is curious, as Heidegger has pointed out, that modern science reproduces the classical metaphysics and classic epistemology—a fact already discussed here in the study of the cognitional paradigm. The object of science is the present-at-hand (*Vorhandenheit*). But what is universally present is not being as present-at-hand, but rather language. Thus the world constituted by language is far more universally available than any form of objectivity studied by the natural sciences. As Gadamer has noted, the human sciences, such as theology and religious studies, have their existence within this larger horizon of language—a reason compelling enough in itself to reject the systematic theologies that attempt to move themselves into the model world of the natural sciences and thus to seek a dominion over a certain aspect of being. Assuredly the procedures of the natural sciences have signalized themselves in the realm of pure intellectual dominance and have likewise generated a realm of discourse with rigorous rules accessible to anyone willing to submit to specialized and defined procedures. Assuredly too this one linguistic thought and mode plays a role in religious studies, as, for example, in the historical-critical method exercised in the literary, historical, and comparative operations. So too does the methodology of the natural sciences serve as a propaedeutic in the theological operation. But the theological operation intrinsically involves the being of the interpreters, more precisely their relationship to the subject matter as well as their reaction to the subject matter they are currently investigating.

At this point the tradition being studied offers the interpreters a possible way of understanding their existence. Religious studies is constituted not primarily by a relationship to aspects of being-present-at-hand, being which can be dominated, but rather is religious studies established by a form of being to which the interpreter either submits or which he rejects. Religious traditions are constituted by the larger world of linguistic experience, which always includes the existence of the interpreters and their involvement in this linguistic world. Hints of transcendence may be found within the interpreters and the community. But there are no a priori principles from which the existence of this transcendent world may be deduced. Into this ambiguous environment the affirmation or denial of the interpreter enters and thus becomes creative. But the choice and the environment into which the choice is inserted should be subjected to the highest and most continuous rational scrutiny. In the midst of the ambiguity that results from the plurality of the religious and secular worlds and of the nature of the transcendent world, one comes face to face with the ultimate ambiguity—the ambiguity of the human spirit. Mortal, finite, and limited—or at least so it would seem—the human spirit would be immortal, infinite, and unlimited. Given but a portion of time and space and starting anew with each birth, the human spirit seeks to move beyond itself and yet has the feeling that maybe it cannot. So the spirit seeks to affirm by faith and belief a creativity that seems indigenous and compulsive and surrounded with ambiguity. Human birth and development suggest the transformational power of faith, hope, and love, and call attention to the growth of language and symbolism, which seem to have almost no other end than the joy of converse movement into ever expanding worlds, and the creation of heuristic visions. It is with this creativity, this forward motion, and these heuristic visions that religious studies deals. The renewed articulation of the motion toward transcendence is largely the work of the theological operation, which is carried along and nurtured by an interpretative cycle constituted by the historical, the literary, and the comparative operations. The hermeneutic field, the heuristic visions of transcendence, is the horizon of understanding within the context of the human world. So may the interpreter move to the music of the dance.

NOTES

Introduction

1 Carl Becker, *The Heavenly City of the Eighteenth-Century Philosophers* (New Haven: Yale University Press, 1932), p. 17. The climate described by Becker is not exclusively a product of the Enlightenment period but goes back to the Renaissance during which the foundations for historical scholarship were established. Cf. the excellent book by Donald R. Kelley, *Foundations of Modern Historical Scholarship: Language, Law, and History in the French Renaissance* (New York: Columbia University Press, 1970).

Ebeling's essay on the historical-critical method's challenge to theology and established belief is as pertinent today as when it was written. "The Significance of the Critical Historical Method for Church and Theology in Protestantism," *Word and Faith,* trans. James W. Leitch (London: SCM Press, 1963), pp. 17–61. To this must be added the newly developing literary dimension. Cf. the fine work of Robert Alter, *The Art of Biblical Narrative* (New York: Basic Books, 1981).

2 "The constant factor in Troeltsch's understanding of the modern world may be simply stated: The modern world had its beginning in the Enlightenment, and not in the Protestant Reformation . . . he had independently arrived at a conclusion that he shared with Wilhelm Dilthey, namely, that the thought of the Reformation is basically medieval in character" (Benjamin A. Reist, *Toward a Theology of Involvement* [Philadelphia: Westminster Press, 1966], p. 20). Troeltsch, as well as many others, overemphasizes the influence of the Enlightenment. Historical consciousness as well as literary concern as thematized issues can be better located in the Renaissance period. See here Kelley cited in note 1.

3 The literature here is extensive. A useful sketch, particularly of that which pertains directly to hermeneutics, is available in Hans-Georg Gadamer

and Gottfried Boehm, *Seminar: Philosophische Hermeneutik* (Frankfurt am Main: Suhrkamp Verlag, 1976). Note particularly the bibliography. Part of the reason for the initial success of the history of religions was its early affinity for "phenomena susceptible to mechanical and mathematical treatment," thus fitting the discipline into the tenor of the time (Rollo May, *The Meaning of Anxiety* [New York: W. W. Norton & Co., 1977], p. 23). The effort was "to extend the application of the methods of mechanics and mathematics to as many areas of experience as possible . . ." (ibid., pp. 23–24).

4 Particularly necessary for understanding historicity are not only the works of Heidegger but also the discussion that followed in the late twenties. Cf., for example, Gerhard Noller, ed., *Heidegger und die Theologie* (Munich: Chr. Kaiser Verlag, 1967).

5 A similar and more extensive attempt, but in the field of science, has been made by Michael Polanyi, *Personal Knowledge: Towards a Post-Critical Philosophy* (New York and Evanston: Harper Torchbooks, 1962). That the theoretical consideration of the relationships between the history of religions and theology rests on a whole series of concrete social confrontations between religions and encounters of the religions with the culture is clear. Cf. Ernst Benz, *Ideen zu Einer Theologie der Religionsgeschichte* (Mainz: Akademie der Wissenschaften und der Literatur, 1961), a series of lectures given in the United States.

6 Paul Ricoeur, *Freud and Philosophy: An Essay on Interpretation,* trans. Denis Savage (New Haven and London: Yale University Press, 1970), p. 118. This is an excellent hermeneutical reflection on interpretation. Cf., also, Stanley A. Leavy, *The Psychoanalytic Dialogue* (New Haven: Yale University Press, 1980).

7 Joachim Wach, *The Comparative Study of Religions* (New York; Columbia University Press, 1958); Ninian Smart, *The Science of Religion and the Sociology of Knowledge* (Princeton: Princeton University Press, 1973); idem, *The Phenomenon of Religion* (London: MacMillan, 1973); W. C. Smith, *The Meaning and End of Religion* (New York: New American Library, 1962). All of these authors attempt to define religion, religious studies, the history of religion, and theology. Wach's great work on the history of understanding is far more productive than the very brief and sketchy work, *The Comparative Study of Religions.* Smart remains mostly on the descriptive level. Smith's emphasis on the individual and his faith as criteria of scientific research is motivated by long experience and outstanding success in the field of religious studies. But the emphasis tends to limit severely the objective dimensions of a religious tradition and would, if carried to its logical outcome, make theology impossible. On this point see Ugo Bianchi, *The History of Religions* (Leiden: E. J. Brill, 1975), pp. 18–19, 22–23, n. 9. (The reader should be forewarned against the incredibly poor translation of Bianchi's book.) Smith's error is epistemological and consists precisely in failing to see that a tradition has an

objectivity all its own and does not basically depend for its existence on whether or not a particular individual or group momentarily or transiently deny it. Cf. Peter L. Berger and Thomas Luckmann, *The Social Construction of Reality* (Garden City, N.Y.: Doubleday & Co., 1967) chapters 2 and 3, the contrast between objective and subjective reality. For a more nuanced position of Smith, cf. "Interpreting Religious Interrelations: An Historian's View of Christian and Muslim," *Studies in Religion* 6:5 (1976–1977) 515–26. We shall later suggest that a prior relation of the interpreter to the subject matter of religion plus sound historical-critical method will insure the accuracy of the interpreter's understanding.

8 Erik Erikson, *Life History and the Historical Moment* (New York: W. W. Norton & Co., 1925), p. 206.

9 May, *Meaning of Anxiety,* p. 37.

10 Bernard Lonergan, *Collection,* ed. F. E. Crowe (New York: Herder and Herder, 1967), p. 241.

11 Polanyi, *Personal Knowledge.* Also, *Knowing and Being,* ed. Marjorie Grene (Chicago: University of Chicago Press, 1969). For a striking instance of the involvement of the knowing subject in the natural sciences, cf. Bultmann's observations about atomic investigations (Rudolf Bultmann, *Glauben und Verstehen* III [Tübingen: J. C. B. Mohr (Paul Siebeck), 1960], pp. 108–9).

12 Walter Ong, *The Presence of the Word* (New Haven: Yale University Press, 1967). The larger question of how technologies restructure the human psyche and more specifically relate to religious practice and thought is a largely underdeveloped area. Here we can only allude to it. For a slightly more detailed presentation, cf. Norman E. Wagner, "System Theory, Cybernetics, Old Testament Tradition," *Studies in Religion* 6:6 (1976–1977) 597–605. The seminal work here, of course, is Harold A. Innis, *The Bias of Communication* (Toronto: University of Toronto Press, 1951).

13 Bianchi, *History of Religions.*

14 Ibid., p. 13.

15 Ibid.

Chapter 1: Historicity

1 Martin Heidegger, *Being and Time,* trans. John Macquarrie and Edward Robinson (New York and Evanston: Harper & Row, 1962), pp. H 44f. (all references with H are to the pagination of the German edition and are shown in the outer margins of the English translation), 54–57, 64, 105, 111, 121, 129f., 134, 143f., 148, 150f., 160, 165, 199f., 226, 242, 297, 311, 336.

2 Ibid., p. H 57.

3 Ibid., p. H 64.

4 It is clear that definitions of person in the Western tradition arise in a context of differentiating persons in the Trinity. Cf. the perceptive comments of W. J. Ong, "Second Edition: Secular and Religious," *The Center Magazine* 8 (1975) 69–77.

5 Heidegger, *Being and Time,* p. H 114.

6 Ibid., p. H 129.

7 Ibid., section 29.

8 Ibid.

9 Ibid., section 31.

10 Ibid., section 32

11 Ibid., section 33.

12 Ibid., section J 4, p. H 133.

13 Ibid., p. H 143.

14 Thomas Langan, *The Meaning of Heidegger* (New York and London: Columbia University Press, 1959), p. 16. For the radical shift in thinking which such a distinction involves, cf. Rudolf Bultmann, *History and Eschatology* (Edinburgh: The University Press, 1957), particularly chapter 7.

15 David Tracy, *The Achievement of Bernard Lonergan* (New York: Herder and Herder, 1970), pp. 206–7. Heidegger conceives historicity and historical consciousness more radically.

16 Langan, *Meaning of Heidegger,* p. 17.

17 Ibid., p. 40.

18 Bultmann, *History and Eschatology,* p. 103.

19 Ibid., p. 104.

20 Ibid., p. 105.

21 Ibid.

22 Ibid., p. 14.

23 Ong, *Presence of the Word,* passim.

24 For more on differentiation of consciousness, cf. Bernard J. F. Lonergan, *Insight* (London, New York, Toronto: Longmans, Green & Co., 1958) and *Method in Theology* (New York: Herder and Herder, 1972). For the historical development, cf. Bultmann, *History and Eschatology.* For the concrete relation of historical consciousness, historicity, and hermeneutic, cf. Gadamer and Boehm, *Seminar: Philosophische Hermeneutik;* Leavy, *The Psychoanalytic Dialogue.*

25 Cf. Henri F. Ellenberger, *The Discovery of the Unconscious* (New York: Basic Books, 1970); Marthe Robert, *The Psychoanalytic Revolution,* trans. Kenneth Morgan (New York: Harcourt Brace, 1966); Ernest Jones, *The Life and Work of Sigmund Freud,* 3 vols. (New York: Basic Books, 1953–57); Daniel Yankelovich and William Barrett, *Ego and Instinct* (New York: Random House, 1970).

26 May, *Meaning of Anxiety*, p. 34. Cf. Yankelovich and Barrett, *Ego and Instinct*, pp. 52–87; Paul Ricoeur, *Freud and Philosophy*, pp. 3–58.

27 Hans-Georg Gadamer, *Wahrheit und Methode* (Tübingen: J. C. Mohr [Paul Siebeck], 1965), p. 261, my translation.

28 C. G. Jung, *The Undiscovered Self*, trans. R. F. C. Hull (Boston and Toronto: Little, Brown & Co., 1958), p. 5.

29 Ibid., p. 6.

30 Ibid.

31 Cf. John C. Murray, *We Hold These Truths* (New York: Sheed and Ward, 1960), pp. 8–18. I have described what is meant by civil conversation in the concrete in the context of the IAHR meeting in Lancaster, 1975 ("Mélanges," *Studies in Religion* 5:4 [1975–76] 404–7).

32 Charles Davis, "The Reconvergence of Theology and Religious Studies," *Studies in Religion* 4:3 (1974–75) 205–21 (a series of responses follow the article). Cf., also, Bernard Lonergan, "Religious Studies and/or Theology"(Paper delivered for the Donald Mather Memorial Lectureship, Kingston, Ontario, 1976). Lonergan here suggests or hints at the reasons behind reconvergence, which is, of course, the issue.

33 Becker, *Heavenly City*, p. 19.

34 Carl Becker, "What Are Historical Facts," *The Philosophy of History in Our Time* (New York: Doubleday Anchor, 1959), p. 135.

35 C. P. Snow, *The Two Cultures and the Scientific Revolution* (New York: Cambridge University Press, 1961). "Perhaps it will be, not the Snow-like guilt about intellectual indifference to the vast riches of scientific progress, but a shared sense of mutual impoverishment, that will lead to some reconciliation in the conflict of the Two Cultures" (François Bundy, "Notes and Topics: European Notebook," *Encounter* 48:3 [March, 1977] 69).

36 Gordon D. Kaufman, *An Essay on Theological Method* (Missoula, Mont.: Scholars Press, 1975). Cf., also, Kaufman's *Systematic Theology: A Historicist Perspective* (New York: Scribners, 1968) and *God the Problem* (Cambridge, Mass.: Harvard University Press, 1972). Kaufman takes very seriously the influence of historical consciousness. My present study is only remotely related to the precise question of theological method; my central point is the foundational basis for the relations of the history of religions and theology to each other and to the field of religious studies. I am concerned, therefore, with the background against which methodological questions will be developed.

37 Kaufman, *Essay on Theological Method*, p. 33.

38 Northrop Frye, *Anatomy of Criticism* (Princeton: Princeton University Press, 1957), p. 141.

39 Alter, *Art of Biblical Narrative*, p. 12.

Chapter 2: A Cognitional Paradigm

1 To appreciate the extent and depth of this disagreement, one need only turn to the German discussions of the subject during the later nineteen twenties and the early thirties. See also studies in the sociology of knowledge which now constitute an independent discipline and owe their origin to the early German theoreticians. Cf. Peter L. Berger and Thomas Luckmann, *The Social Construction of Reality* (New York: Doubleday & Co., 1967).

2 Roger Aubert, *Le Problème de l'Acte de Foi* (Louvain: Warny, 1958), especially pp. 265–72 and the section on the theology of the manuals, as well as pp. 576–87.

3 Robert F. Harvanek, "The Community of Truth" (Bellarmine School of Theology, North Aurora, Ill., 1965).

4 Friedrich Ohly, *Schriften zur mittelalterlichen Bedeutungs-forschung* (Darmstadt: Wissenschaftliche Buchgesellschaft, 1977), p. 7.

5 Ong, *Presence of the Word.*

6 Robert W. Funk. *Language, Hermeneutic, and Word of God* (New York: Harper & Row, 1966), p. xiii.

7 Ignace de la Potterie, *La Vérité dans Saint Jean* I (Rome: Biblical Institute Press, 1977), pp. 170–241. The use and implications of verbs of hearing employed in the sense of understanding and acting on this understanding in the New Testament is reasonably well-known. Hearing is the figure of speech used for interiorization. Ignace de la Potterie, *La Vérité dans Saint Jean* II (Rome: Biblical Institute Press, 1977), pp. 492–514, particularly p. 507. For verbs of seeing cf. pp. 540, 577, 671. In the Amithabha Scripture, those in the Buddha-land hear the sounds of trees and nets, "like a hundred thousand kinds of music arising at the same time" (W. T. Chan, I. Faruqi, J. M. Kitagawa, P. T. Raju, eds., *The Great Asian Religions,* [London: Collier-Macmillan, 1970], p. 197). Those who hear the music are led to contemplation of the Buddha, the law, and the order. The process by which all becomes one's *Atman* pervades the Upanishads. One moves through the field of sensation to integrality which is an internalized state, a becoming one with consciousness.

8 De la Potterie, *La Vérité* I, pp. 170–241.

9 Harvanek, "The Community of Truth," p. 6. This is accepted by societies such as the International Association of the History of Religions. The IAHR, according to the first statutes of the association, "is a world-wide organization which has as its object the promotion of the academic study of the history of religions through the international collaboration of all scholars whose research has a bearing on the subject" (C. J. Bleeker, *The History of Religions* [Lancaster: University of Lancaster, 1975], p. 3). "Descartes' classi-

cal phrase, 'I think, therefore, I exist,' shows the emphasis on rational processes as a criterion of existence, but it also implies that one arrives at belief in one's own existence *in vacuo* as far as the community is concerned" (May, *Meaning of Anxiety*, pp. 24–25).

10 Harvanek, "The Community of Truth," p. 6. This position is rooted in Peirce, Mead, and Royce. Royce, in *The Problem of Christianity* (Chicago: University of Chicago, 1968), describes the individual *substantia* as modified by the social cooperation which takes place in a community. The result is the *natura secunda* of which the social scientists speak. The community that shapes the individual is itself brought into existence by common language, customs, and religion (p. 239). The community "is essentially a product of a time process. A community has a past and will have a future. Its more or less conscious history, real or ideal, is a part of its very essence" (ibid., p. 243). In affirming the temporality of the individual and the community, Royce is maintaining a position quite like that of Heidegger. Similarities continue when Royce notes that the past of a community and its orientation to a future involve a hermeneutic that is defined as interpretation and understanding. The community of memory (remembrance of the tradition) and expectation (hope of tradition) is based on the interpretation of a common past and future (p. 252). It is this tradition in the community that confers identify on the individual. The triadic nature of knowledge is elaborated in part 2, particularly chapters 12–14. For a different presentation of the historicity of knowledge, cf. Michel Foucault, *Archäologie des Wissens*, trans. Ulrich Köppen (Frankfurt: Suhrkamp, 1973).

11 Philip Wheelwright, *Metaphor and Reality* (Bloomington, Ind.: Indiana University Press, 1975), pp. 25–26. See also Gerhard Ebeling, *Introduction to a Theological Theory of Language* trans. R. A. Wilson (Philadelphia: Fortress Press, 1971).

12 One, for example, looks at a bibliography, e.g., Jacques Waardenburg, *Classical Approaches to the Study of Religion*, 2: Bibliography (The Hague: Mouton Press, 1974); reads the excerpts of the most important authors: Max Müller, Cornelis P. Tiele, Chantepie de la Saussaye, etc., and comes up with a definition of religious studies from the words of these writers and from the reader's interpretation of the words. The beginner normally proceeds in this fashion. Later experience and reflection may modify earlier accepted definitions. Strikingly new understanding is usually published. The process as triadic is clear. There is an identifiable community of which Royce speaks. It is possible, however, to assume unconsciously the Cartesian paradigm of knowledge with its inherent dyadic structure and to consider the definitions of religious studies as the *res extensae* of Descartes, the sensible bodies of classical intellectualism. This very often seems to be the case of those who would exclude theology from the university because of its definition in

terms of a classical culture and a period of history that are no longer present.

13 Helmer Ringgren and Ake V. Strom, *Religions of Mankind,* trans. Niels L. Jensen, ed. J. C. G. Grieg (Philadelphia: Fortress Press, 1967), p. xix. That this opinion conflicts somewhat with our earlier citation of Bianchi is clear.

14 Cf., for example, John B. Noss, *Man's Religions* (London: Macmillan Company, 1970³). Or consider Ninian Smart's *The Religious Experience of Mankind* where the author tries to go beyond exegesis of the subject matter in beginning with the religious experience and noting that the study of religions "requires a sensitive and artistic heart" (p. 4). This is, of course, a requirement for any successful study of subjects that deal with people. As such it is implying that the study of religion belongs to the fine arts. So too the requirement is reminiscent of Schleiermacher's empathy. The primary issue is how does one come to a state where one does, as a matter of fact, sensitively and artistically study religions.

15 Rudolf Bultmann, "The Problem of a Theological Exegesis of the New Testament," *The Beginnings of Dialectic Theology,* ed. James M. Robinson, trans. Keith R. Crim and Louis De Grazia (Richmond, Va.: John Knox, 1968), p. 241.

16 P. Joseph Cahill, "The Theological Significance of Bultmann," *Theological Studies* 38 (1977) 238.

17 Ibid.

18 Ibid.

19 Bultmann, "The Problem of Theological Exegesis of the New Testament," p. 251.

Chapter 3: Hermeneutics and Understanding

1 Gadamer and Boehm's *Seminar: Philosophische Hermeneutik* gives a good account of hermeneutics in its early stages. For hermeneutics in the modern context and for an excellent bibliography, cf. James M. Robinson, "Hermeneutic Since Barth," *The New Hermeneutic* II, ed. James M. Robinson and John B. Cobb, Jr. (New York, Evanston, and London: Harper & Row, 1964), pp. 1–77. For hermeneutic in a theological context, as well as for a brief history, cf. René Marlé, *Le Problème théologique de l'Hermeneutique: Les grands axes de la recherche contemporaine* (Paris: Editions de l'Orante, 1963). Virtually all the works of Ricoeur are relevant to our point. Cf., likewise, *The Journal of Religion* 55 (1975), which is entirely devoted to hermeneutics and contains a brief bibliography.

2 Cf., for example, James Barr, "Story and History in Biblical Theology," *The Journal of Religion* 56:1 (1976) 1–17.

3 A failure to understand the native, in this instance the Amerindian,

generally arises from the conflicts between symbolic consciousnesses characteristic of an aural-oral period and a literate period. I have documented this in "An Amerindian Search: Propaideutic to the study of religion in transition," *Studies in Religion* 5:3 (1975) 286–99. The contrasts in consciousness are evident in the works of Vine Deloria, which I have examined in "Vine Deloria: An Essay in Comparison of Christianity and Amerindian Religions," *Journal of the American Academy of Religion* 45: Supplement (June, 1977) 419–46.

4 Gadamer, *Wahrheit und Methode*, p. 249.

5 Lonergan, *Method*, p. 212.

6 Langan, *The Meaning of Heidegger*, p. 3.

7 Gadamer, *Wahrheit und Methode*, p. 249.

8 William J. Richardson, *Heidegger: Through Phenomenology to Thought* (The Hague: Marinus Nijhoff, 1967), p. 47.

9 Langan, *The Meaning of Heidegger*, p. 23.

10 Richardson, *Heidegger*, p. 67.

11 Heidegger, *Being and Time*, p. H 232.

12 Ibid.

13 Bultmann, "Welchen Sinn hat es von Gott zu reden?" *Glauben* I, pp. 26–37; "Das Problem der Hermeneutik," *Glauben* II, p. 211–35; "Ist voraussetzungslose Exegese möglich," *Glauben* III, pp. 142–50.

14 Paul Ricoeur, "Philosophical Hermeneutics and Theology," *Theology Digest* 24:2 (1976) 154–5.

15 Wheelwright, *Metaphor and Reality*, p. 154.

16 Ricoeur, "Philosophical Hermeneutics," p. 155.

17 Ibid., 161–2.

18 Heidegger, *Being and Time*, p. H 37.

19 Ibid., p. H 37.

20 Ibid., p. H 37.

21 *Karl Barth-Rudolf Bultmann Briefwechesel 1922–1926,* ed. Bernd Jasper (Zurich: Theologischer Verlag, 1971), p. 80.

22 For the context, cf. my article, "The Theological Significance of Rudolf Bultmann," *Theological Studies* 38:2 (1977) 231–74.

23 Bultmann, "The Problem of a Theological Exegesis of the New Testament," *Beginnings*, pp. 236–56.

24 Wheelwright, *Metaphor and Reality*, p. 26.

25 Oscar Wilde, "The Critic as Artist," *The Norton Anthology of English Literature* II, ed. M. H. Abrams et al. (New York: W. W. Norton & Co., 1968), p. 1394.

26 Gadamer, *Wahrheit und Methode*, p. 15.

27 Ibid., pp. xx, xxi, etc.

28 Ibid., p. xvi.

29 Cf. J. D. Crossan, ed., *Semeia* 4 (Missoula, Mont.: Scholars Press, 1975).

30 Hans-Georg Gadamer, "On the Scope and Function of Hermeneutical Relection," trans. G. Hess and R. Palmer, *Continuum* 8 (1970) 92.

31 Ibid., p. 81.

32 B. J. F. Lonergan, *Insight, A Study of Human Understanding* (London: Longmans, Green, 1958), p. 635.

33 Ibid., p. 546.

34 For one example, cf. *The Complete Works of Saint John of the Cross,* trans. and ed. E. Allison Peers (Glasgow: The University Press, 1974). From a different standpoint but leading to the same conclusion, cf. William James, *The Varieties of Religious Experience* (New York: New American Library, 1958).

35 Wheelwright, *Metaphor and Reality,* p. 37.

36 Erikson, *Life History and the Historical Moment,* pp. 172-3.

37 I have developed myth as a necessary and valid carrier of meaning in "Myth and Meaning: Demythologizing Revisited," *No Famine in the Land,* ed. James W. Flanagan and Anita Robinson (Missoula, Mont.: Scholars Press, 1975), pp. 275-92.

38 Documentation is too extensive to cite in detail. A careful reading of some classic biblical commentaries, e.g., Gunkel's *Genesis,* is very informative. There is, moreover, an excellent anthology that is an aid in following mythography during two crucial centuries: Burton Feldman and Richard D. Richardson, *The Rise of Modern Mythology 1680-1860* (Bloomington, Ind.: Indiana University Press, 1972). For a more dramatic account of the eighteenth century's preoccupation with myth, cf. Frank E. Manuel, *The Eighteenth Century Confronts the Gods* (Cambridge, Mass.: Harvard University Press, 1972).

39 An illustrative instance is the understanding of original sin.

40 Northrop Frye et al., *Myth and Symbol* (Lincoln, Nebr.: University of Nebraska Press, 1970). C. G. Jung et al., *Man and His Symbols* (New York: Dell, 1970), pp. 3, 4, 41, 80. Paul Ricoeur, *The Symbolism of Evil,* trans. E. Buchanan (New York: Harper & Row, 1967); idem, *Freud and Philosophy,* pp. 3-28, 494-553. Norman Perrin, "Eschatology and Hermeneutics: Reflections on Method in the Interpretation of the New Testament," *Journal of Biblical Literature* 93 (1974) 3-13: "I want, therefore, to define literary criticism so as to include consideration of the ways in which literary forms and types of language *function,* and a consideration of the nature of response they evoke from the reader or hearer" (p. 10). This article represents a belated catching up with Bultmannian hermeneutics. John J. Collins takes up Perrin's idea in Wheelwright's context: John J. Collins, "The Symbolism of Transcendence in Jewish Apocalyptic," *Biblical Research* 19 (1974) 5-22. Modern interpretation of religious literature is beginning to stress the double intentionality of the symbol, to which corresponds an enlarged notion of

interpretation. Bultmann had years earlier stressed the double intentionality of the act of interpretation without, however, providing a systematic explanation of the double intentionality of the symbol as the basis for the multiple intentionality of all interpretation. The literal interpretation was grasped by exegesis of the subject matter; the second intentionality by criticism of the subject matter. A full account of all the implications of criticism of the subject matter remains to be written. The basic difference between Catholicism and Evangelical Christianity in Germany seems to be found right here, rather than in particular stances on justification or any other specifically religious or theological issue. Nor has there to my knowledge been any specific consideration given by historians of religion to criticism of the subject matter as opposed to exegesis of the subject matter. The excellence of Bianchi's accounts of the history of religions is found in the way he exercises, without theoretical justification or explanation, criticism of the subject matter, even though his analysis of the positive-inductive method he proposes is woefully short of what he intends to say. For a brief unfavorable review of Bianchi's *History of Religions,* cf. Hans H. Penner, *Journal of the American Academy of Religion* 45:1 (1977) 126-7. The poor translation of Bianchi's book may account for some of the venom in the review.

Articulations of cognitional structure and process such as those provided by Heidegger and Lonergan are important not only in themselves but also in the light such developments throw on criticism of the subject matter. Cf., especially, Lonergan, *Method in Theology,* pp. 150-73. Bultmann's early consideration of exegesis of the subject matter and criticism of the subject matter led directly to his essays in hermeneutics. Cf. Bultmann, "The Problem of a Theological Exegesis of the New Testament," *Beginnings of Dialectic Theology,* pp. 236-56. This essay was originally published in *Zwischen den Zeiten* in 1925 and represented a decisive turn not only in Bultmann's thinking but in biblical interpretation as such.

41 Lonergan, *Method,* pp. 153-74. Ricoeur likewise uses the term *Sache,* which is the subject matter. "The 'Sache' is the referent in human experience." Paul Ricoeur, "Biblical Hermeneutics," *Semeia* 4, *Paul Ricoeur on Biblical Hermeneutics,* ed. J. D. Crossan (Missoula, Mont.: Scholars Press, 1975), p. 92. The movement from the broad dimensions of hermeneutics to the more precise activity of literary interpretation within the biblical context has been brilliantly outlined by Ricoeur in *Essays on Biblical Interpretation,* ed. Lewis S. Mudge (Philadelphia: Fortress Press, 1980).

Chapter 4: Tradition

1 Ronald Hayman, "Cartography of Discourse," *Encounter* 47:6 (1976) 74, quoting Foucault.

2 "For persons need no determination or definition or formulation. They are there, given realities—mysterious and impenetrable, but for all that the most real things we know" (Walter J. Ong, "Second Edition: Secular and Religious," *The Center Magazine* 8[1975]76).

3 Cf. Royce, *Problem of Christianity,* pp. 235-52.

4 Gordon W. Allport, *Becoming* (New Haven: Yale University Press, 1955), p. 19.

5 Mortimer J. Adler, "World Peace in Truth," *The Center Magazine* 11:2 (March/April, 1978) 56.

6 Wheelwright, *Metaphor and Reality,* p. 111.

7 This outline will be found in the works of Lonergan, Polanyi, and Popper to which I refer.

8 David E. Linge, "Dilthey and Gadamer: Two Theories of Historical Understanding," *Journal of the American Academy of Religion* 41 (1973) 536-52, especially 544.

9 Horst Bürkle, *Einführung in die Theologie der Religionen* (Darmstadt: Wissenschaftliche Buchgesellschaft, 1977), p. 2. The author provides an excellent bibliography for the more general confrontation of Christianity with world religions. Other instances of what we are talking about are found in the writings of G. Ebeling, particularly *Word and Faith.* When defining tradition in the Protestant communities, he sees it as the ongoing *discursus fidei* through the generations. This *discursus* takes place on two levels, the *existentiell* and the *existentiell,* the ontological and the ontic. I have given an example of this approach in "Scripture, Tradition and Unity," *Catholic Biblical Quarterly* 27 (1965) 315-35.

10 Ichiro Hori, *Folk Religion in Japan,* ed. J. M. Kitagawa and A. L. Miller (Chicago and London: University of Chicago Press, 1974). If Hori's procedure illustrates the assimilation of one's own tradition, an instance of the assimilation of an alien tradition is illustrated by Langdon Warner, *The Enduring Art of Japan* (New York: Grove Press, 1958).

11 For the influence of tradition in physics, cf. Werner Heisenberg, "The Great Tradition," *Encounter* 44 (1975) 52-58.

12 For most of these terms I am indebted to Freud and Lonergan.

13 For a prethematic explanation of how one actually goes about understanding a tradition, the works of J. G. Herder (1744-1803) still provide probably the best model.

14 W. J. Ong et al., "Knowledge in Time," *Knowledge and the Future of Man* (New York: Holt, Rinehart, and Winston, 1968), p. 22.

15 Lonergan, *Method in Theology,* pp. 57-99.

16 Harvanek, "Community of Truth," p. 13.

17 Ibid., p. 15.

18 Ibid., p. 16.

19 What has been radically altered in both the history of religions and theology is not the object of study or the aspects by which the disciplines pursue their studies but rather the context in which the study must take place. In addition to the works already cited, the following works are basic to the relation of understanding and historicity: Wilhelm Dilthey, *Gesammelte Schriften* I, *Einleitung in die Geisteswissenschaften* (Göttingen: Vandenhoeck & Ruprecht, 1959); VII, *Der Aufbau der geschichtlichen Welt in den Geisteswissenschaften*, 1958; XI, *Vom Anfang des Geschichtlichen Bewusstseins*, 1960. Wilhelm Dilthey, *Pattern and Meaning in History*, ed. H. P. Richman (New York: Harper & Row, 1962). Ernst Troeltsch, *Der Historismus und seine Überwindung* (Berlin: Pan Verlag Rolf Heise, 1924). Albrecht Rischl, *Die Absolutheit des Christentums und die Religionsgeschichte* (Tübingen: J. C. B. Mohr [Paul Siebeck], 1912). Max Weber, *The Methodology of the Social Sciences*, trans. and ed. Edward A. Shils and Henry A. Finch (Glencoe: Free Press, 1949). Rudolf Bultmann, *Glauben und Verstehen*, 4 vols. (Tübingen: J. C. B. Mohr [Paul Siebeck], 1933–65). Historicity plays so large a role in Bultmann's thought that one must recommend virtually the entire corpus. Gerhard Ebeling, *Word and Faith*, particularly essays 1, 10, 11, 14; idem, *The Problem of Historicity*, trans. Grover Foley (Philadelphia: Fortress Press, 1967). R. G. Collingwood, *The Idea of History*, ed. Phil Snyder (Ithaca, N.Y.: Cornell, 1958). Fritz Stern, ed., *The Varieties of History* (New York: Meridian Books, 1960). Hans Meyerhoff ed., *The Philosophy of History in Our Time* (New York: Doubleday Anchor Books, 1959). Karl Rahner and Herbert Vorgrimler, *Theological Dictionary*, ed. Cornelius Ernst, trans. Richard Strachan (New York: Herder & Herder, 1965). Karl Rahner, *Theological Investigations* VI, trans. Karl H. and Boniface Kruger (Baltimore: Helicon Press, 1969), p. 178.

Historicity has entered the long faith-reason controversy: "The proof of the matter is apparent in the fact that for modern thought religion itself is properly a subject for observation and comment precisely as are all the other phenomena that make up human experience and accordingly come before human scrutiny" (Reist, *Toward a Theology of Involvement*, p. 23). Taken seriously this statement must mean that theology inevitably becomes a rubric of religious studies, no matter how strong past definitions of theology.

20 Bultmann, "The Problem of a Theological Exegesis of the New Testament," *Beginnings of Dialectic Theology*, pp. 250–51. Even when historians explicitly deny the relevance of the present for the past or vice versa, they must operate from a particular understanding of the present.

21 Ibid.

22 Royce, *Problem of Christianity*, part 2.

23 The validity of this statement and the degree to which it is true varies from country to country. On the political level a striking instance of both

dissonance and material identity is found in Canada's puzzlement about how the provinces, particularly Quebec, are related to the larger structure—whatever that may be.

24 Hori, *Folk Religion in Japan,* p. 18.

25 These shifts are particularly noticeable in the later works of Lonergan and his commentators.

26 See, for example, L. Gilkey, "Empirical Science and Theological Knowing," *Foundations of Theology,* ed. Philip McShane (Dublin: Gill and Macmillan, 1971), pp. 76–101. Also, Lonergan, *Method in Theology,* where the author describes the unity of faith conceived of in the culture of classicism as the "shabby shell of Catholicism," a statement that could be applied *a pari* to other denominations and religions. One may agree with the observation; but one must also note the ambivalence and ambiguity of the tradition, not to mention the responsibility of believers to do something about the situation in which they find themselves. Apropos of this point is the striking consideration of Luther's activity in Jaroslav Pelikan, *Spirit Versus Structure* (New York: Harper & Row, 1968).

27 I am confining my remarks to the Cree and Blood though I think the generalization goes beyond these groups. I have dealt with the issue in "An Amerindian Search: Propaideutic to the Study of Religion in Transition," *Studies in Religion* 5:3 (1975) 286–99.

28 Paul Ricoeur, "The Specificity of Language," *Semeia* 4, (Missoula, Mont.: Scholars Press, 1975), p. 132.

29 Bernard Lonergan, "Aquinas Today: Tradition and Innovation," *Journal of Religion* 55:2 (1975) 165–80.

30 John W. O'Malley, "Reform, Historical Consciousness, and Vatican II's Aggiornamento," *Theological Studies* 32:4 (1971) 582. The Enlightenment's emphasis, continuing the Greek tradition, on a common unchangeable human nature, the same at all times and in every place—a supposition that makes diversity difficult to understand and that suggests studies that would terminate in a single, unified structure—is misleading. For detailed development of this idea cf. Isaiah Berlin, *Against the Current* (New York: Viking Press, 1980).

31 Garry Wills, *Bare Ruined Choirs* (Garden City, N.Y.: Doubleday & Co., 1972). This theme likewise permeates the now largely obsolete "death of God" theology. That such lamentations, products of hopes disappointed, would take place was perceived early on: cf. the rather remarkable polemic of Antonino Romeo, *L'Enciclica 'Divino Afflante Spiritu' e le 'Opiniones Novae'* (Rome: Libreria Editrice della Pontificia Università Lateranense, 1960).

32 Cf. note 26. Also, P. J. Cahill, "Vine Deloria: An Essay in Comparison of Christianity and Amerindian Religion," pp. 419–46.

33 V. S. Naipaul, *India's Tragic Flaws: A Wounded Civilization* (New York: Knopf, 1977).

34 Gerhard von Rad, *Wisdom in Israel* (Nashville and New York: Abingdon Press, 1972), pp. 3–4.

Chapter 5: Comparative Religion or the History of Religions

1 In addition to the standard introductory books, see also Feldman and Richardson, *The Rise of Modern Mythology 1680–1860.*

2 Cf. Richard M. Dorson, "The Eclipse of Solar Mythology," *Myth: A Symposium,* ed. Thomas A. Sebeck (Bloomington and London: Indiana University Press, 1971), pp. 25–63.

3 Ibid., p. 26.

4 Feldman and Richardson, *Rise of Modern Mythology,* p. 41.

5 Ibid.

6 Ibid., p. 100.

7 See Bianchi, *History of Religions,* pp. 27–29 for more details.

8 Mircea Eliade, "Comparative Religion: Its Past and Future," *Knowledge and the Future of Man,* ed. Walter J. Ong (New York: Holt, Rinehart, and Winston, 1968), p. 251.

9 Albert Jepsen, "The Scientific Study of the Old Testament," *Essays on Old Testament Hermeneutics,* ed. Claus Westermann, ed. and trans. James Luther Mays (Richmond, Va.: John Knox Press, 1963), p. 247.

10 Walter H. Capps, *Ways of Understanding Religion* (New York: Macmillan, 1972).

11 Ibid., pp. 135–67.

12 Ibid., p. 166.

13 Mircea Eliade, *A History of Religious Ideas* I, *From the Stone Age to the Eleusinian Mysteries,* trans. Willard R. Trask (Chicago: University of Chicago Press, 1978), p. xiii.

14 Capps, *Ways of Understanding Religion,* p. 188.

15 Eliade, *Patterns of Comparative Religions,* pp. 25–30.

16 Cf. Charles Y. Glock and Phillip E. Hammond, eds., *Beyond the Classics* (New York: Harper Torchbooks, 1973). J. Milton Yinger, *The Scientific Study of Religion* (London: Macmillan, 1970). Jacques Waardenburg, *Classical Approaches to the Study of Religion* II, *Bibliography* (The Hague: Mouton, 1974).

17 Capps, *Ways of Understanding Religion,* p. 287.

18 Alter, *The Art of Biblical Narrative,* p. 12.

19 For a survey, cf. C. J. Bleeker, *The History of Religions* (Lancaster: University of Lancaster, 1975). The quote is from Simon's presidential address circulated in mimeographed form.

20 Ibid.

21 F. Schuon, *The Transcendent Unity of Religions,* trans. Peter Townsend

(New York: Harper & Row, 1975). Cf. Richard C. Bush, "Frithjof Schuon's *The Transcendent Unity of Religions:* Con," and Huston Smith, "Frithjof Schuon's *The Transcendent Unity of Religions:* Pro," *Journal of the American Academy of Religion* 44:44 (1976) 715–20; 721–24.

22 Schuon, *Transcendent Unity,* p. xxiv, from the introduction by Huston Smith.

23 Schuon, *Transcendent Unity,* p. 8.

24 Ibid., pp. 14–15. "No religion, ideology, culture, or tradition can reasonably claim to exhaust the universal range of human experience. Thus a *pluralism* distinct from the mere coexistence of a plurality of worldviews is a present-day necessity" (Raimundo Panikkar, "Have 'Religions' the Monopoly of Religion?" *Journal of Ecumenical Studies* 11:3 [1974] 516).

25 Ibid., p. 19.

26 Mortimer J. Adler, "World Peace in Truth," *The Center Magazine* 11:2 (March/April, 1978) 56–64.

27 Ibid., p. 59.

28 Ibid.

29 Ibid., p. 60.

30 Ibid., p. 61.

31 Ibid., p. 63.

32 Ibid.

33 Wheelwright, *Metaphor and Reality,* p. 92

34 Michael Polanyi, *Personal Knowledge,* p. 285.

35 Ibid., p. 280.

36 Ibid.

37 Ibid., p. 281.

Chapter 6: Theology and the Constitutive Operations in Religious Studies

1 Roger A. Johnson, *The Origins of Demythologizing* (Leiden: E. J. Brill, 1974), p. 70.

2 Ibid., p. 59.

3 Ibid., p. 59. For the influence of Herrmann on Bultmann, cf. Bernard Dieckmann, *"Welt" und "Entweltlichung" in der Theologie Rudolf Bultmann's* (Munich: Verlag Ferdinand Schoningh, 1977).

4 Ibid., p. 62. "Herrmann thinks that behind metaphysics there is a practical motive, the desire of man to find his orientation in the world. This desire is satisfied not by metaphysics but by religion" (John MacQuarrie, *Twentieth-Century Religious Thought* [London: SCM Press, 1963], p. 84). This

idea exercised a profound influence on the Protestant theology of the early twentieth century.

5 Johnson, *Origins of Demythologizing*, p. 68.

6 Ibid.

7 Ibid., p. 69. Johnson does not touch the real problem evident in Kant's assumption that knowing is almost the same as seeing. His epistemology is built on a visual model which can reach phenomena but cannot, by definition, reach interiors or noumena. Nor do we know how much the assumption that the natural locus of the word is space, the printed page, influenced the philosophers of the time of Kant. "How much of the problem Kant poses is really in the understanding or intellectual process itself and how much of it is in the model for understanding which the history of his culture made available to him" (Ong, *Presence of the Word*, p. 74). Following the Kantian problematic one must find a source of the really real. That would be the *Erlebnis* and *Gefühle*, which are not consigned by Kant to the work of *Geist*, which deals with exteriorized reality, the phenomena, and that which is seen (understood).

8 Johnson, *Origins of Demythologizing*, p. 75.

9 Ibid., p. 84.

10 Smart, *Divided Mind*, p. 31–37.

11 "Die Theologie des 19. Jahrhunderts ist im grossen und ganzen keine Glanzerscheinung in der Geschichte der Theologie" (Johannes Beumer, *Theologie als Glaubenverständnis* [Würzburg: Eschter Verlag, 1953], p. 132).

12 Lonergan, *Method in Theology*, pp. 249–50. At each point the data must be understood and judged. Comparison is a sophisticated and complex process requiring careful self-analysis. The interpreter must have a relationship to the subject matter of religion, and this relationship, if the interpreter is to engage in comparison, must become a matter of reflective consideration and analysis. The interpreter does not have the same experience as those whose religions he or she compares but rather has a similar relationship to the subject matter, intentionality directed to ultimate transcendence, which then places the individual in a new situation. Bianchi's *History of Religions* contains the best prescriptions for the historical operation but lacks the requisite reflections on hermeneutical self-appropriation. Without this, historical methodology will succeed only accidentally, by virtue of the talent and concern of the individual interpreter. For an instance of what I mean by a prior relationship to the subject matter and by an articulation of this relationship, see J. W. Rogerson, *Myth in Old Testament Interpretation* (Berlin and New York: De Gruyter, 1974), pp. 64–65, for the controversy between Gunkel and Fraser. What is at issue is the different self-understandings of two interpreters who are dealing with one and the same subject. In other terms, the

conflict centers about the tacit component of knowledge. Cf. Michael Polanyi, *Personal Knowledge* and *Knowing and Being,* ed. Marjorie Greene (Chicago: University of Chicago Press, 1969), particularly chapter 11. For a simple explanation of the art of comparison in the case of Near Eastern parallels to Old Testament passages, see Stan Rummel, "Using Ancient Near Eastern Parallels in Old Testament Study," *The Biblical Archaeology Review* 3:3 (1977) 3–11.

13 Heinz Robert Schlette, *Towards a Theology of Religions,* trans. W. J. O'Hara (New York: Herder and Herder, 1966). What is missing in this work is a serious exercise of the historical operation. The normative assumption of the absolute value of one religion is not made on historical grounds, indeed cannot be made on these grounds, but rather by a personal decision. The author provides no serious grounds for an evaluative hermeneutic nor does he distinguish between exoteric and esoteric.

14 I accept the now common distinction in which faith is the ultimate orientation of the believer and in which faith grounds the body of religious beliefs. These beliefs are available for study. One may also distinguish the religious experience that constitutes the faith and therefore grounds the religious belief or belief system. See Lonergan, *Method,* p. 123.

15 Bultmann, *History and Eschatology,* p. 124.

16 René Marlé, "Chalcedoine reinterrogé," *Rechersches de Science Religieuse* 65 (1977) 24.

17 I have in mind here the more recent works of Hans Küng and agree with the following perceptive and brief evaluation of Küng's theology: Küng has not yet taken historicity seriously enough on the critical level, (John Bossey, "Hans Küng's Theology," *Encounter* 50:1 [January, 1978] 41–45).

18 Jepsen, "The Scientific Study of the Old Testament," *Essays on Old Testament Hermeneutics,* p. 247.

19 Bernard Lonergan, *De Deo Trino* (Rome: Apud Aedes Universitatis Gregorianae, 1961); idem, *De Constitutione Christi* (Rome: Apud Aedes Universitatis Gregorianae, 1956); idem, *Method,* pp. 305–12.

20 Longergan, *Method,* pp. xi, 124.

21 Jaroslav Pelikan, *The Christian Tradition: The Emergence of the Catholic Tradition,* 100–600 (Chicago: University of Chicago Press, 1972) p. 206.

22 Ibid.

23 Ibid.

24 "Welte claims, rightly I believe, that by and large the Bible is a narrative of events" (B. J. Lonergan, "Theology and Praxis," *Proceedings of the Thirty-Second Annual Convention* [New York: Catholic Theological Society, 1977], p. 12). The very fact that one relates theology and praxis indicates a prior separation of the two. This dichotomy is hardened by the traditional

mediatorial role assumed by the church and its sacramental system in the transmission of revelation. This mediatorial role insulated the church from the works of the historical-critical method until 1943. "Human Generis" of 1950 can be considered an attempt to restrain the method approved in 1943.

25 Pelikan, *Christian Tradition,* p. 196.

26 Ibid., p. 198.

27 Ibid.

28 Rudolf Bultmann, "Das Problem der Hermeneutik," *Theologie und Kirche* 47 (1950) 47–69.

29 Cf. Mary Gerhart, "Genre Studies: Their Renewed Importance in Religious and Literary Criticisms," *Journal of the American Academy of Religion* 45:3 (1977) 309–26. Her diagram on page 325 is informative and illustrates the fact that the normal reader is quite distant from the text. Cf., also, Charles R. Strain, "Ideology and Alienation: Theses on the Interpretation and Evaluation of Theologies of Liberation," *Journal of the American Academy of Religion* 45:4 (1977) 473–90.

30 "Religious communication generally must overcome a long addiction to the discursive, the rationalistic, and the prosaic" (Amos N. Wilder, *Theopoetic* [Philadelphia: Fortress Press, 1976]; see also, idem, *The New Voice* [New York: Herder and Herder, 1969]).

31 P. Joseph Cahill, "The Joannine Logos as Center," *Catholic Biblical Quarterly* 38 (1976), 54–72.

32 *Shakespeare's Sonnets,* ed. Stephen Booth (New Haven: Yale University Press, 1977), p. xiii. Cf. E. D. Hirsch, *Validity in Interpretation* (New Haven: Yale University Press, 1967). Hirsch is correct in stressing the need to recover the intended meaning of the author but incorrect in his criticism of Gadamer who focuses rather on the meaning of a text in its toal literary and historical environment. For two similar perspectives on potential ambiguity in interpretation cf. Frank Kermode, *The Genesis of Secrecy: On the Interpretation of Narrative* (Cambridge, Mass.: Harvard University Press, 1979), and Stanley A. Leavy, *The Psychoanalytic Dialogue,* particularly Leavy's discussions of ambiguity, p. 37, and latent intention, p. 46.

33 Northrop Frye, *Anatomy of Criticism,* p. 51.

34 Cf. Isaiah Berlin, *Against the Current* (New York: Viking Press, 1980).

35 Bruno Snell, *The Discovery of the Mind,* trans. T. G. Rosenmeyer (New York: Harper Torchbooks, 1960).

36 Hans-Georg Gadamer, *Truth and Method,* trans. Garrett Barden and John Cumming (New York: Seabury Press, 1975).

37 Isaac Asimov, "A Cult of Ignorance," *Newsweek* (January 21, 1980) p. 19.

38 Sample expected lifetime average salaries: Lawyer: $54,516; accountant: $41,880; engineer: $28,847; professor: $25,890; schoolteacher: $24,176; car-

penter: $23,510; supermarket cashier (BC): $18,358, *Canadian Association of University Teachers Bulletin* 27:3 (May, 1980) 36.

39 Northrop Frye, *The Critical Path* (Bloomington, Ind.: Indiana University Press, 1971), p. 29.

40 Northrop Frye, *The Stubborn Structure* (Ithaca, N.Y.: Cornell University Press, 1970), p. 81. The operations are complementary.

41 Ibid., p. 82.

42 Ibid., p. 74.

43 Ibid., p. 75.

44 Ibid., pp. 6–7.

45 Robert D. Denham, *Northrop Frye and Critical Method* (London: University Park, Penn.: Pennsylvania State University Press, 1978), p. 55.

46 Ibid., p. 55.

47 Frye, *The Critical Path,* passim.

48 W. B. Yeats, *Selected Criticism* (London: Macmillan, 1964), p. 33.

49 Wheelwright, *Metaphor and Reality,* p. 45–69.

50 Leonard Bernstein, "The Norton Lectures 1973: The Unanswered Question" IV, "The Delights and Dangers of Ambiguity." Columbia Records.

51 Wheelwright, *Metaphor and Reality,* p. 92. For a brief but accurate discussion of symbol in the larger context, cf. Otto Friedrich Bollnow, "Die Welt der Symbole," *Leben und Tod in den Religionen,* ed. Gunther Stephenson (Darmstadt: Wissenschaftliche Buchgesellschaft, 1980), pp. 1–14.

52 Paul Ricoeur, *The Rule of Metaphor,* trans. Robert Czerny with Kathleen McLaughlin and John Costello (Toronto: University of Toronto Press, 1979).

53 Norman Perrin, *Jesus and the Language of the Kingdom* (Philadelphia: Fortress Press, 1976). Joseph M. Kitagawa, "Primitive, Classical, and Modern Religions: A Perspective on Understanding the History of Religions," *The History of Religions* I, ed. Joseph M. Kitagawa (Chicago: University of Chicago Press, 1967), pp. 39–66.

54 Marcel Griaule, *Conversations with Ogotemmeli* (New York: Oxford University Press, 1975), p. 138.

55 Hermann Gunkel, *The Legends of Genesis,* trans. W. H. Carruth (New York: Schocken Books, 1970), p. 3.

56 Ibid., p. 1.

57 Ibid., p. 11.

58 Quoted by Nathan Scott, "Criticism and the Religious Horizon," *Humanities, Religion, and the Arts Tomorrow,* ed. Howard Hunter (New York: Holt, Rinehart, and Winston, 1972), p. 39.

59 Ricoeur, *Rule of Metaphor,* p. 67. Thus the need for diverse operations.

60 The emphasis on literature is meant to include other symbolic systems

as well, for example, that of pictorial mediation which likewise functions through symbolic presentation. What I am saying of literature is applicable to other symbolic mediators of religious tradition such as the visual arts and music, with appropriate modification according to genre. The literary operation, in the largest sense, will work with the historical operation.

61 Lonergan, *Method in Theology*, pp. 355–68.

62 David Tracy, "Grace and the Search for the Human: The Sense of the Uncanny," *Proceedings of the Thirty-Fourth Annual Convention of the Catholic Theological Society of America* (Washington: Catholic Theological Society, 1980), pp. 64–77.

63 1 Timothy 1:4; 4:7; 2 Timothy 4:4; 2 Peter 1:16.

64 Wolfhart Pannenberg, *Theology and the Philosophy of Science*, trans. Francis McDonagh (London: Darton, Longman and Todd, 1976), pp. 7–8.

65 Ibid., p. 8.

66 Burton Feldman and Robert D. Richardson, *The Rise of Modern Mythology, 1680–1860* (Bloomington, Ind.: Indiana University Press, 1972) Vico 50–62; Herder 224–40.

67 Edwin Hatch, *The Influence of Greek Ideas on Christianity* (New York: Harper Torchbooks, 1957). One of the very best books on the writing of history is by Jacques Barzun and Henry F. Graff, *The Modern Researcher* (London: Harcourt Brace Jovanovich, 1977).

68 Bultmann, *History and Eschatology*, p. 6.

69 Bultmann, "The Problem of a Theological Exegesis of the New Testament," *Beginnings*, p. 242.

70 Gadamer, *Truth and Method*, p. 179.

71 Ibid., p. 180.

72 Frye, *The Stubborn Structure*, p. 81.

73 Arnold Toynbee, *A Study of History*, rev. ed., A. Toynbee and Jane Caplan (New York: Oxford University Press, 1972), p. 30.

74 Ibid., p. 32.

75 Ibid.

76 Hugh Trevor-Roper, "History and Imagination," *Times Literary Supplement* 4035 (July 25, 1980) 135.

77 Ibid.

78 Ricoeur, *Rule of Metaphor*, p. 82.

79 Frye, *Anatomy of Criticism*, p. 35b.

80 René Wellek and Austin Warner, *Theory of Literature* (New York: Harcourt, Brace & World, 1970), pp. 57–69.

81 "In diesem Sinne könne wir von einem Lernprozess sprechen, der das theologische Verständnis einer fremden Religion begleitet" (Bürkle, *Einführung in die Theologie der Religionen*, p. 3). The same is true of comparison within a religious tradition. An interesting long-range program, funded

by the Canada Council, is underway at McMaster University in which the intention is to find the self-definition process at work in the period of early Christianity.

82 Ricoeur, *Symbolism of Evil.*

83 For example, Eliade, *Patterns in Comparative Religion.*

84 Cf. Ebeling, "The Significance of the Critical History Method for Church and Theology in Protestantism," *World and Faith,* pp. 12–61.

85 Ibid., p. 58.

86 Ibid., p. 40.

87 Hatch, *Influence,* p. 58.

88 I have already cited Hans Küng as one instance.

89 P. J. Cahill, "Myth and Meaning: Demythologizing," *No Famine in the Land* (Missoula, MT: Scholars Press, 1975), pp. 275–91.

90 Eliade, *Patterns in Comparative Religion,* p. 29.

91 Gerhard von Rad, *Old Testament Theology* I (New York: Harper & Brothers, 1960).

92 Roland de Vaux, *Ancient Israel: Social Institutions* I (New York: McGraw Hill, 1965).

93 Ong, *Presence of the Word;* idem, "Maranatha: Death and Life in the Text of the Bible," *Journal of the American Academy of Religion* 45:4 (1977) 419–49.

94 Meyer Schapiro, *Late Antique, Early Christian and Medieval Art* (New York: George Braziller, 1979) 34–47.

95 Rudolf Wittkower, *Architectural Principles in the Age of Humanism* (London: The Warburg Institute, 1949). Cf. a review by John Collidge, *The Magazine of Art* 43 (1950) 317. I owe this reference to Professor Larry Cook, Department of Music, University of Alberta.

96 Jaspert, *Briefwechsel,* p. 80.

97 Ernst Benz, "On Understanding Non-Christian Religions," *The History of Religions: Essays in Methodology,* ed. M. Eliade and J. M. Kitagawa (Chicago: University of Chicago Press, 1973), p. 121. "Here the problem arises as to whether a given phenomenon or a given system (for example, the Buddhism of the 'Small Vehicle') deserves the term 'religion' or 'religious,' not in relation to the concept of 'true' religion and the 'truly' religious in the philosophical and theological sense (as opposed to 'false' religion and 'false' religiosity) but in relation to historical-phenomenological 'analogy' to which we have already referred, which is the special object of the history of religions" (Bianchi, *History of Religions,* pp. 5–6, 32). Cf. W. C. Smith, "Religious Atheism? Early Buddhist and Recent American," *Comparative Religion: The Charles Strong Trust Lectures 1961–1970* (Leiden: E. J. Brill, 1972); Smith maintains that Nirvana, according to the Buddha and early followers, had qualities of what we would call the divine. And the concept Dharma

"is also, and indeed more, akin to the notion of God in the West" (ibid., p. 57).

98 Jaspert, *Briefwechsel,* p. 80.

99 A documentation of this tendency can be found in Wolfhart Panneberg, *Theology and the Philosophy of Science,* trans. Francis McDonough (London: Darton, Longman and Todd, 1976).

Chapter 7: The Theological Operation and the Hermeneutic Field

1 W. B. Yeats, *The Collected Poems of W. B. Yeats* (New York: Macmillan, 1979), p. 214.

2 Richard W. Murphy and the Editors of Time-Life Books, *The World of Cézanne 1839–1906* (Alexandria, Va.: Time-Life Books, 1977), p. 76.

3 Ibid., p. 84.

4 Georges Dumézil, *Archaic Roman Religion* I, trans. Philip Kropp (Chicago: University of Chicago Press, 1966), p. xiii. In an earlier article Eliade had contrasted the approach of the historian of religion to that of the theologian, somewhat to the detriment of the theological operation. He claimed that the historian of religion "is preoccupied uniquely with *religious* symbols . . . the historian of religions uses an empirical method of approach" (Mircea Eliade, "Methodological Remarks on the Study of Religious Symbolism," *The History of Religions,* ed. Joseph M. Kitagawa [Chicago: Chicago University Press, 1973], p. 88). If one holds clearly and permanently in mind that all religions—archaic, ancient, and modern—have "representations of divinity" or transcendence and thus have a theology, then the relation between the history of religions and theology becomes clear.

5 Gustave von Grunebaum, *Medieval Islam* (Chicago: University of Chicago Press, 1953), p. 258.

6 Jonathan Culler, *The Pursuit of Signs: Semiotics, Literature, Deconstruction* (Ithaca, N.Y.: Cornell University Press, 1981), p. 66.

7 Paul Ricoeur, *The Symbolism of Evil,* trans. Emerson Buchanan (New York: Harper & Row, 1967). Cf. also, idem, *Freud and Philosophy.* For the context, cf. David M. Rasmussen, *Mythic-Symbolic Language and Philosophical Anthropology.* For the larger background, cf. the articles on theology, history of religions, science of religion, and comparative religion in *Die Religion in Geschichte und Gegenwart.*

8 Culler, *The Pursuit of Signs,* p. 48.

9 Thomas R. Martland, *Religion as Art: An Interpretation* (Albany, N.Y.: State University of New York Press, 1981,) p. 84.

10 Ibid., p. 10.

11 Ibid., p. 13.

12 Ibid., p. 6.

13 Cf. Walter J. Ong, "Maranatha: Death and Life in the Text of the Bible," *Journal of the American Academy of Religion* 45 (1977) 419–49. The futurity that Ong seems to confine to the Bible is equally characteristic of the Koran, the Bhagavad Gita, the I Ching and all religious literature.

14 Erich Auerbach, *Scenes from the Drama of European Literature* (New York: Meridian Books, 1959), p. 52.

15 Ibid., p. 12.

16 Northrop Frye, *Creation and Recreation* (Toronto: University of Toronto Press, 1980), p. 60.

17 Kermode, *Genesis of Secrecy*, pp. 18–21.

18 Jung, *Psychology and Religion*, pp. 5–6.

19 Erwin R. Goodenough, *Jewish Symbols in the Greco-Roman Period* IV, Bollingen Series XXXVII (New York: Pantheon Books, 1954), p. 39.

20 Jacob Neusner, "Religious Studies: The Next Vocation," *Bulletin: The Council on the Study of Religion* 3:5 (December, 1977) 119.

21 Martland, *Religion as Art*, p. 18.

22 Ibid., p. 34.

23 Ibid., p. 25.

24 Bultmann, *History and Eschatology*, p. 115.

25 For further analysis of community, cf. Lonergan, *Method*, pp. 78–81.

26 I find the sophisticated and attractive analysis of human thinking and its consequent application to theological procedures proposed by Lonergan unconvincing. None of the eight activities (research, interpretation, history, dialectic, foundations, doctrines, systematics, and communications) really distinguishes the activity of the theologian. The position of systematics, which would leave behind or transcend rhetorical expression, is suspect. The inverse chiastic found in the *oratione obliqua* and the *oratione recta* are models of intellectual distinction. The human mind, however, tends to work within ever expanding hermeneutic circles and not in the linear mode, however often repeated. Nor am I convinced that we can usefully invoke conversion at critical points of understanding.

27 Bowman, ed., *Comparative Religion*.

28 Gadamer, *Truth and Method*, p. 401.

29 Ibid., p. 402.

30 Ibid., p. 408.

31 Ibid., p. 422.

32 Ibid., p. 405. The study of semiotics has taken the insights of Gadamer a large step forward and is therefore not only useful for the literary enterprise but also for the existential analysis we have proposed.

INDEX